WEYERHAEUSER ENVIRONMENTAL BOOKS

Paul S. Sutter, Editor

WEYERHAEUSER ENVIRONMENTAL BOOKS explore human relationships with natural environments in all their variety and complexity. They seek to cast new light on the ways that natural systems affect human communities, the ways that people affect the environments of which they are a part, and the ways that different cultural conceptions of nature profoundly shape our sense of the world around us. A complete list of the books in the series appears at the end of this book.

THE ORGANIC PROFIT

*Rodale and the Making
of Marketplace Environmentalism*

ANDREW N. CASE

UNIVERSITY OF WASHINGTON PRESS
Seattle

The Organic Profit is published with the assistance of a grant from the Weyerhaeuser Environmental Books Endowment, established by the Weyerhaeuser Company Foundation, members of the Weyerhaeuser family, and Janet and Jack Creighton.

University of Washington Press
www.washington.edu/uwpress

Library of Congress Cataloging-in-Publication Data
Names: Case, Andrew N., author.
Title: The organic profit : Rodale and the making of marketplace
    environmentalism / Andrew N. Case.
Description: 1st Edition. | Seattle : University of Washington Press, [2018] |
    Series: Weyerhaeuser environmental books | Includes bibliographical
    references and index. |
Identifiers: LCCN 2017026612 (print) | LCCN 2017051724 (ebook) |
    ISBN 9780295743028 (ebook) | ISBN 9780295743011 (hardcover : alk. paper)
Subjects: LCSH: Rodale (Firm)—History. | Rodale, J. I. (Jerome Irving), 1898–
    1971. | Organic gardening—United States—History. | Physical fitness—
    United States—History.
Classification: LCC SB453.5 (ebook) | LCC SB453.5 .C36 2018 (print) |
    DDC 338.7/6107050973—dc23
LC record available at https://lccn.loc.gov/2017026612

The paper used in this publication is acid-free and meets the minimum requirements of American National Standard for Information Sciences—Permanence of Paper for Printed Library Materials, ANSI Z39.48–1984. ∞

CONTENTS

FOREWORD

The Organic Citizen Consumer

PAUL S. SUTTER

For most of American history, all agriculture was organic. Farmers did not use chemical pesticides, and those who chose to maintain the fertility of their soils did so by laboriously returning plant, animal, and human wastes to them, and by planting leguminous cover crops that could fix atmospheric nitrogen. That began to change in the late nineteenth and early twentieth centuries, as farmers, gardeners, and orchardists turned to arsenical compounds to control pests, and as they sought out concentrated sources of the essential chemical elements of soil fertility—nitrogen, potassium, and phosphorous in particular—to alleviate the labor demands of traditional soil husbandry. Nonetheless, as late as the 1930s, it made little sense to distinguish an American agriculture that was organic from one that was not. Indeed, the dominant environmental critique of American agriculture during the New Deal era was one of frontier wastefulness and impermanence—of Americans skimming the land of its fertility and moving on—not of Americans polluting the land, and themselves, with synthetic chemicals. Before World War II, "permanent agriculture," not "organic agriculture," was the rallying cry of environmentally minded reformers.

So how did the "organic," once the unexamined rule of American agriculture, quickly become the reformist exception? The answer lies largely in the profound changes in American agricultural production during the middle decades of the twentieth century, and in an acute sense after World War II that our food system was dangerously hooked on industrially produced fertilizers, a new generation of powerful pesticides, and a panoply of artificial additives in the processed foods we ate. The modern organic movement was forged in this crucible of chemical concern, and consumers were critical to its success. In fact, one could argue that the rise of a robust market for organic products has been one of the great success stories of politicized consumer activism in postwar American history. But there is another side to this story, another explanation for the rapid rise of the "organic": during the last decades of the twentieth century, consumer markets fragmented as Americans searched for products, and even entire lifestyles, that could differentiate them from the masses. In this context, "organic" became a signifier of an elite consumer status: to buy organic was to express in the consumer marketplace one's privileged affinity for nature and natural living. Seen this way, the "organic" movement seems more a marketing success story than a triumph of environmental politics and popular reform.

No one had more to do with the rise of the "organic" ideal in the United States and the movement that would bring it into the consumer mainstream than did the Rodales—the idiosyncratic Jerome I. Rodale and his son, Robert. After establishing a modestly successful electrical manufacturing business and dabbling in publishing, Jerome Rodale bought a farm in Emmaus, Pennsylvania, in 1942 and simultaneously launched a new magazine, *Organic Farming and Gardening*, designed to be the mouthpiece of his burgeoning organic crusade. Rodale did not invent the organic ideal; he was influenced by the British agricultural reformer Sir Albert Howard, and by the various American back-to-the-land advocates of the interwar years. Still, Jerome and, later, Robert Rodale outshined all others in their efforts to champion and popularize it. Jerome Rodale initially focused his critique on artificial fertilizers and his sense that these denatured chemical additives impoverished the soil and the health of those who consumed its products. His organic crusade thus began as a gospel of compost, a prophecy that the organic health of the soil was critical to personal health. But as the 1940s gave way to the 1950s, and as Robert joined his father in advocacy, the Rodales increasingly critiqued chemical pesticides as well. In doing so, the Rodales made a connection that would be critical to postwar environmentalism: that bodies and environments were intimately linked, and that fears for one's personal health could be powerful motivators for supporting environmental protection. As such, one could make a strong case that the Rodales ought to be much more prominent figures in the American environmental pantheon.

Andrew Case makes just such an argument in *The Organic Profit*, his fascinating cultural and environmental history of the Rodales and their publishing enterprises. But this is much more than a book about the origins of organic agriculture. Case is, in fact, more interested in the marketing side of the story, in how the Rodales organized and mobilized consumers to embrace the organic ideal for both reformist and lifestyle reasons. Case asks a series of questions about the relationship between business, consumerism, and environmental activism that could not be more relevant to us today. While the Rodales were principled leaders of the organic agriculture movement in the United States, they were also businessmen who sought to make money from their organic crusade and thus progenitors of today's organic marketplace. How, Case asks, do we make sense of the Rodales as prophets who sought to make profits? How do we assess an environmental movement that took corporate form? And what were the implications of anchoring efforts at systemic agricultural reform in a consumer movement that prized personal health and self-improvement?

Case convincingly argues that those Americans who responded to, and reshaped, the Rodale message, which cascaded forth in a steady stream of postwar publications, did so as both activists and as consumers. Case is no starry-eyed proponent of the power of green capitalism to change the world, and he can be incisively critical of consumerism as a path to meaningful environmental change. But he nonetheless insists that we have missed an important part of the story of the modern environmental movement by too quickly assuming that business and environmentalism are necessarily oppositional forces and that green consumerism is merely therapeutic escapism. As this history of the Rodales and their readers reveals, what Case aptly calls "marketplace environmentalism" is a much richer phenomenon.

While the Rodales hoped that they could directly influence modern agricultural production with their organic message—and Case suggests that they ultimately did with the sweeping if deeply compromised Organic Foods Production Act in 1990, which established the federal "organic" standards that we live with today—the more important part of their story is how they worked with and through consumers to push for reforms to the food system. As the Rodales built a publishing business, they forged an organic community not of alternative farmers but of health-conscious consumers. In building that community, the Rodales were not simply purveyors of information, and their readers were not merely passive consumers of it. Rodale publications—which included not only various iterations on *Organic Farming and Gardening* but also the company's more successful health magazine, *Prevention*—were forums in which readers could share their personal experiences, and the Rodales themselves constantly calibrated their message based on these interactions with readers.

As a result, the Rodales built a social movement by—to use the old saw of second-wave feminism—making the personal political. They pulled together and politicized a group of readers who initially experienced their anxieties about the postwar American food system in their bodies, their homes, and their gardens. For example, readers largely drove the growing alarm in Rodale publications about powerful pesticides and their potential health and environmental effects, preparing the seedbed for the sweeping critique of pesticides that Rachel Carson offered in *Silent Spring*. By highlighting the innovative organizational role played by the Rodales and their publications, Case gives to us a dynamic and politicized variant on green consumerism, one in which a business gave birth to an activist community. When readers subscribed to Rodale publications, or bought the carefully curated assortment of natural products advertised therein, they were not just making themselves feel better or defining themselves as particular kinds of consumers—they were also getting a purchase on political power.

Nonetheless, as Case brilliantly shows, the Rodale model for mobilizing citizen consumers had profound tensions at its core. Unlike most leaders of the postwar environmental movement, the Rodales were not scientific experts. They were aggregators and collators of the experiential and anecdotal who empowered consumer feelings and preferences and sowed a deep suspicion of expertise among their readership. Postwar American consumers had a right to be suspicious of experts at a moment when some of the most powerful products of modern science and medicine seemed to threaten human and environmental health. Indeed, environmentalism as a social movement thrived on a healthy skepticism of this powerful postwar scientific consensus. But the

Rodales empowered the impressionistic and the speculative in troubling ways, they showed only modest interest in scientific evidence or rigorous experimentation to support their organic prescriptions, and, in the process, they edged too easily into therapeutic quackery.

The consumer marketplace, it turns out, can be a poor arbiter of quality, of what is true and what is effective, and therein lies one of the most powerful lessons of *The Organic Profit*: that marketplace environmentalism is as capable of producing conspiratorial anti-vaccine activism or championing unproven and ineffectual health supplements as it is of challenging the indiscriminate use of dangerous pesticides or transforming the American food system. It is not that the consumer marketplace is structurally incapable of producing meaningful political activism. The Rodale story contains important examples to the contrary, as Case clearly demonstrates. Rather, the central lesson of *The Organic Profit* is that marketplace environmentalism—with its tensions between prophecy and profit, universal scientific truth and individual consumer experience, the public world of political engagement and the private world of self-improvement—is as mercurial as it is full of potential.

In the end, Andrew Case wisely resists giving us either of the two stories that we might expect from a study of the Rodales: a triumphant narrative of heroic prophets moving the organic ideal from the fringes to the mainstream, or a declensionist narrative in which a business enterprise profits from encouraging banal consumer self-realization. Instead, Case insists that the Rodales gave us something messier and more profound: a marketplace environmentalism in which business leaders and citizen consumers together built an organic community as capable of achieving political reform as it was susceptible to misguided therapeutic nostrums. The Rodales and their publications, by launching both an organic movement and an organic marketplace, tried to convince Americans that improving themselves and improving the world could be complementary activities. *The Organic Profit* is an admirably critical engagement with that project that, paradoxically, may help to redeem it in the end.

ACKNOWLEDGMENTS

This book exists due to the generosity of a number of colleagues, scholars, as well as friends and family. At the University of Wisconsin–Madison, I had the good fortune of working with Bill Cronon, whose inexhaustible kindness has been a model for me as a teacher, scholar, and citizen. Bill saw the potential for this project from the beginning, and although a reader will not find Bill cited anywhere, it is safe to say his ideas and influence run through every one of these pages. Likewise, Nan Enstad's enthusiasm and insights into cultural history were crucial to this project. From its earliest incarnation as a thesis about the fluoridation, Gregg Mitman has been generous with his guidance, feedback, and friendship. I would like to thank Susan Lederer and the late James Baughman for their contributions as well.

At the University of Washington Press, Marianne Keddington-Lang was an early champion of this project, and Regan Huff and Catherine Cocks helped steer the manuscript toward completion. Paul Sutter's comments and kind encouragement have been invaluable—this book is far clearer and more compelling as a result of his efforts. Thank you as well to two outside readers and their much-needed critiques. The research at the core of this book could not have been completed without the assistance of staff members of the Rodale company, particularly Mark Kintzel. Thank you as well to Carlton Jackson, who wrote the first book on J. I. Rodale that J. I. did not write himself.

I am immensely proud to call this book a product of the Center for Culture, History, and Environment at UW–Madison. Over the years I enjoyed many great conversations (and afternoon jams) with Andrew Stuhl, Rob Emmett, Mitch Aso, Brian Hamilton, Kellen Backer, Alex Nading, Rachel Gross, and many more. Conversations—and ongoing friendships—with Todd Dresser, Kendra Howard, Amrys Williams, and Anna Zeide were also formative to this project. Thanks also to Crystal Marie Moten, Jennifer Holland, Libby Tronnes, Charles Hughes, Doug Kiel, and Megan Raby for tackling the draftiest of drafts.

Various parts of this book have been presented to audiences both large and small. Panels at the American Society for Environmental History, the Association for the History of Medicine, the Business History Association, and many others were central to the development of this project. I would also like to thank Roger Horowitz and the Hagley Library's Research Seminar for a fruitful conversation about my work. Likewise, thanks to everyone over the years who has asked a kind (or even an unkind) question about this book or shared a story about their own garden or told me about a family member who used to clip articles from *Prevention*.

There are many friends both near and far who deserve thanks as well. I miss not being able to walk two blocks to visit Vanessa and Adi Walker-Gordon, but I have happily followed them to Haifa, New Orleans, Cincinnati, and Amherst to enjoy their company. Danny and Jillian Festa remain good friends I wish I could see all the time. Abby Neely helped me confirm that tea and fig bars are the secret ingredients to writing, and that friends, roasted vegetables, and bourbon create a balanced approach to scholarly life. Family dinners with Abby, Todd, and Amrys on Mifflin Street will always be fond memories. Aaron Ruesch used to listen to me ramble about fluoride and organic food, and still humors me in some of my digressions. It is not entirely accidental that I chose to write a book that took me back to Pennsylvania, if only for a brief time. While they are not sure what I was doing in college all those years, Rob Hain, Jerry Hain, and Marthe Chensel make it a pleasure to come back home.

Over many years my family has provided gentle encouragement even when I would have rather not talked about "how that book was going." Thanks to my sister, Sarah Reigel, and her family. My mother, Shahan McCracken, might not admit it, but she once owned a copy of *Stocking Up*, so she bears some responsibility for inspiring this book. She and George McCracken have been unfailing in their support, and I love them for it. I am also immensely grateful to my grandmother Stella McIntyre for her example of a life well lived. Thanks also to my extended family—Jim and Cathy Sommerfeld, Lisa and Carl Schultz, and Rod and Cathy Case.

This book and so much more would not be a reality without my wife, Amanda Sommerfeld. Amanda has lived with the ideas in this book over many meals and during many miles on trail. Her relentless pursuit of a more equitable world, her love for life, her love for learning, and her patience have inspired me to "get behind the mule" on many days when I would have rather not. We might struggle to keep plants alive in our own garden, but we have cultivated a life together and started growing a family of our own with the addition of our wondrous daughter, Lena. With buckets of love and gratitude, this book is dedicated to them.

NOTE TO READERS

Readers should know that in researching and writing this history, several barriers limited what this book could and could not uncover. The unpublished papers of J. I. and Robert Rodale and the archives of the Rodale company are not currently available to the public, but I was given an unprecedented amount of access with the help of Rodale staff and associates of the Rodale family. The papers of both J. I. and Robert are housed in a private family archive in Emmaus, Pennsylvania, but they were not cataloged, which made finding correspondence and specific materials a considerable challenge. I was unable to use this archive freely, but boxes of materials that J. I. Rodale had collected for his own autobiography, the company's extensive clippings files, documents from the firm's Federal Trade Commission trial, its pamphlet collection, and its remarkable in-house library were made available to me. Because detailed information about subscribers and the company's finances were not made available, any financial details described here comes from published accounts. Readers should also know that at no point have I asked for or received any funding for this research from the Rodale family or the Rodale company nor have they asked to review any of the research or writing for this book. The company has generously permitted republication of the images in this book.

THE ORGANIC PROFIT

BACK TO THE GARDEN, THROUGH THE MARKET

ON A WARM EVENING IN NEW YORK CITY IN JUNE 1971, J. I. RODALE sweated nervously as he waited to go on stage. The seventy-two-year-old was no stranger to the streets of Manhattan, but this experience was something new. Rodale was about to be a guest on Dick Cavett's television show; he was stepping into the bright lights after years of waiting in the wings. He had been invited on the show because he had just been featured in a cover story of the *New York Times Magazine*, and because the subjects he had spent the last thirty years promoting—natural health, organic food, and farming—were making headlines across the country in the early 1970s.

With his bushy beard and dark glasses, the slight-statured and neatly dressed Rodale was sharp-witted, self-deprecating, and idiosyncratic. He was, for the lack of a better term, a character. He could talk a blue streak about what sugar did to the mind and what natural food could do for the health of the body. He made acerbic claims about what doctors thought of his ideas and declared he had been ahead of the times in writing about the dangers of chemicals in food and medicine. Since he began writing and publishing in the 1930s, he had churned out books about matters like the merits of hawthorne berries and self-financed a theater company to produce his own allegorical plays about good health. All the while, he maintained a wry sense of

Jerome Irving (J. I.) Rodale (1898–1971), n.d. Courtesy of the Rodale Family Archives.

humor that gave away his ethnic roots in the Jewish enclave of New York's Lower East Side.

In print, as on television, J. I. Rodale could happily play the charming health nut, but his work was also serious business. Since the 1940s his company, the Rodale Press, had produced the magazines *Organic*

Gardening and Farming and *Prevention* as well as scores of books about natural methods of gardening and health. Even as he made wisecracks, Rodale also called attention to the potential hazards of artificial chemicals that were seeping into daily life in the decades after 1945. Scrutinizing the safety of fertilizers and pesticides, Rodale questioned how these substances might be accreting in plants, foods, bodies, and the broader environment. He did not simply ring alarm bells; he told his readers how to protect themselves, and how to change their lives by gardening, eating, and living more naturally. Remarkably, Rodale began writing about the hazards of synthetic chemicals two decades before these issues entered the national spotlight with the publication of Rachel Carson's *Silent Spring* and the emergence of the environmental movement in the 1960s.

Yet J. I. Rodale would have been hard to peg as part of the environmental vanguard of the Earth Day generation. Not only had he grown up in the tenements of New York City, but he lacked any education or training in farming or ecology and had only a layperson's education in scientific matters. Before he became a publisher and natural health "guru," he was an electrical parts manufacturer who ran a company that made products like lamps, switches, and fuses. He was more comfortable as a man of business than as a man of the great outdoors. He did not crusade for wild spaces or fight to protect ecosystems, but instead worked to change the more personal landscapes of the body through eating and health practices. Whether by consuming vitamins and supplements or by developing habits that safeguarded the body from chemicals, he argued that natural methods were the path toward a better version of the *self*.

J. I. Rodale also stands out from other leading environmental figures because his passion also produced a corporate enterprise. Unlike many environmental reformers, his mission to make modern life more natural was fundamentally a commercial one. He and his publishing company cultivated a niche for natural health products in the 1950s, helped organize the emerging marketplace for organic foods in the 1960s, and produced an endless supply of advice books on diet and health in the process. That mission was taken up and expanded by J. I. Rodale's son, Robert, who would lead the family publishing company through its remarkable growth and expansion into a media powerhouse in the

1970s and 1980s. Over the years, the publications of the Rodale Press created a space where natural health *ideas* and natural *products* could find one another, and where reforming the environment began at the checkout counter. That distinct legacy of advocacy and profitability remains today. Still led by Rodale's heirs, the firm supports a nonprofit institute that serves as a hub for research in sustainable food systems. At the same time, the company grosses over $500 million each year with magazines like *Men's Health, Women's Health, Runner's World, Prevention,* the venerable *Organic Gardening,* and a still-unending supply of advice books that teach consumers how to feel better, live longer, and how to make their homes and their bodies more natural.[1]

Looking back from our own time in the early twenty-first century, when it is a popular aphorism of the "green" economy that a company should make a profit while also helping the environment, it can be hard to recognize just how far out of the mainstream the Rodales once were. The type of consumer-centered advice that used to fill the columns of Rodale magazines in the 1950s and 1960s today packs books, blogs, and websites that instruct Americans in how to clean their homes, freshen their breath, and live their lives without relying on artificial chemicals. Moreover, just as Rodale magazines were once filled with ads for natural supplements and compost kits, today's "green" consumer media is fused with an array of products. From green-lifestyle mavens who endorse products for their followers on social media to natural health activists sponsored by organic food companies, the marketplace for advice about what to do and what to buy to make your life more natural is more abundant than ever.

My guess is that this landscape—the consumer one—is one most readers have experienced—after all, this landscape is where many Americans today most often find themselves making choices that reflect their environmental values and their health concerns. What foods to eat, what type of personal care products to buy, what type of lives to live are increasingly how those of us in the more privileged corners of the world choose to enact our values, including our environmental values. In this way, on top of alerting us to the merits of compost and the evils of white sugar, the Rodales are timely guides for understanding the green marketplace that surrounds us today. Ultimately, the story of J. I. Rodale, Robert Rodale, and the company that bears their name demonstrates how far "green" entrepreneurs and consumers have come over the decades, as well as the limits of the marketplace as an agent of systematic environmental reform.

The Rodale story helps us make more sense of the green consumerism and green businesses of our time, but it also helps widen the scope we use to understand the environmental movement's history. For some time now scholars have been working to show that environmentalism's history in postwar America should not be limited just to those activists and scientists who fought to protect wild lands and natural resources.[2] Scholars now frequently point to a range of "environmentalisms" that emerged from varying political and social groups as well as a range of different environmental concerns. Indeed, to speak of environmentalism as a movement sparked solely by Rachel Carson's *Silent Spring* or a single turning point like a particular oil spill or Earth Day 1970 is now passé among scholars. Yet there is still more work to be done in expanding our understanding of environmentalism and its complexities. Toward that end, the story of the Rodales and their readers helps further incorporate other figures, other concerns, and other avenues for reform into the stories we tell about environmentalism's emergence. The publication and public reaction to *Silent Spring* was undoubtedly a pivotal moment. But Carson and the debate over synthetic chemicals did not come from nowhere. The Rodale story provides some important context to where consumer concerns about chemicals came from and at the same time puts a focus on how both commerce and sometimes-questionable personal health anxieties shaped environmental sentiments in the postwar years. Environmentalism undoubtedly relied on the insights of ecological science, but as in the marketplace it often elevated personal experience over scientific evidence. The Rodales—as well their devoted army of composters and natural health enthusiasts—help us add a vital yet often neglected layer to the fuller picture of the multiple and often conflicted ways environmentalism emerged in postwar America.

But the case made by this book is not simply that we should add the Rodale company's logo to environmentalism's "Hall of Fame." We also need to take seriously the *type* of environmentalism the Rodales promoted and explore it as a site of critical inquiry. Although environmental historians have long argued that consumer society explains the emergence of environmentalism in the postwar era, a focus on social movements and political action has often obscured how the consumer marketplace served as a site of environmental thought and action. Likewise, historians have generally depicted businesses as foils to environmentalism. Following the Rodales and their company over the decades reveals how they, along with their readers, crafted a marketplace environmentalism that provided an open space for critiquing material ecology, contesting scientific and medical understandings of health and the environment, and creating personal styles of living that reflected changing environmental values.[3] Marketplace environmentalism did not emerge solely from a business or a group of consumers, but instead from those two entities working in tandem. The Rodale story demonstrates that the marketplace—created by a firm *and* its consumers—was not a sideshow to the "real" environmental reform of social and political movements, but a site where Americans navigated the changing ecology of daily life in the postwar decades. To fold the marketplace into our understanding of environmentalism's past requires taking seriously the types of ideas, products, and practices that circulated through Rodale's commercial universe as places of environmental thought and action.

Of course, taking that marketplace seriously does not mean ignoring its faults. The Rodale Press deserves credit for giving a voice to "little old ladies in tennis shoes," whose concerns were often disregarded by medical and scientific experts. But the company's publications also fostered a popular marketplace of ideas, products, and personalities that frequently strained credulity. The great virtue of marketplace environmentalism, for both businesses and consumers, was that it did not require a PhD or peer-reviewed results to gain entry. Yet that virtue also proved to be its vice. If the Rodales helped make compost bins and organic foods part of daily life for those concerned about the environment, they also helped make an ocean of nutritional advice and waves of diet regimens and lifestyle choices of questionable scientific merit part of environmentalism as well. The Rodales and their readers staked out the garden, the home, and the body as front lines for resisting environmental harms, but they did so by often elevating firsthand experience and folkloric knowledge production over scientific evidence. The Rodales used their magazines and the marketplace as tools for carving out a critique of agricultural and medical science in the 1950s and 1960s, but they did so by foregrounding personal choice over public health. In this way, the Rodale story highlights the dissonance between environmental concerns addressed in the marketplace and the normative values defined by the expert world of environmental science and policy. That dissonance now rattles through environmental and health issues ranging from childhood vaccination, to genetically modified crops, to raw milk. And that tension—between the consensus of the marketplace and that of science—has been a shaping force in environmentalism's history rather than just a by-product of the age of social media.

In addition to helping us widen the scope of environmentalism's history and developing the marketplace as a vital if contested site of environmental thought and action, the Rodale story also challenges some common assumptions about the history of green consumerism. Scholars and critics point to organic foods and natural health-products as evidence of how late twentieth-century consumers sought to insulate themselves personally rather than reform the environment more broadly. The sociologist Andrew Szasz has developed the notion of "inverted quarantine" to suggest that consumers in the 1980s and 1990s adopted natural products to shelter their bodies at the expense of larger reforms. Julie Guthman has argued that the embrace of organic foods and other "green" consumption habits in recent decades has been the result of an ideology of "healthism" that doubles as a method of policing acceptable social, economic, racial, and bodily norms.[4] In showing how the Rodales taught consumers how to use natural products to protect an idealized notion of their own bodies and their own backyards, this book largely agrees with those critical assessments. Yet the Rodale story demonstrates that there was also a form of power in the marketplace, which emerges when we view both the company and its consumers in historical context. Rodale's readers and subscribers used the company's publications as tools to buy books, gardening widgets, and nutritional supplements that could help them create natural oases out of their bodies and homes. They also used the marketplace to develop a network of what the historian Lawrence Glickman has called "long-distance solidarity."[5]

For many organic and natural health enthusiasts, J. I. Rodale was a prophet and pioneer who raised a cautionary flag about chemicals in both foods and daily life more broadly. For his detractors, Rodale and his company put an all-natural veneer on selling untested health advice. The tension between those perspectives is captured by the title of this book, *The Organic Profit*. The title's corny play on words is not just an homage to J. I. Rodale and his humor, it captures two divergent ways of seeing both Rodale and marketplace environmentalism. The Rodale Press advanced important critiques of the modern food system and its impact on human health and the environment. But the company also learned how to sell consumers on the promises of natural foods and health and made money from its environmental commitments. *The Organic Profit* asks readers to see the Rodales and their marketplace as a complex and overlooked part of the history of environmentalism. Rather than simply venerating or debunking, this book centers on the tension—between the mission of a prophet and the motive of profits— to highlight both the possibilities *and* the limits of the marketplace the Rodales created.

For the most part historians have had little to say about J. I. Rodale or the type of environmentalism that flourished in his company's publications. Historians of science and medicine in the 1970s and 1980s viewed the Rodales as contemporary examples of the food and health faddism that has cycled through American culture since the nineteenth century.[6] More recently, J. I. Rodale's status as the "apostle of the compost heap" has become less of an insult and more of an honorific. Rodale received favorable mention in Michael Pollan's best-selling books about food in the mid-2000s, and popular attention to issues of food, health, and the environment in the past decade has certainly made the ideas the Rodales promoted in the middle of the twentieth century seem perhaps not so faddish after all.[7]

Signaling this changing perspective, more scholars have been exploring both Rodale and the history of organic food, farming, and natural health.[8] Yet much of the scholarship on the history of the organic movement suffers from what Paul Sutter has characterized in his history of the wilderness movement as a "detached idealism," where an overriding sense of the movement's inherent rightness obscures the more complex and contingent nature of its past. In much the same way that historians once assumed "wilderness" was an enlightened idea whose key proponents had the gift of prescience, many assume that early enthusiasts like J. I. Rodale were visionaries who grasped the deep truth of an idea.[9] However, ideas like "organic," "natural," "green," or "sustainable" are—like any other analytical categories—not ahistorical, platonic ideals whose "rightness" has been steadily uncovered, but ideas and categories that have been created, contested, and changed over time.

But the Rodale story is not just about organic food and farming. It is also about the broader array of products, practices, and ideas that circulated in what we now call the "green" marketplace. The Rodale story demonstrates that green consumption's impact runs deeper than marketers responding to the arrival of the baby boomers in the 1980s with their credit cards and running shorts. Green consumption was not simply an outgrowth of the environmental turn of the late 1960s and 1970s, but a formative element of that turn as well.[10] More recent historical assessments of green consumerism carve out a prominent place for J. I. Rodale. Increasingly, both Rodale and the early organic movement constitute a space where postwar environmentalists adopted consumerism to "shelter from the storm of corporate capitalism."[11] Yet even when such analyses have taken Rodale seriously as a formative voice in green consumerism, they have often done so by neglecting Rodale's commercial aims and the commercial context within which the Rodale Press operated.

Likewise, even the best assessments of the organic marketplace's history mistake Rodale as a visionary agriculturalist and leader of a social movement who undertook a "sacred mission" to put society on a path toward an "organic nirvana."[12] Not only does that type of interpretation parrot Rodale's own depiction of himself as a visionary prophet, it is frankly difficult to square with the fact that Rodale owned an electrical manufacturing company throughout the years he produced his writings about soils and health. J. I. Rodale rarely, if ever, placed his hands in the soil, and the very ground of his own business would later become an EPA Superfund site. Moreover, many assessments often hold Rodale's words about soils in high esteem while ignoring the dubious natural products and advice—indeed the quackery—that Rodale also circulated. Few, if any, scholars have investigated *Prevention* or the business side of the Rodale firm, or explored how these pioneers of organic gardening were also pioneers in the marketing of books, magazines, and lifestyle trends. Some have been eager to sanctify Rodale's organic critique without critically considering his links to a more questionable history of popular health reform. Rodale can certainly be discussed alongside Aldo Leopold as a visionary of ecological agriculture, but we need to also consider what he and his company had in common with the likes of Bernarr Macfadden and Charles Atlas. Most analyses do not consider J. I. Rodale's other writings and pay little attention to the link between *Men's Health* and *Organic Gardening and Farming*. Fully understanding Rodale and his impact on environmentalism means not ignoring his links to health faddism, which earlier historians highlighted. Viewed together, those parts of the story reveal the tension between the profits of businesses and the desire for environmental reform that rests at the heart of the green marketplace today.

Scholars have also generally given short shrift to J. I.'s son, Robert, who dropped out of college at age nineteen to take over as editor of what was then called *Organic Gardening* and became president of the company in 1954. In the 1950s J. I. was focused on *Prevention* and many other endeavors, while Robert and other editors did the work of producing stories about compost each month and keeping readers engaged. Robert steered the publishing company toward profitability in the late 1950s and fought off attempts by the Federal Trade Commission to restrict the company's operations in the 1960s. It was also Robert who cemented his father's legacy as a prophet by untangling organic methods from some of J. I.'s more questionable ideas and moving the company and organic foods toward mass-market success. Focusing on Robert Rodale in addition to the company and its readers helps widen the lens beyond the funny food faddist who appeared on Dick Cavett's television show in 1971. Scholars are increasingly enriching our understanding of green entrepreneurship as something that originated well before the 1990s, and Robert Rodale was a key figure among those "who believed business could help create a more sustainable world."[13] Robert applied his company's profits to develop and sustain research in organic methods and made his company's operations a reflection of his organic living philosophy. Likewise, this broader focus brings the marketplace into the frame and opens it up as a site for critical inquiry.

The Rodale story also demonstrates how the environmental effects of businesses in the twentieth century were not limited to resources consumed and wastes emitted into the environment. Scholars are increasingly interested in "analyzing the business response to environmental challenges"; while the Rodales did not pioneer sustainable practices in the publishing industry, we can view them as important precursors for today's green capitalists.[14] A firm like Rodale certainly printed tons of glossy paper and mountains of direct-mail circulars that ended up in landfills, but the story told here points less to material flows of natural resources and more to flows of information that defined the emergence of the late twentieth-century knowledge economy. Rodale's history thus suggests that the interface between a firm and the environment can be not only material, but cultural as well.[15]

Rodale's marketplace environmentalism ultimately bears the distinct marks of the postindustrial chemical and nuclear age that Ulrich Beck labeled the "risk society." The risk society emerged in the decades after 1945 in places like the United States and other developed countries where concerns about the "dark sides of progress" came to outweigh concerns about the equitable distribution of the benefits of industrial society.[16] In products of the Rodale Press we can see a commercial culture of the risk society sustained in the most benign of places: gardening books, natural food stores, self-help manuals, and direct-mail circulars.[17] Importantly, even as they argued for simpler, more natural ways of living and the value of firsthand experience, these are not texts that sought an outright rejection of modernity. J. I. and Robert Rodale could certainly be skeptical and ambivalent about some of the defining features of modernity—science, technology, biomedicine, and expertise—but they relied on the very modern tools of mass media and consumer culture to spread their critique and to create their community of consumers. Similarly, even if they were uneasy with some parts of modern capitalism, the Rodales and their company were a part of capitalism's order and the consumption habits on which that system has been sustained.

One caveat to bear in mind is that even as these texts challenged the material ecology of the postwar world, they, along with marketplace environmentalism, were also highly selective about the risks addressed. The Rodales and their readers feared the pesticides that rained down from airplanes over the landscape, but had less to say about the farm workers who labored below. Devoted readers relied on Rodale's advice to avoid the doctor, but likely not because they lacked health insurance. The company crafted its products to reflect the anxieties of middle- and upper-class consumers who could afford not just vitamins, but special types of naturally produced vitamins. To put it more simply, these were anxieties of those who could afford to join the marketplace. Like much of the green marketplace in our own time, the Rodales and their readers are generally silent about the persistent social and economic inequalities that influenced *whose* homes and *whose* bodies were most at risk due to environmental hazards.

The chapters of this book roughly flow from decade to decade, from the late 1930s through the early 1990s, with the lives of J. I. and Robert Rodale alongside turning points in postwar environmentalism. The first chapter introduces the question of how an accountant and owner of an electrical manufacturing company first aspired to become a reformer of agriculture and human health. By exploring J. I. Rodale's early publishing efforts in the 1930s and how he turned to readers to help develop the organic method in the 1940s, the chapter highlights how the world of publishing provided Rodale with an avenue to become a soil reformer and to carve out a space for himself and his firm.

Chapter 2 introduces readers to the overlooked history of *Prevention* magazine and the making of a marketplace in the 1950s and 1960s for ideas and products that fell outside of mainstream medical understandings of health, nature, and the body. *Prevention* reflected J. I. Rodale's interest in personal health and soon outstripped *Organic Gardening* as the firm's most important asset. The magazine housed a lively trade in all manner of natural accoutrement and provided a key outlet for natural vitamin sellers to reach their desired consumers. Yet that asset was also an Achilles' heel. In a trial that pitted the FTC against the Rodale company in the 1960s, both its advertising practices and the ability of the marketplace to challenge scientific consensus were put to the test.

If the early history of the Press turns on J. I. Rodale and his ideas, its evolution centers on Robert Rodale and the business strategies he adopted to grow the market over time. Robert took the reins of the company just as more and more Americans grew concerned about synthetic chemicals in the 1960s. As chapter 3 discusses, he turned *Organic Gardening and Farming* into a network for connecting readers across disparate locations. In this way, the marketplace provided an outlet for organic gardeners and allowed them to take their actions beyond their backyard compost piles. By the start of the 1970s, public awareness of environmental issues spawned an array of competitors for the Rodale Press. Chapter 4 demonstrates how the Press recast organic as a *style of living* and used new tools and technologies to secure its place among "green" consumers in an increasingly crowded marketplace. Chapter 5 concludes the book in the place where most scholars would begin the story of the green marketplace—the 1980s. The company generated a presence in the mass market in the 1980s, which it used to study and advocate for reforms of the nation's food system. At the same time, however, the company became increasingly centered on health and personal fitness as therapeutic methods for improving the body. The 1980s would ultimately reveal both the potential and the limits of the marketplace as a path for changing how foods were produced, distributed, and consumed.

Of course, by putting a spotlight on the Rodales, this narrative neglects others. There were untold numbers of activists, writers, scientists, growers, and organizers who also worked to draw attention to the impact of modern food production on the health of the human body and the natural world. Nonetheless the Rodales prove to be useful guides for helping us make sense of the commercial landscape we so frequently encounter in early twenty-first-century daily life. While flipping through a magazine or walking around the controlled environment of the supermarket today, it is nearly impossible *not* to notice the vast array of products telling consumers how to improve their consumption habits to benefit both themselves and the environment. Likewise, more and more businesses describe themselves as driven by a mission of environmental reform. This is the landscape that the Rodales help us understand. It is not a landscape of prairies and bison, or old-growth trees and reintroduced wolves; it is not a sublime mountain or a tropical Eden. It is the landscape of glossy magazine covers at the checkout counter, it is mail-order books full of natural gardening and home-improvement advice, it is the aisles devoted to organic foods, natural vitamin supplements, and the businesses whose products promise to help us fight global warming. Even with his hoary jokes and exhortations about bone meal and liver tablets and books about sleeping positions and white sugar and maintaining a healthy prostate, J. I. Rodale has something to teach us about how ideas and products brought together a community of consumers.

Likewise, Robert Rodale's understated cultivation of green consumers and their changing interests, not to mention his marketing skills, helps us see how organic became as much about a *style* of living as a type of food to consume. The Rodale Press was certainly not alone in the lively commerce of environmental awareness in the second half of the twentieth century, but its history is one of the best guides for which we could ask. The Rodales blazed a trail for taking Americans back to the garden—a trail that wound its way through the marketplace.

ONE

PAY DIRT

Making a Method and a Market

ON DECEMBER 15, 1950, J. I. RODALE TRAVELED FROM EMMAUS, PENN-
sylvania, to Washington, DC, to testify before a congressional committee investigating chemicals in food products. In less than a decade,
Rodale had made a name for himself by founding a magazine on farming
and gardening without chemicals and publishing three books on the
relationship between soils and health. With these credentials, Rodale
presented himself to the committee as the leader of the organic movement in the United States, which was still in its infancy in the early 1950s.
The committee, commonly referred to as the Delaney Commission after
James Delaney, the House member who led the hearings, was charged
with investigating the safety of chemicals used in food production. The
first testimony of the day came from the widow of Harvey J. Wiley, the
former head of the Food and Drug Administration and one of the pioneers of the early twentieth century's battle against adulterated substances in foods and drugs.[1] Mrs. Wiley was followed by Dr. William J.
Darby, a biochemist and nutritionist from Vanderbilt University who
represented the American Medical Association's Council on Food and
Nutrition. The council, formed in 1931, had been concerned about chemical additives in foods for some time according to Darby, but had only
recently been forced to grapple with the "importance and immensity of
the problem," given the rapid rate of new additives introduced to food
production after 1945.[2] Following Dr. Darby was Eugene W. Brockenbrough, president of the Institute of Shortening and Edible Oils, a trade

association of refiners and producers of food oils, who argued that some of the new chemical emulsifiers being used as bread softeners had not been adequately tested for their "complete harmlessness."[3]

Despite the fact that Rodale called himself the leader of the *organic* movement, given how new the use of that term was with respect to food and farming and given Rodale's background, many members of the committee surely had never heard of his ideas or the movement he claimed to represent. By the end of the 1940s, Rodale had a monthly readership of around sixty thousand subscribers, but his name was largely unknown outside the rarified set of gardeners who adopted his ideas about gardening with composts. He began his prepared statement by describing how he had learned about the organic method by reading the work of British agricultural reformer Sir Albert Howard, and how, after seeing the remarkable results on his own farm, he decided to publish a magazine to tell others. "The purpose of my talk," he told the commission, "is to show that it seems that science today has only one ammunition. That is chemicals. What the reason for that is open to conjecture but there are other things that are being neglected."[4]

What was being neglected, Rodale felt, was attention to the quality of foods raised with the use of chemical fertilizers versus those raised with biologic or *organic* matter added to the soil. Rodale told the committee he recognized Howard as the first scientist to question how food was raised. Physicians, he claimed, "up to this time took food as an accomplished fact, studying carbohydrates and proteins and vitamins and calories, but never questioning whether a carrot was grown in a cinder bank or in highly fertile soil."[5] He added that, given all the data he had accumulated over the last decade, there was undoubtedly "something to" how organic methods improved the health of soils, as well as the plants, animals, and humans nourished from those soils. Rodale stated that his purpose was not to argue for any legislation, but to advocate for a series of tests at agricultural colleges and experiment stations to research the organic method alongside those fertilizers synthesized by chemists. Closing with a note of warning about the state of the nation's health, he reminded the committee of the weak state of draft-eligible men just as the country was going to war in Korea.[6]

Rattling off facts and figures about soils and nutrients in front of a congressional committee as the editor of *Organic Gardening* magazine and the president of the esteemed-sounding Soil and Health Foundation, Rodale likely hoped that his audience would forgive the fact that he was an outsider in the world of agricultural and nutritional science—and lacked any training in science at all—but that was not the case. The hearings treated neither J. I. Rodale nor his claims about growing foods with organic methods as serious matters. Although Chairman Delaney expressed interest in the subject and commended Rodale as a "pioneer," other members of the committee were less considerate. When the committee turned to asking him questions, rather than debating whether organic matter could be applied at large scales or questioning the health effects of consuming organic food, they focused on Rodale's shaky credentials and expertise. Congressman Thomas Abernathy, after pointing out that Rodale had only bought his farm in 1940, asked if he had any other training in the field of agriculture other than what he had learned by owning a farm. Abernathy went on to outline salient points in Rodale's biography: how he had grown up in New York City and worked as an accountant, and how he had written the "word finder" books in the 1930s. Abernathy asserted that Rodale's principal experience had been in the editing and accounting field, "and the manufacture of electric wire." Knowing he was being disregarded, Rodale defended himself as "a man of general intelligence" and claimed that Abernathy's attempt to belittle him would only provide fuel to opponents of the organic method.[7]

The congressman's attempt to take Rodale down a peg reflected how agricultural scientists and policy makers viewed organic ideas. Yet Abernathy's question about how Rodale got *here*—in front of Congress, testifying about matters of soils, science, and nutrition, and as the publisher of a magazine and the self-styed leader of a "movement" to reform food production—touched on an abiding and important question. What had in fact brought J. I. Rodale and his ideas about soils and health to *this* place?

Rodale made a name for himself as a reformer of food and agriculture not by racking up academic credentials or running for public office, but by using the tools of the marketplace. Building on his acumen and his interest in self-improvement regimes, Rodale ventured into publishing in the late 1930s and early 1940s to make a name for himself and to market his ideas about health. The marketplace lent Rodale a foothold for entering a larger debate about soils and health, and it gave him the tools to bring his readers together into a nascent movement. Crucially, those connections also gave him the means to gather and develop evidence from the experience of readers. Without access to research laboratories and agricultural experiment stations, which were closed off by scientists and policy makers uninterested and at times hostile to organic ideas, the marketplace offered Rodale and the earliest generation of organic enthusiasts a method for attempting to create a science of their own.

A focus on Rodale's early life and his path to becoming an agricultural reformer demonstrates how the marketplace offered a forum for views about nature and health that fell outside of, and challenged, scientific consensus in the mid-twentieth century. The organic ideal that Rodale promoted contrasted with prevailing scientific opinion about agriculture and how to improve both crops and agricultural production. By the early 1940s, when J. I. Rodale became interested in agriculture, agricultural researchers in the United States had spent decades exploring how improved crop varieties, mechanization, and the application of synthetic fertilizers could boost agricultural production. The organic ideal emerged in the 1940s as a reaction to these trends, even as agriculture was on the cusp of adopting an even more potent set of chemical tools to protect crops from insects. Indeed, by suggesting that farms could produce food without relying on the tools of chemistry, Rodale's organic ideal was anathema to the consensus of agricultural science and the industry it supported. Furthermore, by questioning how foods raised with chemical fertilizers might be producing poorer human health, Rodale and his readers confronted established understandings of the body and the natural world. In this way, *Organic Gardening* proved to be more than a monthly magazine full of gardening tips. It was a site where Rodale made a name for himself and where his ideals, despite being anathema to agricultural science, could be tested— in both the backyard and the marketplace.

YOU CAN'T EAT THAT

J. I. Rodale began his life in a place where we might least expect a reformer of health and agriculture to come from: the crowded enclave of New York City's Lower East Side. Born in 1898 as the child of immigrants, Rodale knew firsthand the poverty and poor health that often went hand in hand in urban tenements of the early twentieth century. A childhood of bad health in an unhealthy environment lay at the root of Rodale's life story and how he would later narrate his unlikely journey toward being a champion of alternative ideas about soils and health. But the narrative of a "city man" who set out in search of health in the countryside does not explain how and why Rodale chose to become a publisher, writer, and agricultural reformer. To better understand that aspect of Rodale's story requires considering the mass culture of self-improvement in the early twentieth century, and how the marketplace of words and ideas provided a space for Rodale to craft himself as an entrepreneur. J. I. Rodale may have stumbled into debates about soils, but becoming a publisher was part of an ongoing process of making himself a man of both business as well as ideas.

It is difficult to find J. I. Rodale in the yearbook pages of DeWitt Clinton High School from 1913. He was not a particularly strong student or an athlete, and he was still known by his birth name, Jerome Cohen. He would later claim that it was his poor eyesight and illness that affected his grades in school. He also spent a great deal of his time studying for the rabbinate at the insistence of his father, which kept him inside much of the time and which he later felt had exacerbated his poor health. When his father passed away suddenly in 1914, Jerome was freed from the pressure of becoming a rabbi, but his father's death made the Cohen family's unsure finances all the more insecure and forced Jerome into sundry jobs in his high school years. One of these positions was as a stock runner on Wall Street, a job that sparked his interest in the world of finance and the nuances of markets. After completing school in 1916, Cohen held a series of jobs as a bookkeeper for small firms and briefly took night courses in accounting at New York University.[8] After a few classes, he began looking for full-time employment as an accountant and gained the bulk of his experience by taking care of the books for small firms. Decades later, as he became a public figure and critiqued agricultural and medical science, the fact that he did not hold a degree in accounting or any other subject would be a source of both pride and acrimony. His lack of professional credentials gave detractors a reason to dismiss his claims and at times label him a fraud.[9]

Jerome Cohen found avenues beyond the classroom where he could remake himself. Like many eager neophytes in the early twentieth century, what he could not find through formal education he found in consumer culture. Correspondence courses and study-at-home guides for subjects ranging from Western philosophy to shoe repair filled the back pages of popular magazines at the time. Targeting young immigrants and people like Jerome Cohen who lacked the means and access to higher education, mail-order firms sold the promise of both improved skills and respectability. Language courses were particularly prevalent, and many popular guides offered etiquette lessons for those trying to learn the century's rapidly changing social mores. Systems for improving the health of the body also filled the mail-order pages of magazines. Indeed, "popular health reform" in the early twentieth century consisted of an untold variety of dietary systems, exercise regimes, and schools of treatment for all manner of bodily ills and mental ailments. Pills and tonics had long been a staple of consumer culture, and at the end of the nineteenth century cheap magazines made offers for these types of self-improvement systems even more common.

Jerome Cohen was the type of consumer about whom advertisers of these systems dreamed. An avid reader of any and all materials he could get his hands on, Cohen recalled that he "was a great ad-answerer" for systems that could teach him how to be healthy and successful.[10] While still a high school student in 1915, he subscribed to the Alois P. Swoboda's system of "conscientious evolution" and sent twelve dollars for a "free" book claiming to improve mental and physical strength. The Swoboda system's exercise routine claimed to be easy on the heart and promised to develop both confidence and stamina, concerns that J. I. Rodale would later focus on in his health writing.[11] In his late teens and early twenties, he visited health clinics with names like the Neurological Institute and the Life Extension Institute. Never dogmatic about any particular system, he dropped routines as easily as he picked them up. In his twenties Cohen began what he called a "systematic quest" to find ways to improve his poor health. Years later he recalled, "I took up tennis and went at it like a demon, but all it did was give me a heart murmur. I then became a vegetarian, but that did not accomplish the task. Over the next twenty years I experimented with M.D.'s, osteopaths, chiropractors, Turkish baths, Swedish massage, diathermy, and everything else on the popular health agenda."[12] Each system of improvement invariably fell short of his hopes, and then, like many consumers of diet and health advice, he would turn to another.

His search for a system to improve his body came second only to Cohen's efforts to improve his capital position. Like young entrepreneurs before and after him, Cohen rolled the dice with a host of different moneymaking plans. In addition to working as an accountant in his late teens, Cohen bought and sold penny stocks and tried to turn vacant lots into investment properties. On more than one occasion he could not resist the mail-order ads for investment schemes that also filled the magazines and newspapers he read.[13] Like a failed diet regimen, his investment hopes often came up short, and he learned the hard way about the promises and perils of investing. After a handful of bad stock picks, Cohen adjusted his focus away from the quick-money ads and started reading financial newspapers and bulletins more closely. Beginning a process that would become central to how he digested, analyzed, and reproduced information, he clipped articles from financial papers and built an idiosyncratic system for indexing the clippings to help him make better-informed investments.[14]

Cohen gleaned a great deal about the world of business through his work as an accountant for small firms. That knowledge grew exponentially when he took a job with the recently created Internal Revenue Service and moved to Washington, DC, in 1919. While living in the nation's capital, Cohen carried on much like a bachelor of the time would be expected to—he lived in rooming houses, went to concerts and parks, traveled with friends to the outskirts of the city, danced waltzes, went to the circus, and spent a fair bit of his time and energy pursuing romantic interests. But Cohen's time was not all devoted to merrymaking. At work he pored over piles of audits at the IRS and studied the details and variations in investment strategies and their good and bad outcomes.[15] He frequently devoted his evenings to studying in the Library of Congress and schooled himself in the basics of corporate organization and the nuances of patent law. Jerome's letters from the time reveal that he was prone to a bit of dreamy woolgathering about his future prospects, but he was also busy making serious plans. It was at this time that Cohen concluded that despite his personal advancements, he would always be limited in the business world by his last name. Like many children of immigrant families, he decided that improving his prospects required casting off an old label and embracing an Anglicized replacement. Cohen settled on Rodale, a derivation of his mother's maiden name, Rouda.[16] Indeed, the name Rodale—which decades later became synonymous with the culture of self-improvement—was the product of Jerome Cohen's search for ways to better himself.

Cohen dove further into the world of business when he took a position with the accounting firm Robertson, Furman, and Murphy in Pittsburgh. In that city, Rodale worked as an accountant for several steel firms and for the first time found himself welcomed into the rarified rooms that overlooked the factory floor. Rubbing elbows with owners and financiers, Rodale later recalled fondly his interactions with the millionaires who employed him. In a scene that would not have been out of place in a Horatio Alger story in which a young boy learns that a captain of industry has a heart of gold, Rodale claimed he discovered that his impression of millionaires had been mistaken. From his humble origins in the immigrant warrens of Manhattan, Rodale had expected the worst of the wealthy mill owners but recalled that, instead, he "found millionaires as a class, insofar as I was privileged to know them, to be more humble, more pleasant and more democratic than the general public."[17] These industry leaders were also leaders in civil society who contributed to the advancements of the arts, sciences, and education—to the improvement of the country as a whole—something a young accountant full of dreams could only hope to emulate someday.

Rodale became a man of business in his own right when he returned to New York City in 1923 and joined his brother Joseph in a business venture. The firm he and his brother acquired, which they renamed the Rodale Manufacturing Company, made electric plugs, switches, sockets, and a variety of electrical wiring devices. The brothers chose the firm because they were speculating on the booming market for electrical appliances in the 1920s and found methods of cheaply copying and reproducing the products of other companies. Applying some of his self-acquired knowledge on the finer points of patent law, Rodale and his brother reverse engineered more electrical products than they created.[18] Before he sold magazines and books, the marketplace for consumer products made all his other pursuits possible.

As he settled into adulthood, Rodale's search for paths to improve himself expanded beyond the world of business. One area he hoped to make his mark was as a writer. Rodale married and started family with Anna Andrews in 1927, and consequently found he had more time to indulge his always-expansive set of reading interests and also tried his hand at writing.[19] In the early 1920s he had dashed off a few letters to the editor and even had a small pamphlet published by the National Association of Cost Accountants about adjusting taxes for wartime depreciation of equipment in steel mills. Yet, as he tried to become a writer, Rodale discovered he lacked "a way with words" and the verbal dexterity of his favorite authors. Just as he had taught himself about investing by scrutinizing manuals and company profiles before creating his own, Rodale approached improving his writing by systematically studying the words of others and eventually developing his own manual. Rodale became a writer by engaging in the most literal form of textual deconstruction. He physically cut words out of printed books and articles and arranged them around common verbs, eventually filling hundreds of envelopes with the clipped words. This process went on for the better part of a decade, eventually requiring the outside help of high school students and a professor from Muhlenberg College to complete the task. In 1937, Rodale published the results as *The Verb Finder*, which became the first in a line of thesaurus books that some writers still use to improve their prose.[20]

Rodale became more fully engaged in writing when he moved his family and his business to Allentown, Pennsylvania, in 1930. Like many firms in the early 1930s, the Rodale Manufacturing Company saw its sales decline precipitously after the market crash of 1929. In moving the firm out of New York, Jerome and his brother hoped they could lower their capital costs and operating expenses. The town of Emmaus, located a short distance from Allentown, sealed the deal for the firm with an offer of low rent on a shuttered silk mill downtown.[21] It is striking that Rodale sought to become a writer and publisher at a time when he had two young children and a business struggling through the Great Depression. The electrical business, however, bored Rodale. He would later write that his heart was with the company for its first three or four years in New York, but he found he could never devote 100 percent of his attention to the firm. Although being in business kept his feet "firmly planted on the ground," Rodale spent his spare time making his dream of writing and publishing a reality.[22] Shortly after moving to Emmaus in 1930, he published his first magazine, *The Humorous Scrapbook*, a digest of comical short stories and news clippings. Like many of his projects, the magazine was short-lived, and he soon tried again with another humor magazine, *The Clown*. After initially sending out his magazines to be printed, he soon acquired his own equipment for each stage of magazine production.[23] With extra space in the Rodale Manufacturing building and some minimal hired labor, he produced these magazines on a modest scale. Owning his own equipment made it easy to create a new title, send out a trial run, and then reformat or discontinue the title if it did not draw subscribers. In the years between 1935 and 1940 he had several magazines going at once, including *Fact Digest, Everybody's Digest, Biography, Science and Discovery, Health Guide, You Can't Eat That, You're Wrong about That, True Health Stories*, and *Modern Tempo*.[24]

Without exception, these were digest-style magazines pieced together from previously published material. As a genre, the digest magazine had existed for decades, but in the 1920s and 1930s *Reader's Digest* emerged as a nationwide mass-market publication that culled articles from other sources.[25] In addition to the convenience of pieces shortened for quick reading, the digest had several advantages over those that published original content. Not paying a staff of writers was one benefit, and a novice publisher like Rodale could select articles and reproduce them at little or no cost. Just as Rodale created his "word finder" system by literally cutting apart sentences in books, he spent hours clipping and marking up articles on any number of topics that formed the content of his magazines. These magazines enjoyed circulations of a few thousand, were always sold and advertised through the classifieds of penny papers, and frequently lost Rodale more money than they made him.

Rodale's publishing endeavors were more than just a hobby. Like those millionaires he had met in Pittsburgh who supported the arts and civic organizations, a writer and a publisher of even the most modest books and magazines produced something more significant than a set of electrical products. Then, as now, writing rarely produced actual capital, but the *cultural capital* of being a writer—or even just being thought

Contents

Table of contents from *The Writings of J. I. Rodale*, n.d. Rodale Press Pamphlet Collection. Courtesy of the Rodale Family Archives.

of as a writer—paid off in other ways. Even his prosaic digest magazines of the 1930s that retold old jokes and recycled true crime stories nonetheless gave Rodale a stake, however small, in the cultural economy of ideas. Rodale enjoyed corresponding with famous columnists and critics in asking permission to reprint their work. Something of an autograph hound, he carefully saved this correspondence as evidence of his efforts. With his credentials as a member of the press, he delighted in having full access to all the exhibits at the 1939 World's Fair in New York.[26] More than just a hobby, being a publisher, a writer, and person of ideas was a path that could open doors to places Rodale was eager to explore.

Whether they were spent assembling a digest magazine or study-ing how to reverse engineer an electrical appliance, the years before J. I. Rodale became a reformer of soils are telling. Just as ads in the back pages of magazines created avenues for self-improvement, so, too, did the market for digest magazines give Rodale a place to remake himself. With his accounting skills, Rodale knew how to combine his idiosyn-cratic pursuits with systematic rigor, and the marketplace offered opportunities that were otherwise closed off to him. Like a character in the Horatio Alger novels he loved, publishing and writing showed that he could improve himself not only through his "pluck" on the factory floor but also by staying up late at night and devoting himself to science and the finer points of the liberal arts. Making a mark for himself—in the business world and the world of ideas—was a goal that J. I. Rodale would not give up easily. Reforming agriculture and health may have been an unlikely pursuit for a kid from the Lower East Side, but in the midcentury debate about soils and health, Rodale saw an opportunity to remake soils and himself.

THE ORGANIC FRONT

To say that the world changed in the 1940s would be an understate-ment. From the horrors of a war that transformed lives and landscapes around the globe, to the revival of the US economy after the Depres-sion of the 1930s, to the rearrangement of global power and the new realities of the atomic age—few things looked or felt the same at the end of the decade as they did at the start. The 1940s also augured a transformation in the material ecology of daily life. New synthetic materials that had been developed during the war years made their way into consumer goods, and pesticides and fertilizers along with a host of new materials transformed how foods were grown and produced in the United States. Whether they were designed to boost nitrogen in soils or kill off pests, these new chemicals helped American farmers produce more food than ever before and facilitated new advances in food processing and preservation.

Those chemical tools helped further transform the very structure of the agricultural economy as well as its impact on environments and farming communities. By the middle decades of the twentieth century, the American farm economy was well on its way toward larger and larger growing operations that relied on fossil-fueled machines and chemical tools more than the work of human muscles. In decades to come, the majority of farms would look less and less like those small, diversified, and family-run operations that surrounded J. I. Rodale in Pennsylvania Dutch Country, and more and more like the large-scale monocultures of California's Central Valley. Chemicals and machines allowed farms to raise their productivity and squeeze more out of every acre of land, leaving smaller producers unable to compete. Agricultural scientists, policy makers, and corporate interests avidly supported these macroscale trends. This transformation was still gathering steam in the 1940s, but applying the tools of science and resources like fossil fuels along with manufactured fertilizers and pesticides to increase the scale of production was the seemingly inexorable course on which American agriculture was set.[27]

The 1940s were also transformative for J. I. Rodale. At the start of the decade he was running a modest firm with his brother and publishing his digest magazines to little notice. By 1950 he was testifying in front of Congress about what he saw as the hazards of all those new materials used in food production. Over the course of a decade he purchased a farm and became the publisher of the magazines *Organic Gardening*, the short-lived *The Organic Farmer*, and the newly created *Prevention*. He published three books on the relationship between soils and health between 1945 and 1950, and he considered himself the leader of the "organic movement" in the United States. That rapid transformation— from humble businessman to crusader for health—provided the foundation for how Rodale narrated his discovery of the organic method. But this transition was far more intentional than accidental. Rodale made himself into a reformer of soils on the heels of a popular conversation about soils and the "back to the land" movement of the 1930s. Indeed, in the years following the Dust Bowl, there was a market for *ideas* about soils, and it was a time when even someone with no experience might make a mark. Dovetailing with his lifelong interest in systems of self-improvement, Rodale's transformation was in many ways as much about remaking his own life as it was about reforming soils and health.

Rather than a son of the soil answering his true calling, Rodale discovered soils as a place to make his mark and, indeed, build an enterprise.

It might seem strange that soils were once a hot topic for conversation, but in the wake of the Dust Bowl and the Depression of the 1930s many voices sought to reform the management of soils. Of course, soil management had long been a basic riddle for agricultural societies as they grappled with how to put back into soils what farming removed. Biophysically, soils exist at the interface of the lithosphere, hydrosphere, and atmosphere, and as a result, they are a complex mixture of solids, liquids, and gasses. Created by the slow erosion, deposition, and accretion of rock and mineral fragments, soils are often described as the brief resting places for rocks as they make their way from the mountains to the sea. Halting, or at least slowing, that movement to sea is a key element of soil management, as is enriching soils. Soils develop in the thin layer of the earth known as the biosphere, and from plants, animals, microbes, and fungi—both dead and alive—they build up nutrient-rich biologic, or *organic*, content. Growing plants for agriculture invariably wears down a soil's available nutrients, a challenge that becomes more formidable with intensive cultivation. Over the last ten thousand years, well before scientists isolated specific nutrients, societies have worked out all sorts of methods to restore the fertility of their soils. Everything from burying fish, to crop rotation, to harvesting fossilized bird droppings, to packing up and leaving were common methods of restoring the depleted ledgers of the land's fertility.[28]

For the first century or more of US history, it had been easier to find a new patch of soil in the United States than to invest in the improvement of an old one. Indeed, the search for more fertile soil has long been one of the great drivers of human resettlement, and the North American continent was no exception.[29] By the early decades of the twentieth century, however, it appeared as if that story might be changing, and the end of "new" land suggested a need for different farming methods. A central text in the modern search for a set of stable or "permanent" agricultural practices was the American soil scientist F. H. King's 1911 book *Farmers of Forty Centuries: Permanent Agriculture in China, Korea, and Japan*. Much like George Perkins Marsh had done several decades before, the book drew from King's travels in the Old World to critique natural resource management in the New. However, the Old World farming practices that King studied at the turn of the twentieth century were those of Asian countries rather than Europe. In the book's introduction, the American agricultural reformer Liberty Hyde Bailey noted that "agricultural wealth" was so great in the Americas because "our soil is fertile and new, and in large acreage for every person."[30] Yet the availability and fertility of soil in the United States would not last, according to King. In crafting his travelogue of visits to farms and experiment stations in China, Korea, and Japan, King hoped the methods and insights of these centuries-old agricultural systems could be applied to the West. King wrote at great length about water-management practices, but it was waste management in particular that he felt was the key to how farmers of the East solved the riddle of maintaining soil fertility to create a "permanent" agriculture. "The wastes of the body, of fuel, and of fabric worn beyond other use are taken back to the field," King wrote. "Before doing so they are housed against waste from weather, compounded with intelligence and forethought and patiently labored with through one, three or even six months, to bring them into the most efficient form to serve as manure for the soil or as feed for the crop."[31] By transforming wastes into a productive resource, King suggested that these farmers had learned how to halt and, indeed, reverse the slow ebbing of soil fertility.

Scientific and technological advances in farming and fertilization practices largely overshadowed the insights of F. H. King's book. In arguably one of the most important transformations in the relationship between humans and the environment, the calculus of soil fertility changed dramatically in the 1920s. Although other types of manufactured fertilizers like superphosphates had been created in the nineteenth century, the German scientists Fritz Haber and Carl Bosch upended the equation by developing a process of synthesizing ammonia from the atmosphere and producing nitrogen fertilizers. Bolstered by artificially derived sources of nitrogen, soils could sustain and increase yields like never before. The process spread from Germany to other industrialized nations in the 1930s, and like any new technology it had both its supporters and detractors. Some worried about the costs of these new materials, while others were focused on the quality of foods produced using them. Others worried about how these new fertilizers might hasten the hollowing out of agrarian societies. Then, as now, these new "artificial" substances proved to be a lightning rod for a range of often-disparate concerns.[32]

One of the earliest and most strident critiques of artificial fertilizers was the one put forward by Sir Albert Howard. Acting as F. H. King's most prominent heir in the 1930s and 1940s, Howard was the agricultural reformer that J. I. Rodale cited for enlightening him about the relationship between soils, food, and health.[33] In 1905 Howard received an appointment as a botanist at the Agricultural Research Institute in Pusa, India.[34] King's writing inspired Howard to incorporate Chinese methods of composting at the experimental fields he oversaw and to explore scientifically the type of age-old methods about which King had written. Howard felt his Indian research had uncovered methods that Western agriculture had either forgotten or ignored. Howard called the method of preserving and composting farm waste he developed the "Indore process," which became the composting scheme J. I. Rodale first learned of, and the first of many, many methods that organic enthusiasts adopted in the twentieth century.[35] After returning to England, Howard became a prominent critic of modern farming methods and developed his critique in *An Agricultural Testament* (1940), which became a foundational text of the organic movement in England as well as the United States.

Howard was not simply interested in the reform of soils but the reform of societies as well. He was one among many in the 1930s who saw reforming agricultural practices as a means of stabilizing both domestic and global economies. These sorts of claims resonated in the United States in the 1930s, where some agricultural reformers feared that the stored capital of the nation's soils had not only been depleted but dried up and blown away. Amid the crisis of the Dust Bowl, proponents of alternative agriculture in the United States emerged as part of larger efforts to reform both farming and market practices of the nation's agricultural economy. As in western Europe, mechanization had transformed agriculture in the first decades of the twentieth century, increasing the amount of land under cultivation and the scale and scope of production. American farmers had benefited greatly from the combination of cheap land, easy credit, and new technologies, which allowed them to purchase new farm implements and save on labor. However, following the boom years of World War I, American agriculture entered a period of combined financial and ecological crisis.

The dust storms, the global depression of the 1930s, and a host of other political and social calamities gave rise to grim writings about soils and the fate of societies. These discourses about soils—what the historians Randal Beeman and James Pritchard have called "soil jeremiads"— came from diverse political, social, and scientific sources. However, a common thread they shared pointed to poor soil management as indicative of a larger set of failures besetting Western civilization.[36] In many jeremiads, the slow, imperceptible wearing away of soils that precipitated a crisis represented the social, economic, or moral decline of the nation. Such jeremiads coincided with New Deal–era attempts at agricultural reform and frequently argued for soil conservation efforts as part of a centralized, planned, and scientific approach to agriculture that would head off crises in the future. Grappling with how to conserve soils in areas like the American South pushed many scientists to see the close link between rural poverty and erosion and the need for conservation strategies that did more than just secure soils.[37]

Concerns about soils and the fate of societies created space for a number of critical voices and popular figures in the 1930s and 1940s, including those who argued against the use of synthetic fertilizers and for a return to *natural* farming methods. One such voice was that of the American writer Louis Bromfield. Born in Ohio, Bromfield attended Cornell before expatriating to Europe before World War I. In the 1920s Bromfield enjoyed a successful career as a novelist, winning the Pulitzer Prize for fiction in 1927. Bromfield and his family fled occupied France in 1939 and returned to the United States, taking up residence near where he had grown up in Ohio.[38] Renaming the land Malabar Farm in honor of his travels along the coast of India, Bromfield set about restoring the land and making the farm a model for rural revival and ecological permanence. An avid reader of Howard, he experimented with making composts and various methods for improving soil fertility without artificial fertilizers. At the same time, Bromfield saw his farm as a model for how an agrarian culture could be an alternative to the precarious forces of industrialization, centralization, and modernity. Echoing the Jeffersonian agrarian ideal, Bromfield depicted farmers as the steely salt of the earth who, when "working with

Nature rather than fighting or trying to outwit her," could have all the security and independence they desired.[39] Bromfield also advocated crop rotation and cover planting, as well as increasing the organic content of soils to halt erosion. Cover crops and no-till methods were a cause célèbre in the years after the Dust Bowl, even as drought eased and agricultural markets rebounded with wartime demand. In 1943 Edward Faulkner, a former agricultural agent, created a stir with a book that claimed plowing methods had decimated American soils. *The Plowman's Folly* became something of a media sensation, and Faulkner's "trash mulching" system of farming was widely debated in agricultural and scientific circles.[40]

The conversation about how to reform soils had a relatively low barrier of entry, so even a devoted amateur like Rodale might have his say. When J. I. Rodale purchased a farm and started writing about soils in the early 1940s, he was likely inspired by the ideas of Howard, but he was also eager to claim a spot in that debate. Louis Bromfield's farm specifically, and his celebrity more generally, provided a model J. I. Rodale hoped to emulate. Bromfield's writing appeared frequently in national magazines like *Reader's Digest* and the *Saturday Evening Post*, and his novels had been turned into screenplays. Something of a literary gentleman farmer, Bromfield was well traveled and well off; like other reformers who did not rely on the land to make their living, he could afford to tinker. Bromfield's farm, in addition to serving as a makeshift experiment station for "ecological agriculture," was also something of a scene for literati and celebrities. Humphrey Bogart famously married Lauren Bacall at Malabar in 1945.[41]

The fact that even someone without much experience working with soils could become a well-known personality certainly appealed to J. I. Rodale. In a 1973 interview about his father's life, Robert Rodale explicitly pointed to Bromfield's celebrity and Malabar Farm as part of what inspired J. I. Rodale's entry into the world of farming: "He was quite envious, I think[,] of Louis Bromfield. Who made a tremendous reputation as a novelist and then when he got his farm—Malabar Farm—and then started writing about farming, suddenly overnight, Bromfield was a great expert on agriculture in the U.S."[42] Indeed, just as being an accountant allowed him to rub elbows with millionaires and being a publisher gave him access to the World's Fair, buying a farm of his own in 1942 and writing about soils gave Rodale an avenue into an important and even fashionable conversation of the time.

Rodale also bought his farm at a time when it was popular to go "back to the land." Writers and publishers in the 1930s "responded to the buzz" during the Depression years and produced scores of books on the renewed interest in "country life."[43] One of the most prominent homesteading advocates—and another voice that clearly influenced J. I. Rodale—was Ralph Borsodi, who began his career as a marketing and accounting consultant but in the 1910s became dissatisfied with city life. With his wife, Myrtle Mae, and their two children, Borsodi purchased a home and seven acres of land in Rockland County, New York, in 1920. The Borsodis grew and canned their own vegetables, raised and processed their own meats, and made a system of home-based production central to their family life.[44]

Borsodi's impact on Rodale was more oblique than that of Louis Bromfield or Sir Albert Howard. The model of self-sufficient homesteads that Borsodi advocated called for limited outside inputs and thus eschewed manufactured chemical fertilizers. Likewise, Borsodi emphasized the health values of fresh foods over those purchased through far-flung distribution channels. Like Louis Bromfield, Borsodi was another educated, cultured personality with a modicum of popularity on whom Rodale modeled his own transformation. The publishing boom in back-to-the-land titles during the Depression era continued through the 1940s and the immediate postwar years. Homesteading literature allowed Rodale to cast his decision to purchase a farm as part of a broader movement, one that was taking people out of the city and reviving life in the countryside.

Yet Rodale's transformation into a soil reformer was also linked to his affinity for the popular health ideas of Bernarr Macfadden. In addition to publishing the popular *Physical Culture* and *True Stories* magazines as part of his publishing empire in 1920s, Macfadden purchased the more bookish *Liberty* magazine in 1931. Macfadden used the editorial pages of this magazine to argue for government support for back-to-the-land colonies. Between 1931 and 1933, Macfadden printed fourteen articles and editorials on homesteading as a solution to the economic crisis.[45] Macfadden is commonly remembered as an advocate and entrepreneur of personal fitness as well as diet and exercise regimens, yet his promotion of homesteading demonstrates the popular appeal of going back to the land as a path for improving both individuals and society in the 1930s. Robert Rodale claimed his father was an avid reader of Macfadden's magazines; furthermore, given that J. I. Rodale routinely experimented with various popular heath regimens, it seems unlikely he would have escaped the mass popularity of Macfadden's work in that area as well.[46] Moreover, as the millionaire head of a publishing empire—built on self-improvement, health, and diet and exercise regimens—Macfadden surely inspired Rodale's ambitions.

Ultimately, Rodale's decision to purchase a farm in 1942 served as a turning point in his life story. It helped him explain why he transformed himself from an accountant into an agricultural and health reformer. Rodale routinely told readers and audiences the story of how discovering Sir Albert Howard's *An Agricultural Testament* inspired him to buy a farm and then grow and consume as much organic food as possible. Rebecca Kneale Gould argues that such a "conversion narrative" serves as a "persistent trope" among the back-to-the-land enthusiasts.[47] Rodale's conversion did not end with the purchase of a farm. After buying that farm and experiencing what an organically grown diet did for his health, he knew he needed to tell people about it—namely, by starting a magazine and publishing books on farming and health. Describing the "healthy corn" from the first harvest on his farm, Rodale wrote in his autobiography, "When I saw this I felt I had to share this information with the rest of the country. I started publishing and editing a magazine called *Organic Farming and Gardening*. . . . Little did I realize what I was touching off—that I would be the one to introduce this great movement to the United States."[48] Like any prophetic claim, Rodale's decision to write about what he learned about the organic method was not something he chose to do, but something he *had* to do.

Viewed against the backdrop of soil jeremiads and popular figures of the 1930s and 1940s, Rodale's transformation into a leader of the organic movement appears far more planned than Rodale let on in his writings. Both historians and enthusiasts have neglected what Rodale did before his moment of conversion and ignored the fact that he had long been in search of ways to make a name for himself. Likewise, Rodale was inured in the culture of self-improvement and popular health reform before he learned about soils. Publishing and writing gave Rodale the tools to transform himself into a movement leader, and the freedom of the marketplace allowed him to popularize the organic method as a fix for what ailed modern food and farming.

MANUFACTURING A METHOD

Sir Albert Howard provided Rodale with the ideas he needed to make his transformation into a soil reformer. However, transforming those ideas into a reality and convincing others was another matter. Not only did Rodale lack any experience or credentials in science or agriculture, he lacked access to the scientific infrastructure of field stations, test plots, and lab results. But what he did have was readers. *Organic Gardening* launched in 1942, coinciding with renewed popular interest in gardening during the war years. Buoyed by a devoted set of "victory gardeners," in just a few years Rodale could claim fifty thousand monthly readers—a number which showed that, at least among gardeners, there was a receptive audience for Rodale's ideas. Those gardeners and their experience with organic methods in their backyards and in their bodies provided a means for Rodale to assemble evidence and experience outside the formal pathways of science. As he told members of the Delaney Commission in 1950, "Since I have been eating organic food I have been cured of colds and headaches.... My whole family has the same record of less colds, less cavities in their teeth. And we have thousands of readers who are experiencing the same thing."[49] With their ideas largely unwelcomed in the halls of agricultural scientists, Rodale and his readers used his magazine to create not only compost piles and organic gardens, but a community of vernacular science as well.[50]

The fact that a group of gardeners rather than farmers embraced Rodale's ideas should come as no surprise. The agricultural reforms and soil jeremiads of the interwar years largely failed to alter the course of American farming, and by the late 1940s the precipitous decline in the numbers of farmers and the rising use of fertilizers and pesticides was well underway. Gardeners, however, largely existed outside the political economy of agricultural production and the scientific infrastructure that supported it. Gardeners could adopt organic methods by consuming Rodale's magazine and finding community with others who shared those ideas. Uncovering that community requires reading a magazine

Cover of J. I. Rodale's *Pay Dirt: Farming and Gardening with Composts* (1945). Courtesy of the Rodale Family Archives.

like *Organic Gardening* not simply as a text written in stone by an omnipotent writer or editor, but as an "open text" where readers participated in the production of the text in both a literal and a figurative sense.[51] This "openness" became a defining quality of Rodale publications, and one that gave readers a stake in the creation of a community around their gardening practices. Faced with an absence of scientific research on the risks of chemical fertilizers—an absence of knowledge—the magazine became a tool for organic gardeners to create their own. Of course, they created this knowledge through a distinctly commercial medium. While they were building a method, they were also helping Rodale build a market.

Rodale first wrote about agriculture in 1942 with a piece titled "Are Food Crops Fit for Human Consumption?" in one of his early magazines called *Fact Digest*. As he often did, he gauged interest in a subject by how many readers responded; based on the responses he received, he sold the *Fact Digest* and launched *Organic Farming and Gardening* a few months later. Like all of Rodale's early work, the magazine comprised reprints and clippings. The first issue was sixteen pages of rough stock and featured an introduction to the organic method by Rodale, a guide to the Indore composting method by Sir Albert Howard, an introduction to the methods of biodynamic farming by Ehrenfried Pfeiffer, an excerpt from Charles Darwin's *Vegetable Mould and Earthworms*, and several pages of letters from readers of the earlier *Fact Digest* article. The magazine declared itself "A NEW KIND OF AGRICULTURAL MAGAZINE designed to help you build soil fertility in a natural way, and to get crops that are fit for human as well as animal consumption." In his own article, Rodale told readers how he had read Howard's book repeatedly and how it guided his farming methods. He claimed that since July 1941 he had been experimenting with making composts on his newly purchased farm with the manure from twenty steers. In another portion of the magazine, Rodale told a reader that his own results with these compost heaps had at first been a "little disappointing," but that he was sure future results would improve.[52]

As its title suggested, Rodale initially hoped his magazine would reach an audience of farmers. Using a mailing list of farm addresses, he printed and distributed twelve thousand copies of this new magazine but only received a dozen initial subscriptions in response. Few farmers in the United States, it seems, shared his enthusiasm for the labor-intensive process of building compost heaps—particularly at a time when the country faced a war-induced labor shortage. After a handful of issues, Rodale refashioned the magazine in 1943 and fathomed for an audience amid those Americans who were gardening as a part of their efforts to increase domestic food production during the war. Rodale dropped "farming" from the title and used *Organic Gardening* to promote fertilizers made with biological material as a "homemade" means of aiding the war effort. Just as the war created a shortage of labor, it also created a shortage of chemical fertilizers available to home gardeners. The shortage, the magazine concluded, would make gardeners realize the quality and taste they had sacrificed with chemical fertilizers in recent decades. The magazine wagered that many Americans would "realize that the absence of chemical fertilizers will be about the best thing that has happened to gardeners in many a decade. Bloated, unhealthy plant growths will no longer be grown. In their place will come vegetables which are really edible and flavorsome. Gardeners will return again to that fine and ancient art, organic gardening."[53]

Rodale adopted the term "organic," which had been used by other English soil reformers in the interwar years to describe what Howard had called biologic methods of creating fertilizers. Howard was keen on demonstrating that the methods he advocated were scientifically sound, and he was particularly interested in *not* being associated with theories of biodynamic farming. Biodynamics, which grew out of the theories of the German Rudolf Steiner, relied on compost preparations and soil treatments that blended the scientific and spiritual. Reformers like Howard derided biodynamics as "muck and magic," but Rodale often papered over that divide.[54] Once he found an audience, Rodale moved quickly to expand the number of publications he offered to readers. By 1944, Rodale Press publications included small pamphlets based on material already published in *Organic Gardening*. An October 1944 advertising page for materials sold by the Rodale Press included a sixty-four-page pamphlet on how to make compost, several reprints about biodynamic methods, as well as a set of gardener's "companion cards."

The first years of *Organic Gardening* culminated in the publication in 1945 of Rodale's first book devoted to farming and gardening, *Pay Dirt: Farming and Gardening with Composts*, issued by Devin-Adair. The book, according to advertisements, would bring readers "up-to-date on the latest scientific knowledge about composts, and their use from all corners of the world, from the laboratories of leading soil biologists to the everyday experience on farms and gardens."[55] Yet the book assembled this evidence not through laboratory results, but through Rodale's prodigious ability to clip and quote from a crazy quilt of sources. In the introduction to *Pay Dirt*, Sir Albert Howard complimented his inexperienced acolyte's capacity for providing instructions to create composts from animal and vegetable wastes. "What gave me most pleasure," Howard claimed, "was to discover that Mr. Rodale possesses that priceless quality—audacity—without which progress is never made."[56] Louis Bromfield read the book in manuscript form and told Rodale in a personal letter he found it "excellent and very important."[57] In his review of *Pay Dirt* in the *New York Times*, Russell Lord—who had written his own Depression-era soil jeremiad, *Behold Our Land* (1938)—praised Rodale's book as a valuable, if curious, addition to the conversation about soils that was occurring on both sides of the Atlantic. Lord reiterated a common impression that the author was a "city man" who went out and bought a farm after reading Howard's *Testament* and had been trying out the "biodynamic idea" for himself ever since. The book, Lord told readers, was "a recital of experience plus the gleanings of an enormous amount of reading." As for the merits of compost, Lord offered, "Much of the stuff he cites seems to me the outcome of a flaming will-to-believe, and a bit 'screwy': but most of it makes sense, plainly; and there can be no doubt that in plugging for humus, as opposed to mineral powders, Rodale is a much needed makeweight."[58]

As Lord surmised, *Pay Dirt* did indeed reflect an "enormous amount of reading" on Rodale's part. Rodale pulled widely from those writers and reformers who had focused on soils in the 1930s but who would be increasingly marginalized in agricultural science and policy a decade later. In the book's bibliography, Rodale listed magazines of composting clubs from New Zealand, farming newsletters from South Africa and England, the journal *The Land*, as well as *Land and Home*. In addition, he cites several textbooks on soil biology and microbiology, gardening encyclopedias, books about health and homesteading, and the soil jeremiads of writers like Bromfield, Howard, and the writings of English organic enthusiast Lady Eve Balfour. Like the majority of the writing he produced over the next twenty-five years, the text of *Pay Dirt* relied on a profusion of extended quotations. In the span of ten pages in part 3 of the book, "Are Chemical Fertilizers Necessary?" Rodale quotes at length from sources as diverse as an 1825 edition of *The Scotsman's Library*, a 1942 Louis Bromfield article from *Country Life*, Hermann Rauschning's *The Conservative Revolution*, a Sir Albert Howard article already published in *Organic Gardening*, F. C. King's *The Compost*

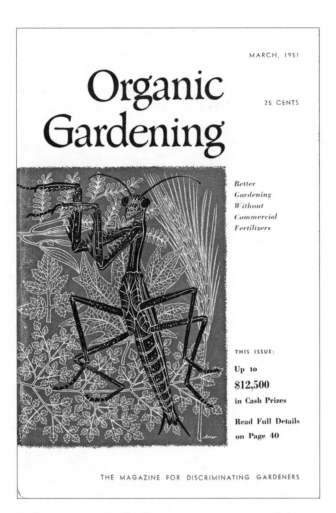

Cover of *Organic Gardening*, March 1951. Courtesy of the Rodale Family Archives.

Gardener, the May 1944 issue of *Science News Letter*, and a letter to the editor of the *New York Times* about fertilizers and strains of Russian wheat.[59] Putting that eclectic mix of clippings to work, Rodale developed his argument that composts could sustain and improve the fertility of soils in both the garden and the farm.

Even as he clipped his way to prove the hypothesis of the organic method, Rodale could not make his ideas into an accepted means for improving soils with his experience alone. Indeed, the pages of *Organic*

Gardening in the 1940s became a place not only to plant the ideas Rodale had cut and pasted, but also to cultivate and harvest the experiences of readers themselves. Howard had conducted numerous experiments with composts, yet composting largely amounted to a miscellany of folk methods rather than a systematic and scientific method. Rodale and his readers needed proof that biologic fertilizing methods could work as well as their chemical counterparts. Moreover, they needed evidence to link the health of plants, animals, and people with the soils that nourished them. While there was an abundance of scientific work on the biological life of soils that he could quote from, Rodale tried and failed at getting agricultural researchers to explore composts in more depth. Lacking access to the infrastructure of science, Rodale opened the pages of his magazine to readers and their experience with the organic method.

After 1945, as *Organic Gardening* expanded, it made more room for the words of readers. The total number of pages grew following the end of wartime restrictions on paper, and by 1948 the monthly publication totaled eighty pages and was full of regular columns, stories, and advertisements devoted to "gardening without chemicals." The "Results" section was just one of a number of places where Rodale and his editors squeezed in more stories from readers about their gardening ideas, their methods, and the evidence from their backyards. Typical of this type of story was one that appeared in April 1948. A. F. Schell of Spartanburg, South Carolina, wrote to *Organic Gardening* to describe how, with the use of organic methods, he had restored the worn-out soils on his property by rebuilding the organic matter in his topsoil. Schell began by trucking in sand, collecting wastes from a local cotton gin, and using "lots of lime and good cow and chicken manure." The result, he wrote, "was one of the finest garden spots I have ever seen." Schell claimed to have been subscribing to *Organic Gardening* for several years, and the more he read, "the more I am interested and the more I am disgusted with some farm agents and colleges and the bulletins they issue." "Why can't men with education and common sense," Schell wondered, "think and see what they are doing to ruin our land and our health by using and recommending commercial fertilizers and sprays?"[60] After experiencing how his own soil could be improved without chemicals, Shell knew there was no use for them on others. Schell's firsthand experience was echoed in similar letters that appeared in *Organic Gardening* each month for decades to come. Taken together, those stories provided proof for Rodale that his ideas could be grounded in evidence. Of course, that anecdotal proof was based on the direct experience of eager gardeners over controlled experimentation. Indeed, the very quality that appealed to Rodale and his readers—the ability to see firsthand results—made the organic method anathema to agricultural science. Although research outposts like Rothamsted in England conducted long-term studies of yields using organic and synthetic fertilizers side by side, there was little if any effort to study biological methods in the United States for many decades, particularly at the land-grant universities that dominated agricultural research.

Of course, what exactly constituted "organic" methods remained poorly defined. To a certain degree, all farming and gardening practices that predated synthetic fertilizers and pesticides could be called organic. What separated the organic method from folk agricultural practices, Rodale claimed, was that Howard had taken age-old techniques and started unearthing the science behind them. In a 1950 piece defending the organic method from its critics, Rodale reminded readers, "We are making a science of the organic method. We are not going to follow a peasant agriculture because history teaches us that the peasant was ignorant of the most elementary aspects of the processes that were in his hands."[61] The organic method, he claimed, meant understanding what was happening in the soil, observing the results, and making changes accordingly.

Without the infrastructure of experiment stations and researchers, Rodale's magazine was the place where the organic method was tested and refined. In his tenth-anniversary reflections in 1952 on why he founded *Organic Gardening*, Rodale reminded readers that he started the magazine as a "means for farmers and gardeners to pool their experiences and mistakes."[62] In August 1947 the magazine asked readers to send in their experiences with applying composting methods at scales larger than the backyard garden in response to a recurring claim of detractors that methods used in the backyard made little sense on large plots of land.[63] Two years later, Rodale published a book titled *The Organic Method on the Farm* that incorporated the ideas that readers had helped gather. Staff writer A. J. Gilardi reminded *Organic Gardening* readers in 1952 that sharing their experiences was the best way to "gradually sift out flaws in the Organic Method." The method, he claimed, was still in a developmental stage, but "in the meantime all organic gardeners are more or less experimenting; by relating their mistakes as freely as their successes they can help each other along and prevent, or at least minimize, repetitions of the same mistakes."[64] Without extension agents to advise them and scientific publications to guide them, the first generation of organic gardeners relied on one another, and Rodale's magazine, to create a community of vernacular scientific knowledge.

Rodale also used his own soil as a site where that accumulated knowledge of organic farmers could be tested. In 1943 Rodale renamed his property the "Organic Gardening Experimental Farm," and it served as the physical site where Rodale and his staff could develop and refine the organic method. After restoring the worn-out soils of the farm with manure, Rodale's workers created various research plots, as well as cement bunkers full of straw and soil and greenhouses with various experiments in chemical-free growing. In early issues, Rodale frequently mentioned his land and shared what experiences he had on his own farm. Similarly, photos of the projects on the farm were included in stories about subjects like building compost boxes or growing sunflowers. By 1946 Rodale was including photos of employees hard at work on the "experimental farm," building heaps and working the various test plots.[65] In truth, the growing plots were small, and the experiments were not carried out with a great deal of care. Rodale frequently struggled to find experienced farm hands to help with his endeavors, and the ones he did hire did not always agree with his methods.[66] Nonetheless, in the pages of the magazine, the experimental farm appeared as the testing ground for the organic method where all the experiences of readers came together.

The larger goal of these research endeavors was to prove not just that compost methods worked, but to demonstrate a link between organic practices and healthier bodies. The plants and animals produced on his farm without chemicals were healthier, he claimed, as were the people who consumed them. The health that the organic method returned to soils, Rodale believed, extended to his own body and the bodies of his family. In an oft-repeated line, Rodale claimed, "After about a year on the farm, eating the food raised organically, we could see a definite improvement in the general health of the family." Headaches, colds, and other common ailments became more infrequent—even the barn rats that had once subsisted on the shriveled spoils of the old farm appeared to Rodale to be fat, healthy, and happy creatures after a few years of eating organic grain.[67] At a time of intense focus on the health and stamina of American bodies during the war years, bodily health was a key source of evidence for Rodale and his readers. When Rodale included a photograph of his wife, Anna, and daughter Nina standing next to a gigantic sunflower in *Pay Dirt*, their bodies provided evidence of how the organic method improved the soil, as well as the health of those fed from that soil.

Yet no amount of anecdotal evidence from his own farm could provide the proof Rodale and other enthusiasts needed. In September 1948, Rodale announced to his readers the planned construction of a laboratory next to the greenhouse on the Organic Gardening Experimental Farm. This laboratory was part of a larger endeavor called "The Soil and Health Foundation," which started in 1947 as a nonprofit research arm of the Rodale Press. The stated goals of the foundation were to foster studies on the effects of organic and artificial fertilizers on soils, plants, animals, and humans. In addition, the foundation claimed it would support farms, experiment stations, publishing houses, and agencies pursuing this type of research.[68] At the same time, Rodale hired Dr. William Eyster, a retired professor of botany, to be the magazine's managing editor. In January 1948, the magazine featured a double-page photo spread of Eyster measuring plants, using a microscope, and testing a hay bale, accompanied by a caption declaring, "Proof guesses won't do at the 'Organic Gardening' Experimental Farm. Dr. William H. Eyster, Managing Editor, wants only proof!"[69] Rodale tried to show readers that he and his staff were investigating the organic method with the skills and tools of agricultural scientists. While these modest experiments would not have passed muster in the pages of scientific journals, for Rodale and his readers they were a step toward verifying what they already intuited about the organic method.

Organic Gardening inducted readers into this effort to produce evidence of the organic method's health benefits. When Rodale asked readers to tell the magazine about their composting tips and tricks, he also wanted to know how eating organically grown foods had changed their health. Writing to talk about how they had restored their soils, readers often eagerly shared anecdotes about how the health of their own bodies had been restored as well. Letters from readers about their results could run the gamut from the philosophical to the practical. In the "Interesting Letters" department in February 1946, the magazine offered the letter of Bingham Small, who claimed, "When even in the matter of our own plot of ground which we garden, science would wish to drown us with poison sprays and chemicals, is it any wonder that we jump at the first hand experience which Organics offers us? Here indeed, we become our own experimenters, studying that original source to which science owes its beginning—Nature." A month later, Louis Sherman of Oakland, California, detailed his own experiments of growing cabbages with "modern treatments" alongside those treated with compost. The cabbage grown with chemicals, he found, became green with lice, while those grown in composts thrived. Comparing the quality of the cabbages, Sherman claimed, "we simply couldn't stomach the modernistic cabbages."[70] Because so many readers "discovered beneficial effects from eating food raised by the organic method," in early 1947 the magazine announced it was collecting such statements in hopes of turning them into a publication. These stories—and countless others of the same variety that appeared in the magazine and then cycled through Rodale's books and gardening manuals in the 1940s and 1950s—provided a foundation of firsthand experience that sustained both the organic method and Rodale's publishing enterprise for decades to come.

Furthermore, as *Organic Gardening* developed, Rodale increasingly welcomed subscribers to be both readers and writers. An editorial note in 1947 stated, "We want you to feel that Organic Gardening Magazine is yours. We desire more contributions from our readers." Introducing a new "seminar" in organic gardening, the magazine told readers, "You need not be a professional writer to take an active part in this garden seminar. We want you to tell us about your most outstanding garden achievement."[71] Some readers submitted occasional articles on their area of specialty, such as primroses or tomatoes; more commonly readers shared their stories about how the organic method transformed their lives and their land. Giving subscribers an active role, the magazine encouraged readers to be a part of the organic movement no matter what their level of skill as a gardener or a writer.

Opening the pages of publications to the bodily and lived experience of readers became a defining feature of the Rodale Press in the decades to come. Indeed, it was through this method of collecting evidence and its two-way relationship with subscribers that *Organic Gardening* began slowly building support for the organic movement. Enrolling readers to be both collectors and disseminators of knowledge and experience with organic methods, the magazine served as an instrument for those readers to spread their enthusiasm. Tying his magazine explicitly to the fortunes of this campaign, Rodale made the strength of *Organic Gardening*'s circulation synonymous with the strength of the movement. Encouraging readers to be active correspondents with the magazine extended to encouraging them to be active correspondents with other publications. Rodale collected and reprinted letters and clippings from his readers, but implored them to send letters and clippings to other outlets as well. An editor's note in 1945 claimed, "If our readers find articles that strike them as having a bearing on our work, we shall be glad to have their ideas. *Send us the clippings* and write to the Editors of papers and magazines who fall down on organic principles. If some of our Answers to Reader's questions seem poor or insufficient, be sure to write us to let us hear the voice of other experiences. Nobody is perfect and every gardener can and does make discoveries that should be communicated to others."[72]

In February 1946, Rodale told readers to "Take the Initiative" and write to organizations on their own to spread the organic idea.[73] Readers kept Rodale informed of developments in their own areas, and they often included clippings from local newspapers and magazines in their correspondence. "This is very valuable work and we trust that the readers will continue to cooperate in this wonderful fashion," Rodale wrote in 1947. "Looking at our mail every day is a thrill because there is always something in it which shows that the organic method is spreading."[74] Rodale claimed that the flow of information back and forth was a sign of the strength of support for the organic method. Even though it could not interest agriculture scientists and policy makers, the *Organic Gardening* community built a vernacular science of their own.

Of course, Rodale was not simply trying to build a community, he was also trying to sell his ideas and grow the number of subscribers. From the outset, reader responses doubled as a bellwether for what drew subscribers' interests and what did not. The number of *Organic Gardening* readers became Rodale's proxy for support of the "organic cause." Rodale also turned to readers to sell subscriptions and offered to make them "agents" by sending them subscription booklets. The magazine frequently reminded readers, "It is important that we tell as many people as possible about the 'goodness' inherent in organic gardening."[75] In 1946 the magazine asked readers to help the organic cause by distributing subscription coupons among "friendly" seed stores, church groups, and garden clubs. Likewise, *Organic Gardening* maintained a half-price gift subscription for schools, doctors' offices, and congressional offices in hopes readers would send the magazine to public places. In 1947 Rodale told his readers that in the past year close to two thousand new subscribers had been added this way.[76] For a brief time the magazine included a chart showing monthly circulation growth so readers could see "how the work collectively of our representatives in the field is helping build our circulation."[77]

Indeed, the Rodale Press created a community around alternative ideas about soil and health with the methods of mass culture. Using readers as subscription agents reached back to antebellum-era periodicals, and mass-market publishers rediscovered this method of growing circulation in the early decades of the twentieth century. This method was particularly effective for *Better Homes and Gardens*, which launched in 1922. The magazine conscripted readers to sign up new subscribers, promising to improve the magazine's quality with the money saved on trying to increase circulation. In their history of magazines in America, John Tebbel and Mary Ellen Zuckerman describe how special interest and "family" magazines in the mid-twentieth century worked to build a "rapport" with their readers: "Through editorials, contests, and various reader-participation schemes, subscribers were made to feel that it was 'their' magazine."[78] A magazine did not have to have an explicit "cause" like *Organic Gardening* to create a community with its readers. Even in the age of mass marketing, giving readers a personal stake in a publication created lasting connections and a viable market.

Getting *Organic Gardening* readers involved in the magazine thus served the dual purpose of building an audience and accumulating evidence to support the organic method. Every letter, story, and photograph of their compost heaps and bountiful gardens that *Organic Gardening* readers sent in created further proof that Rodale was on to something. Just as his own land generated evidence, the backyard experience of readers replicated the results of the organic method. Likewise, in the stories readers told about how their own health had been transformed, Rodale found more proof for the central thesis of the organic movement—that foods grown without chemical fertilizers were nutritionally superior and therefore healthier. While the majority of that evidence was anecdotal and would not stand up to scientific scrutiny, Rodale's community of readers thrived on sharing their stories as well as their tips and tricks gleaned from experience. Moreover, building that community and that body of evidence also served commercial ends. Their clippings and stories provided content for the magazine and the Rodale Press better tuned the periodical to subscribers' interests. As readers shaped the organic method and launched the organic movement, they also helped Rodale create a market. They confirmed his prophecy while allowing him to secure profits.

The fact that *Organic Gardening* and the experimental farm in the 1940s were not simply beneficent enterprises is a reminder that even as he transformed himself into a soil and health reformer, J. I. Rodale never stopped being a man of business. For its first fifteen years, the Press was a division of the Rodale Manufacturing Company, the electrical parts firm Rodale owned with his brother. The firm eked by in the 1930s but saw its fortunes change dramatically in the booming wartime economy of the early 1940s. The types of products the company made—things like plugs, switches, and wiring harnesses—were in high demand. In addition to its electrical parts, the firm worked with Bakelite synthetic resin to produce machine gun mounts and other important pieces of military equipment. The boom in wartime production meant an increase in sales as well as profits. Between 1941 and 1945 the Rodale Manufacturing Company tripled its sales to $1.44 million.[79]

From his experience working for the IRS and accounting for steel firms after World War I, Rodale knew well that excess profits on wartime contracts could be a considerable tax liability. Indeed, Rodale's first published work was on this very subject. Heinrich Meyer, an early editor of *Organic Gardening*, told Rodale's son, Robert, in a 1973 letter that J. I.'s interests in both publishing and organic farming in the 1940s doubled as a shelter for the profits of the manufacturing firm. Meyer worked for J. I. for only a few years, but the two remained friends. To understand those early years, Meyer claimed, one needed to ask why Joseph, J. I.'s brother and equal partner in business, would have allowed J. I. to pursue such "emotional," and also unprofitable, interests in farming and publishing. Outsiders, according to Meyer, always wondered "why he [Joseph] allowed the deficit business of an experimental organic farm and magazine which, though progressing, also involved enormous promises and thereby liabilities toward subscribers." Meyer suggested that many contemporaries could only see the "screwy surface and seeming wastefulness of the operation" and not the obvious "rational underground" of Rodale's projects. The apparent wastefulness continued after the war ended in 1945, when J. I. sank considerable money into a line of clothbound "Story Classics" books. In years to come, even after the press incorporated separately in 1947, Rodale's ever-expanding book, magazine, and other endeavors remained largely unprofitable pursuits. According to Meyer, "The pretty reprints and other matters, the widening trips over the world, and the altogether tax-deductibility of an infinitude of such expenses of professional use . . . might not have stood up successfully if contested, but here the accounting genius of J. I. gave the directions which obviously were satisfactory to the auditors and tax collectors."[80] Rather than simply serving as a path toward reforming soils, Rodale's efforts sprang from more complex, and indeed commercial, motivations.

Meyer's interpretation offers a much-needed corrective to the caricature of Rodale as a prophet somehow inherently drawn to the soil, or as a "city man" who discovered Howard's work and began a "sacred mission" to lead a movement back to the soil. Rodale had his qualms about the fact that chemical companies influenced what type of research occurred in land-grant institutions, but he was hardly antibusiness.[81] Indeed, if Rodale's early life demonstrates anything it is that he knew a good investment when he saw one. Meyer's insight also goes a long way toward explaining why Rodale never conducted the work of farming and gardening himself. Rodale's writings on agriculture are full of observations drawn from his own land; however, that experience came not from his own hands in the soil, but from the labor of hired workers. Not only was his time consumed by running a manufacturing business, he saw himself as more a man of ideas than a yeoman farmer.

This perspective on Rodale's motivations should not overshadow his remarkable ability to conduct research and bring seemingly obscure ideas into the spotlight. Despite his critique of Rodale's publishing operations, Meyer could not help but remark on how impressed he was with Rodale's ability to stay focused on so many proliferating ideas. Meyer states that in his interests in farming and health Rodale demonstrated the scholarly habits he had honed as a young man studying for the rabbinate. Meyer also credited Rodale's upbringing as instilling a "self-centeredness" that allowed him to believe fervently in his own "rightness," as well as an "unlimited generousness and wish to do good."[82] By becoming a publisher, writer, and reformer, Rodale could play a part—however small—in something broader and more important. In the debates about soils and health that he elbowed his way into, Rodale found a conversation to be a part of, one that connected with his long-standing desire to improve himself and improve the world. Even without the celebrity or literary chops of Louis Bromfield, or the titles and training of an agricultural scientist, gardening was a place where even those with little experience could have their say. And in creating a relationship with readers around the organic method, he created space for a critique of new chemical technologies—and, not to mention, a market.

• • •

J. I. Rodale's transformation into an advocate for organic food and farming has been largely mistaken by both scholars and organic enthusiasts. Too frequently Rodale is cast as a visionary who was ahead of his time or someone who was innately drawn to the soil and found his true calling. Caught up in the conversion narrative of a city dweller who found his way back to the soil, it can be easy to overlook the fact that Rodale did not stop being a businessperson once he read Sir Albert Howard. Rather than being intrinsic, Rodale's interests in matters of soil and health were carefully and deliberately acquired. He learned by watching the popular conversations that swirled around the subject of soils in the 1930s, he learned by compulsively reading on and researching the subject, and he learned by searching for even the most picayune details that could confirm his ideas. He learned from the personalities that populated debates about agriculture and health, and he learned how to talk and write like a reformer. He learned that writers, researchers, and publishers occupied a privileged space, and that a producer of even the most ephemeral books and magazines could feel more distinguished than someone who produced electrical parts at a modest profit. He likely also learned that even an unprofitable publishing operation could be an asset. Ever an astute entrepreneur, Rodale combined his search for business opportunities with his desire to reform soils and health.

This facet of Rodale's legacy touches a nerve at the center of the debate between supporters and detractors of organic food and natural health. For critics, Rodale's writings and reform aspirations were always a thin veil for his commercial ambitions. Rodale's background made it that much easier for agricultural scientists to dismiss his ideas. Moreover, the fact that Rodale relied on evidence assembled from untrained gardeners and their firsthand experience—and made sweeping claims about agriculture—meant that a food system adopting new technologies and achieving new economies of scale paid little mind to what Rodale had to say.

However, for Rodale's readers and supporters, the business aspect of his life is a footnote to his insights as a reformer of health and agriculture. The tension between those two views would only grow in decades to come as both the Rodale enterprise and the organic movement grew.

That Rodale assembled, tested, and circulated his ideas about soils and health in the marketplace should come as no surprise. It was the culture he called home. The marketplace of popular culture served as a site where even someone on the outside of scientific and medical practice could carve out a niche. J. I. Rodale was inspired by the work of scientists and reformers, but he also took his cue from the marketplace about what consumers were interested in and what they wanted to read. The readers' shared stories provided evidence to ground the organic method in the 1940s and in years to come pointed to a growing array of consumer concerns about chemicals. In the 1950s Rodale expanded his interests beyond the compost heap and created a forum that highlighted his readers' experiences with the new material ecology of daily life in the postwar world. But he would soon discover that for all the freedom the marketplace offered for his magazine, his ideas, and his public persona, embracing the marketplace produced challenges to both his ideas and his enterprise.

TWO

ADVENTURES IN
SELF-DIAGNOSIS

Science and Experience in the Prevention Marketplace

IN THE PREFACE TO HIS 1967 BOOK, *WALK, DO NOT RUN, TO THE
Doctor*, J. I. Rodale began, as he often did, with a personal anecdote.
In a chapter called "Is It a Disgrace to Be Health-Conscious?" Rodale
aimed "to convince health skeptics that it is good business to be health-
conscious." To illustrate his point, he offered the story of a friend who
had spent many years weakening his body with "reckless eating and
drinking habits." Rodale had tried to guide this friend "in the ways of
good health, because I saw that he was shortening his life." One day the
friend had enough of Rodale's advice and angrily told him, "'Look! You
take care of your cancer and I'll take care of mine!'" A few years later,
the friend died suddenly of a heart attack at the age of fifty-six. "He did
not have the resistance that could have conditioned him against trouble," Rodale claimed. "So he got mowed down by the Grim Reaper long,
long before his allotted time, all because of an unforgivable ignorance
of the simple basic facts of health." The poor soul, he concluded, "could
have lived much longer if he had only been mildly health-conscious."[1]

The remainder of the book's more than four hundred pages chronicled J. I. Rodale's own education in matters of personal health, or what
he called his "adventures in self-diagnosis." Weaving together a story
of his life with the story of his health, Rodale wanted to show readers
why "a healthy life is wonderful" and how they could enjoy their lives as

much as he did. This was the tune Rodale had been singing for years in *Prevention* magazine, the publication devoted to natural food and health he launched in 1950. Rodale described how he had challenged "so many so-called conservative beliefs in medicine and pioneered so many of my own that struck at the cherished viewpoints of the doctors, that they branded me a food faddist." Never shy about brandishing his outsider status, he took the label as a matter of pride, declaring, "In fact, I believe I am America's No. 1 food faddist."[2]

Matters of diet and health had been lifelong passions for J. I. Rodale. Indeed, it was a preoccupation with health that led to his interest in organic methods in the early 1940s. By the late 1940s, however, he was becoming more concerned about threats to human health from sources beyond the soil. Rodale came to see health hazards not just in the fertilizers that bolstered soils, but also in the array of chemicals transforming food, cosmetics, and daily life in the years after 1945. To address these threats, Rodale created *Prevention*, a magazine devoted to conserving "human health" and keeping lay readers in touch with new discoveries of preventive medicine and "medical research workers throughout the world."[3] Building on the critique of contemporary agriculture in *Organic Gardening*, with *Prevention* Rodale widened his lens to challenge doctors and nutritionists with a natural health philosophy. That philosophy was grounded in ideas about using natural practices to protect the body in an increasingly unnatural world. While J. I. Rodale is well known as the creator of *Organic Gardening*, *Prevention* is vital for understanding his critique of modern science and medicine.

From a base circulation of fifty thousand subscribers in 1950, *Prevention* quickly grew to eclipse the circulation of *Organic Gardening*; by the mid-1950s the new magazine was the signature publication of the Rodale Press. Like its organic counterpart, *Prevention*'s system relied on a plethora of excerpted scientific evidence merged with the personal experiences of Rodale and his readers. This process of gathering and sharing was how *Prevention* cataloged concerns about synthetic chemicals and human health—concerns that were largely overlooked, perhaps even outright ignored, by medical professionals and regulators in the 1950s. *Prevention* created a community of like-minded readers and validated their concerns about how new chemical technologies affected their bodies. However, the same firsthand experiences that built community also made *Prevention* anathema to how modern biomedicine gathered and evaluated evidence. One of the cornerstones of biomedicine is a reliance on evidence derived from carefully planned laboratory trials, not the haphazard collection of direct experience. Another cornerstone is a reliance on highly specialized experts whose research is verified by other experts. In both his personal background and his process of gathering information, Rodale ran counter to these core assumptions.

More important, when *Prevention* used personal experience to conclude that individual bodies reacted differently to new chemicals in foods and medicines, the magazine called into question a central tenet of modern medicine. That tenet held that all bodies interacted with the environment in the same way. Indeed, scientists evaluate the safety and efficacy of any new substance—whether a pesticide or an antiperspirant—by testing its effects on a sample of the population and then generalizing toward a relationship of cause and effect. That method relies on an assumption that bodies respond to a substance within a range of normal variation and leaves little room for individual experiences or personal histories. To suggest that one person's body or a group of bodies might experience disparate effects from a new substance called into question that key tenet. It was not only the evidence Rodale relied on that ran counter to biomedicine, but the conclusions he and his readers reached as well.

Of course, Rodale did not just gather evidence and create a community, he also built a business. *Prevention* doubled as a system for buying, selling, and distributing health products that fell outside both orthodox medicine and orthodox business practices. Unlike the organic method, which struggled to find a foothold beyond a circle of committed composters, there was a lively—and indeed profitable— consumer market for natural health products in the 1950s. Responding to concerns about changes in food production and new chemical technologies, Rodale instructed his readers about which "unnatural" substances to avoid. At the same time, he promoted "natural" products. Everything from food supplements produced without chemicals to juicers, orthopedic shoes, natural deodorants, and herb teas filled *Prevention*'s advertising space. The efficacy of these products, like many of Rodale's health ideas, was also grounded in firsthand experience. Natural food supplements and vitamins in particular became the keystone of Rodale's natural health ideas and the marketplace *Prevention* fostered. With the creation of the magazine and an expanding series of books about personal health in the 1950s, the Rodale Press went from being a small, unprofitable side business of Rodale's manufacturing concern to a lucrative conduit that connected producers and consumers of natural health goods. *Prevention* challenged postwar ideas about nature, health, and the body, and it did so by capitalizing on the tools of the marketplace.

Prevention ultimately laid important groundwork for an emerging critique of chemical technologies in the postwar years. Yet the fact that Rodale relied on personal experience and pushed products of questionable efficacy also limited the power of that critique. The magazine proved powerful at highlighting concerns about new chemicals at a time when the benefits of new substances were often accepted with few questions, but it did so by elevating intuition over evidence. And even as Rodale raised questions about biomedicine's assumption of a uniform relationship between bodies and the environment, these questions more often than not came packaged with dubious products and untested health advice. In this way, Rodale's *Prevention* foreshadowed an often-unacknowledged tension that would emerge within environmentalism in the years ahead. Environmentalists raised questions that punctured confidence in postwar scientific advances, but they could also slide into unscientific conclusions that bordered on conspiracy and quackery. Like the questions environmentalists raised, some of the natural health concerns Rodale promoted proved valid, while many others did not. As they battled with authorities, Rodale and his natural health enthusiasts found the marketplace to be nimbler than the scientific method and eager to respond to their concerns about chemicals.

A MEDICAL JOURNAL FOR THE PEOPLE

In 1949 J. I. Rodale began a yearlong series of editorials in *Organic Gardening* called "Is Cancer Related to Artificial Fertilizers?" In the first installment, Rodale compared cancer rates across countries and correlated them with the amount of artificial fertilizers those countries used.[4] Citing a study of organic diets and cancer in mice—which Rodale's own Soil and Health Foundation had funded in 1947—Rodale called for doctors to experiment with the diets of cancer patients.[5] In the editorials that followed, Rodale ranged well beyond composting methods. He discussed the rates of cancer in primitive people, ways to improve protein sources, the role of sugar and salt in conditioning the body for cancer, and many other topics far removed from gardening. By writing as much about constipation as he did about composts, Rodale revealed the extent to which his interests in soils were ultimately about improving personal health and preventing disease. After writing a year's worth of columns, Rodale published his cancer series as a small book in 1950, titled *Cancer: Can It Be Prevented?* Readers of *Organic Gardening* offered mixed reviews of the cancer columns as well as Rodale's increased devotion to matters of health. Some readers found his claims illuminating, others found them distracting, and some even discontinued their subscriptions as a result. Robert Rodale joked in a 1989 interview that his father had always wanted a health magazine rather than a gardening magazine, and those reader responses gave him an excuse.[6] The final page of Rodale's book on cancer announced the launch of a new magazine, *Prevention*, which would go beyond soils and explore human health more generally from a "preventative" standpoint.

Cancer was just the tip of the iceberg for *Prevention*. For Rodale, rising cancer rates were a symptom of something deeply flawed in the health of modern societies and the relationship between bodies and the environment. The synthetic fertilizers and pesticides that remade agricultural production in the 1940s were joined by new chemical technologies applied to foods, medicines, cosmetics, and the very built environment of daily life. This medley included new types of food dyes as well as new techniques for extending the shelf life of food with preservatives. Advances in synthetic chemicals changed the substances that consumers used to brush their teeth, curl their hair, and treat their headaches. Even the fabric of daily life changed after 1945 with the application of synthetic chemical compounds to the clothing, furniture, carpets, and building materials that surrounded consumers. New chemical technologies were the hallmarks of modern life in the postwar era, and many consumers embraced them with little or no hesitation.

By contrast, *Prevention* asked whether the risks these new substances created were greater than their rewards. Rodale found an endless array of questions about what was known and unknown about these materials, and how the chemicals used to make them might influence personal health. Consumers had little extended experience with the new substances in their foods and their medicines, and Rodale appealed to "natural" substances as sources of security and good health. In the same way that "organic" fertilizers only made sense once there was a manufactured alternative, so, too, did "natural" gain purchase with the introduction of consumer products made with newly fashioned compounds. In the years after the world witnessed the awe and terror of atomic power, Rodale and other health enthusiasts put great stock in nature as something that was unchanging and unadulterated. Of course, even definitions of nature do not exist outside of history, and *Prevention* reflected the growing market that sprang up around natural products in response to its artificial counterparts.

In many ways, *Prevention* demonstrated the close link between Rodale's ideas about health and his thinking about soils. What Rodale gleaned from studying soil reformers was that disease—whether a blight on crops, a virus in cattle, or a condition like cancer—was the expression of an underlying deficiency. In his estimation, soils, plants, animals, and people all had a proper diet. Those proper diets were disrupted in the age of chemical fertilizers and pesticides, and the health of people, plants, animals, and soils was breaking down as a result. Rodale's logic held that synthetic chemicals stripped soils of nutrients, which in turn caused animals to wither from grazing on nutrient-deficient plants. Human bodies—at the end of this chain—ultimately became more susceptible to a variety of diseases as a result of consuming those nutritionally deficient foods. By reverse logic, the solution according to Rodale was *prevention*. Organic fertilizers maintained the health of the soil, plants and animals nourished from those soils were better equipped to ward off disease, and human bodies—like soils—built their resistance to disease by consuming a chemical-free diet. Despite the fact that there was little scientific work backing up this assumption, *Prevention* promised to show readers how to build their own bodily resistance to new chemicals and preserve health rather than treat disease: "Many brilliant physicians no doubt have done such experiments but writings of them are lying hidden away unused by the general public. We hereby formally appoint ourselves as the representative of the public to seek out wherever it may be any information that

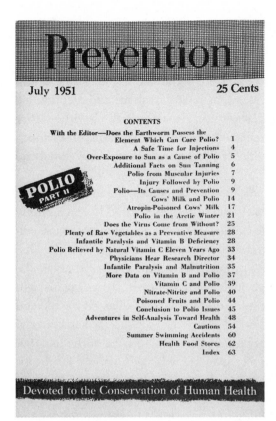

Prevention

July 1951   25 Cents

POLIO
PART II

Devoted to the Conservation of Human Health

Cover of *Prevention*,
July 1951. Courtesy
of the Rodale Family
Archives.

will show people how to prevent themselves from becoming sick and
how to be extremely happy while doing so."[7]

In *Prevention*, Rodale's ideas grew beyond the compost pile into a
systematic approach to personal health that avoided synthetic substances in foods, medicines, and cosmetics. In the magazine's second
issue, Rodale outlined a set of "rules" that would guide the magazine
"to see that our foods are grown properly, without chemical fertilizers, in soils that are full of humus, or organic matter such as manure,
leaves, weeds, etc. This is the essence of prevention—the best that can
be grown and not too much of it." He added, "With such a program
from babyhood, a person should be able to go through life with a minimum of disease or ill-health." Rodale's second rule was not to "overtax"
the body's organs. The third rule, the one that would "be the

constant purpose of this publication to harp on over and over again," was "the principle of which type of foods to eliminate." *Prevention* would tell readers what not to eat, but it also promised to instruct readers on what to consume instead. Rodale claimed the magazine would seek "to reeducate our readers so that when we ask them to cut out some food or other," it would also "show them how to get along without that food and still be happy."[8] *Prevention*'s system not only took certain foods and substances off the table, it offered an ever-growing list of all-natural replacements.

In the same way the organic method was grounded in observations from his farm, Rodale's health ideas frequently cited his own bodily experience as proof. Rodale claimed the magazine would feature evidence drawn from respected medical authorities, and just like OG, parts of many of the articles originated in some type of scholarly or scientific publication. Still, Rodale could not resist including his own experience with health alongside his clipped evidence. At the tail end of an early piece about vitamin E therapy, Rodale inserted an editorial note that described his own vitamin regime: "In spite of the fact that about 60% of my diet is organically raised, without chemical fertilizers, and is of high nutritional value, I have been taking Vitamin E (tocopherex) for years. . . . I take only vitamins that are not made from synthetic chemicals."[9] This brief mention of his personal health was the first of many. Indeed, over the next twenty years Rodale used *Prevention* to chronicle the nuances of his own elaborate set of personal health ideas and experiences. Whether in the multipage editorials he produced each month or in a brief column of miscellany, Rodale's own experience of health and his own body were everywhere in *Prevention*. He chronicled these ongoing investigations in a recurring column called "Adventures in Self-Analysis towards Health." In it, he might share how he cured himself of aches by changing his sleeping position or discovered and tested his hypothesis that his dizzy spells came from eating cherries sprayed with DDT.[10]

At times Rodale inserted his own experiences alongside other writers whose work he was reprinting. In a series of articles on soap in 1951, Rodale blended an article from the *American Druggist* with his own experiences of trying to avoid washing with soap. Rodale offered intimate details, telling readers of his daily washing routine and how he rubbed hot water over his body's various smells, itches, and aches. In addition to describing how soap was not needed to treat his athlete's foot, he noted that for itches in *some* areas soap remained necessary.[11] This level of detail was not limited to *Prevention* but carried over to books as well. In his 1954 book on exercise and the heart, *This Pace Is Not Killing Us*, Rodale published a detailed history of his own pulse, complete with charts and graphs marking the results of his various experiments and exercise regimens.[12] Rodale's focus on his own body and his reliance on personal experience over controlled studies invariably placed him at odds with the medical establishment. Moreover, it made his insights easy for doctors to ignore.

Relying first on his own experiences, Rodale told readers how they could do the same. In a 1954 piece on preventing the common cold, Rodale offered a personal history of his own colds before outlining all the various methods he had tried. Personal experience, rather than accepted medical wisdom, he claimed, was what he had come to rely on in matters of health: "But now I want to show you how important it is not to take any of the popular health concepts for granted. We must question every generally accepted health tenet or dogma, as rooted as it may be in the public mind. You must observe the effect on your own bodily processes of your daily actions. Make your own interpretations."[13] All individuals, Rodale suggested, needed to develop their own methods for managing their health. In this emphasis on personal experience and the search for evidence to support foregone conclusions about diets and health, *Prevention* elevated the anecdotal over the experimental and firsthand experience over medical expertise.

Rodale's focus on both the idiosyncrasies of his body and its reaction to environmental influences was hardly unique in the history of medicine. Indeed, since the early nineteenth century "irregular" physicians such as Thomsonians, homeopaths, and naturopaths had emphasized an empirical experience of health and healing over scientific theory.[14] Outside these defined systems, the personal monitoring of the body and its various fluctuations was a common practice in years before the availability and preeminence of scientific medicine. Self-monitoring often made individuals intimately aware of how their bodies responded to the peculiarities of a surrounding environment and bound one's individual experience of illness and health to local landscapes.[15] Of course, by the time J. I. Rodale began writing about health in the middle of the twentieth century, biomedical authorities had worked to make that type of empiricism a thing of the past. The rise of laboratory-based science, along with the germ theory of disease, located medical knowledge in the hands of experts and their experimental results. In addition, medical treatment based on specific clinical interventions and the development of new tools like vaccines and antibiotics revolutionized modern medicine in the twentieth century.[16]

These developments helped usher in new advances against some of the world's deadliest diseases. However, as acute infections like measles declined in much of the developed world, there was also a corresponding rise in less deadly chronic illness. In what is known as the epidemiological transition, mortality caused by infectious diseases that had once ended lives early gave rise to the prevalence of conditions like cancer and diabetes that predominate late in life. Chronic conditions have been less responsive to clinical interventions and drug therapies, and, unlike pathogens, their cause and effects on the body can vary widely from person to person. Conditions like back pain, bad eyes, bad arches, cavities, hemorrhoids, and acne, as well as conditions that are more serious like heart disease and cancer, can arise from an untold number of causes. Patients often experience these types of conditions quite differently from one another, which can reinforce a subjective or individual experience of the body and its health. For Rodale, the persistence of these chronic conditions was evidence that medical experts still did not have all the answers and that they were overlooking how new chemicals diminished the health of the body.

In providing readers with a system to maintain their personal health and avoid chronic conditions, Rodale promised the wisdom of nature and experience rather than experimental evidence. Rodale undoubtedly was asking legitimate questions about persistent health conditions and matters like diet, synthetic substances, and preventative health that the medical profession largely overlooked in the 1950s. However, the relentless focus on nutrition in the absence of verifiable evidence made both Rodale and his readers easy to discount or outright ignore. What Rodale's food faddism overshadowed was his valid criticism of the reactive and reductive approach of modern medical care. The very title of *Prevention* was meant to reference the adage about "an ounce of prevention being worth a pound of cure," and Rodale routinely told readers that a system that preserved health meant fewer trips to the doctor's office. In his admonitions to "know thyself" and his stories about how to self-monitor the body's various flows and fluxes, he told readers that doctors were there when the body's system broke down and stopped running, but that day-to-day maintenance was up to them. Rodale routinely pointed to the medical profession's fee-for-service model as a core reason for poor health and suggested that alternative models—and a national health service—could deliver better results.

For all his criticisms of medical science, both *Prevention* and Rodale were not explicitly antiscience. Rodale originally planned for *Prevention* to be different from its gardening counterpart by being built solely on scholarly reviewed and "conservative" medical opinion. In his autobiography, Rodale writes that he considered *Prevention* "a medical journal for the people," in that it would distill ideas from widely disparate academic disciplines into an easily readable monthly magazine.[17] Just as soil scientists should not hold a monopoly on ideas about soils, Rodale felt doctors should not have a dominion over ideas about health. Rodale believed that by giving readers the tools to come their own conclusions, he was returning responsibility for health from expert authorities to the people. The empowerment of the individual was a defining feature of how goods were sold in consumer societies, and the popular culture of health was no exception. Even when that type of individual empowerment was not explicitly antiscience, as in Rodale's case, it could nonetheless work toward undermining science as a way of understanding health, disease, and the environment. Armed with their own knowledge and experience, consumers could choose when to accept and when to reject scientific findings. While that knowledge empowered consumers to ask much-needed questions about substances in their foods and medicines, it could also help them choose to ignore sound scientific evidence and conclusions.

As would become common in natural health circles—and indeed among certain strands of environmentalists in the years ahead—the inherent uncertainty of science provided fertile ground for *Prevention*. Rodale launched the magazine with a series of articles on cancer, but the first issue was devoted entirely to polio, a disease whose etiology was still a mystery in 1950. Throughout the 1950s, Rodale published a special issue on polio each summer as outbreaks approached. In the years before the development of the Salk vaccine in 1954, the uncertainty of how polio spread led to endless speculation. Even in respected scientific sources, what would later seem like what the historian David Oshinsky calls "bizarre guesswork" often served to explain polio.[18] In the pages of *Prevention*, such scientific uncertainty translated into an array of possible causes of the outbreaks as well as a variety of ideas for how they could be prevented. Rodale highlighted the uncertainty in medical research over the virus in a 1953 article titled "Does the Polio Virus Come from Without?" Much of the article focused on Ralph Scobey, president of the Poliomyelitis Research Institute, who once hypothesized polio might be a reaction within the body itself and "not imported into it by external contact."[19] As was his practice, Rodale juxtaposed this out-of-context quote with another incongruous quote to support his central claim. Drawing from a bulletin of the International Society of Osteopathic Sacro-Iliac Technicians, Rodale quoted the experience of a doctor who had found a number of cases where victims of polio were stricken a day or two after consuming a large amount of fresh fruit. Always quick to tie an issue back to synthetic chemicals, *Prevention* wondered, "Is it possible that these victims were suffering from the effects of the poisonous spray residues that remained on the fruit?"[20] That simple maneuver was one Rodale performed over and over in *Prevention* and in his health books. By selectively appropriating the words of scientists and speculating in areas of uncertainty, he found evidence to back up one of his core theories—that there was a great deal scientists still did not know. Highlighting what scientists did not know was certainly valuable, but Rodale was also slow to adjust his thinking to new medical knowledge. Even after the poliovirus had been identified and a vaccine developed, *Prevention* continued to suggest nutrition as a key weapon in fighting the disease. Holding on to a preexisting precept rather than adopting new knowledge further distanced Rodale and his readers from accepted medical science.

Pointing to gaps in scientific knowledge as evidence of potential harm, Rodale and natural health enthusiasts routinely questioned the uncertain effects of new chemical technologies that were remaking the built environment of 1950s daily life. Perhaps the best illustration of this process was the debate over the addition of fluoride to public water supplies. Fluoridation emerged as a political issue in the early 1950s as state and local health authorities sought to add compounds to drinking water supplies to improve dental health. Some locales became early adopters without issue, while others experienced vociferous political battles over the government's right to use public water to treat a condition like tooth decay. A separate but related issue in the fluoride debate was the lack of certainty surrounding both the safety and efficacy of the practice. The United States Public Health Service began a set of research trials in Michigan and New York in 1945 that aimed to prove the effectiveness of the compound in strengthening tooth enamel and preventing decay. The trials were planned to span ten years, but advocates in several states pushed to add fluoride ahead of the study's conclusion. Fluoride promoters made confident claims about the compound's safety and efficacy despite a lack of research on daily consumption in drinking water. Scientists had done plenty of work on the effects of high-dose, acute exposure to fluoride but hardly any on the effects of trace amounts consumed over a long time or effects on the body that were subclinical.[21]

Rodale opposed fluoride not because he thought it was an intrusion of the state in matters of health or thought the compound was ineffective in preventing cavities, but because it was a synthetic chemical trying to mimic a natural one. Indeed, Rodale did not doubt fluoride helped prevent tooth decay, but he believed that only "natural" forms of the compound were safe and effective. This type of thinking about chemicals in food, water, and consumer products like vitamins and over-the-counter remedies defined *Prevention*. This type of thinking would also define the conflicted relationship Rodale maintained with medical science over the years and would become a central and contested element of marketplace environmentalism in subsequent years. Scientists could make remarkable advancements in Rodale's estimation, but they could never mimic nature entirely. The problem, then, was not the individual compound per se, but whether a compound was natural. In the same way that Rodale claimed synthetic compounds could not provide soils with nitrogen as well as naturally derived composts could, "man-made" nutrients in the diet could not replace natural ones. One of J. I. Rodale's oft-repeated parables about the limits of science's ability to mimic nature relied on a story about an aquarium in

London with too many fish and too little sea water. A curator, knowing the recipe for sea water, made his own batch, only to find the fish soon died when placed inside. After many failed attempts, another curator came along and made a batch—but to this one added the slightest bit of real sea water—and the fish lived. "It would seem," Rodale wrote, "that the scientist's conception of sea water is defective. According to their own formula, *their* sea water is good for many purposes such as washing one's feet, or cleansing the teeth. But for fish to live in? That is a little detail scientists overlooked."[22] Rodale would ultimately claim that many manufactured chemical compounds were much like that sea water—a close approximation but missing some vital, natural element that science could not re-create. Synthetic substances, created by experts in their laboratories, could not replace those created by nature.

Despite the fact that there was little evidence to support this claim, evidence that synthetic chemicals were not the same as those produced in nature came from another source Rodale trusted: his readers. In 1950, by *Prevention*'s fifth issue, Rodale was no longer relying solely on excerpted medical literature but was asking readers at the end of columns to write to the magazine about their various experiences with soap for his ongoing series on the subject.[23] Reporting a month later on the potential dangers of antihistamines, Rodale drew from a story in the *Annals of Allergy* about adverse side effects in trials with the cold pills. In an editorial note to readers, Rodale asked, "Have you any complaints of different bad side effects after the use of these 'cold killers'? Report them to us if you do."[24] In the same way that the organic method relied on readers' experiences more than laboratory results, in *Prevention* readers' personal experiences testified to the alleged efficacy of natural health practices and products.

The lived experience of *Prevention* readers as described in the magazine contrasts with what has often appeared as unanimous esteem for biomedical science in the middle decades of the twentieth century. After raising standards for medical education in the 1910s, the profession made great strides against infectious diseases with the aid of powerful new sulfa drugs and life-saving technologies in the interwar years.[25] By the 1940s and 1950s, biomedicine enjoyed the heyday of advances in science. Regardless of whether biomedical advances were solely responsible for decreasing infectious diseases, the heroic image of doctors in white coats certainly received most of the credit.[26] To read the pages of popular magazines like *Life* or *Science Digest* was to see a medical world where the ailments of the modern body were being conquered one after the next with new drugs and procedures.[27] However, in the pages of *Prevention* and among the cadre of consumers it reached, the golden age of medicine was far more complicated and far more contested.

The magazine not only thrived on collecting and sharing the lived experiences of its readers, it validated readers' intuitions about synthetic substances. Readers' concerns about everything from aluminum, antibiotics, arsenic sprays, aspirin, barbiturates, chlorine, cigarettes, DDT, diethylstilbestrol, food additives, hair dyes, lipstick, nail polish, parathion, radiation, soft drinks, and white sugar were all routine fare in the magazine.[28] Indeed, a survey of *Prevention* in the 1950s and 1960s is in many ways an index to the emerging anxieties of the chemical age. At the same time that *Prevention* cataloged the conditions, ailments, and concerns of its readers, it also offered a space where readers could share their own methods for preventing health problems. In a special issue in 1954 devoted to preventing the common cold, Rodale edited and excerpted readers' letters into an article titled "Prevention Readers Prevent Respiratory Disorders." Readers like Ruth Blood of Massachusetts confirmed Rodale's suspicion that bread contributed to head colds; although she could eat some in summer months, the rest of the year it was strictly off-limits in her opinion.[29] At other times, Rodale's interest in reader testimonies was broader, asking readers to tell their "health story" to inspire and strengthen the willpower and resolve of other readers. Sharing these stories with the magazine was also important, Rodale claimed, as it "helps our editors to know how you feel about the articles appearing each month."[30] In 1954 *Prevention* began a regular column called "Out of the Mailbag," which published large excerpts of readers' letters. Many of these letters reeled off a long list of conditions and bodily troubles. Just as J. I. Rodale did with his own body, readers described in great detail the aches of joints from arthritis, gas pains and chest pains, skin reactions to chemicals, and the seemingly endless variety of other bodily ills and irritations they experienced. In sharing their concerns, readers at the same time offered their own homespun set of health ideas and personal solutions. Readers might suggest ideas for how to use vinegar instead of cleaning products, ways to avoid DDT sprays, hints for using herbs, or tricks for including bone meal and other supplements in recipes.[31]

Readers wrote to *Prevention* not just to reach Rodale and his editors, but also to connect themselves to a broader community of like-minded health enthusiasts. After having a letter published in *Prevention*, readers reported being swamped by correspondence from other subscribers. Editors found it necessary to remind readers to be patient in waiting for replies from other subscribers, who were private citizens and often unprepared for the avalanche of mail they might receive. Some readers actively used *Prevention* to gather information for their own ends— soliciting fellow readers to contact them with ideas about herbs and health or diets for certain conditions. Others wrote to offer specific advice on organizing local efforts to fight fluoridation or to drum up support for the regulation of chemicals in foods and cosmetics. In general, *Prevention* served as a welcomed respite for those who generally found their ideas about health mocked or derided. As a place to share some gallows humor and Rodale's own jocularity, the magazine provided a place for readers to commiserate over their status as outsiders. Readers joked about being called "health nuts" and turned the mocking they suffered back onto those who made fun of them. Readers told of the "kidding and razzing" they received from coworkers and friends over the foods they ate, and how those folks would eventually come around once they witnessed the good health that resulted from a natural diet.[32]

Rodale's interests certainly steered *Prevention*'s content, but in opening the magazine to the ideas and experiences of readers, it also produced a community of natural health consumers. Rodale's longtime attorney Morton Simon recalled the vast number of letters that poured into Emmaus each month from Rodale's readers. "There undoubtedly is and has been a highly personal, although obviously intangible, relationship in many readers' minds between themselves and J. I. Rodale," Simon observed.[33] That relationship between Rodale and his readers extended onto the pages of *Prevention*. Historians of popular literature have argued that texts such as dime novels and commercial book series often represent not the work of a discrete, autonomous author, but the materialization of a broader "unauthored discourse" that swirls within a culture. Similarly, Rodale and his editors built *Prevention* by what Janice Radway calls "an endless process of circulation or cultural recycling," taking apart texts from scientific literature and cutting, pasting, and recombining them with readers' experiences.[34]

Viewed in historical perspective, it is clear that Rodale and his readers were asking some much-needed questions about chemical compounds that had been introduced with little or no attention to the long-term risks. Some of these concerns—such as diethylstilbestrol or cigarette smoking—would later be borne out by scientific studies. Even some of Rodale's most outlandish ideas about the effects of white sugar on health appear prescient in light of new evidence that sugar companies funded scientific research in the 1950s and 1960s that downplayed health risks.[35] At the same time, other concerns that Rodale publicized— like rimless eyeglasses, the dangers of X-rays, and chlorinated water— never found any scientific backing. Like other aspects of Rodale's career as a reformer, *Prevention* demonstrated both the merits and the limits of assembling conclusions based on firsthand experience. *Prevention* thus demonstrated an emerging sense of uncertainty about the health of the body and its relation to a changing environment in the postwar era, but validated those concerns with a patchwork of science and personal experience.[36] Rodale and his readers asked valid questions, but their conclusions failed to stand up to scrutiny. Moreover, Rodale packaged his unorthodox health ideas with an array of untested and at times suspicious health products, making it all the more difficult for some of his questions to be taken seriously beyond his community of devoted readers. *Prevention* proved to be a lively place for exchanging health ideas, but the fact that it was also a marketplace for buying and selling health products became his company's greatest liability.

A CRUSADE IN THE MARKETPLACE

After a few years of publication, *Prevention* began featuring an occasional article of "Prevention Do's and Don'ts," which recounted the magazine's various positions. Over time, these articles accumulated into a set of practices called "Prevention's Program for Healthful Living." Much like the organic method, the program drew from the research and ideas that the magazine had gathered over time and outlined a set of clearly defined rules.[37] In the foreword to a book-length introduction to the system, Rodale and his editors stated, "*PREVENTION* is not a magazine in the ordinary sense of the word. Rather, it is a system, and to get the best results with it, it is best to follow it as a complete system, with only minor modifications due to personal allergies."[38] Establishing healthy habits required adherence to a system.

The *Prevention* system told readers what to consume and what to avoid. The bedrock of the system was proper nutrition, consuming all foods in as fresh a state as possible, and avoiding processed, packaged, and refined foods. The system limited the consumption of bread, citrus fruits, tobacco and alcohol, as well as liquid milk. Of course, consuming organically grown foods was also a key element. Early on, the magazine drew liberally from its sister magazine, *Organic Gardening*, but this changed after 1951 when J. I. Rodale shifted his focus largely to *Prevention*, leaving his son, Robert, to run OG with a separate staff. Although *Prevention* occasionally gestured toward topics of gardening and farming, the magazine largely stayed focused on the benefits of consuming rather than producing organic foods. The *Prevention* model maintained the unproven assumption that plants grown without chemical fertilizers held onto their natural vitamin content while those sprayed with pesticides lost theirs. Moreover, those foods contained residual amounts of pesticides that chipped away at health. The earliest advertisements in *Prevention* were classified ads for organic foods, and the magazine routinely marketed an *Organic Directory* to help *Prevention* enthusiasts find such foods.[39] "As far as possible," Rodale advised, "make an attempt either to raise your own food organically, which means without chemical fertilizers or poison sprays, or to buy such from advertisers in our magazine *Organic Gardening and Farming*."[40]

But organic food was just one item that *Prevention* told consumers to put in their shopping cart. Indeed, the ideas that proliferated in *Prevention* went hand in hand with an array of natural products that Rodale recommended as key ingredients of maintaining personal health through his system. This marriage of critique and commerce was not always a happy one. Nonetheless, in the 1950s and 1960s *Prevention* expanded its content to become a veritable catalog of advertisements for mail-order firms, making the magazine a conduit for connecting producers and consumers of natural goods. While the marketplace helped *Prevention* raise some important questions about new chemical technologies and their impact on health, the fact that they were sandwiched between ads for products made those questions easy to overlook, and perhaps even outright dismiss.

No products were more essential to the *Prevention* system than natural vitamins and food supplements. As with his critique of fluoride, Rodale argued that vitamins synthesized in a laboratory were not the same as those compounded from natural sources. Enthusiasm for vitamins first swept the country in the 1920s, and the addition of vitamins to breads, cereals, and all manner of foods was fairly standard by the 1950s. Not only the supermarket aisles but also mass-market advertisements touted the benefits of vitamin-enriched foods. Where *Prevention* differed was in its attention to *natural* vitamins and food supplements. *Prevention* advised readers, "Even if you eat the best possible diet, you do not obtain enough vitamins and minerals for robust health from today's refined and chemically fertilized foods. Much of the fresh food you eat has lost most of its vitamin content during the long shipping process before it reaches your grocery. We advise you to supplement your diet with vitamins and minerals from natural sources."[41] The magazine defined natural vitamins as those from plant and animal extracts, which were "the purely-natural ones, present in food . . . not isolated and chemicalized." Synthetic vitamins, by contrast, were those for sale in drug stores rather than food stores, originating in laboratories rather than soils. Regardless of the claims of doctors and nutritionists that there was no distinction, the *Prevention* method maintained that "no combination of known synthetic vitamins satisfies the nutritional requirements of animals and humans."[42] Products like wheat germ capsules, brewer's yeast, cod-liver oil, and rose hips were more effective at improving health, *Prevention* claimed, because they were derived from nature. The efficacy of natural vitamins and many other food products versus their synthetic counterparts remains hotly contested. Cases of acute vitamin deficiency are decidedly rare in developed countries, and medical consensus maintained that a well-balanced diet would take care of most of the body's needs. While *Prevention* eagerly followed research in nutrition, it rarely questioned its own core tenet about the need for supplementing one's diet with natural products. Such products were not an addendum to the *Prevention* system, but rather its very core.

The question of whether a natural substance was more effective than a synthetic one was part of a larger debate about how vitamins themselves should be sold—and regulated—in the marketplace. On one level, this debate stemmed from disagreement among experts over the role of vitamins in proper nutrition. The debate was also rooted in competition in the profitable vitamin market. Pharmacists and grocers spent years battling in both the market and courtrooms over whether vitamins should be treated as food or medicine.[43] Considered as food, vitamins only needed to pass food safety standards; considered as medicine, there was a much higher regulatory bar for testing their safety and efficacy. Despite repeated attempts by the Food and Drug Administration to assert control over the industry, vitamin firms in the 1950s routinely sought out gray areas to avoid restrictions. Largely unable to limit what went into a jar of vitamins, the FDA regulated what that jar could claim.[44] For its part, *Prevention* clung to the belief that vitamins were food and did all it could to protect and grow the marketplace for natural *food* supplements for many years.

The debate over whether vitamins were food or medicine points to a defining feature of *Prevention*'s philosophy and its relationship to commerce. *Prevention* asserted that good health came from maintaining a body that could resist disease, not just relying on medical treatments to treat an ailment. A well-running body, like the engine of a car, came from proper preventative maintenance rather than the cures or interventions of a professional mechanic. This notion of a body that was naturally resistant to disease was common in alternative health circles. J. I. Rodale was no doubt earnest in subscribing to this idea of health, but that philosophy also helped him and his company sidestep the liability of prescribing, or selling, a cure. Telling a reader that sunflower seeds or rose hips could help improve eyesight was very different from promising those products could be used to treat a condition like glaucoma. Just as there was a distinction between selling vitamins as food and selling them as medicine, food and drug regulations made selling advice about how to stay healthy vastly different from selling products that promised a cure. Rodale found it necessary to routinely remind readers that both the ideas and the products the magazine provided did not constitute specific health advice, but rather techniques for maintaining health. *Prevention*'s marketplace operated with fewer restrictions than would a system of natural healing.

Yet Rodale also routinely tested the boundary between selling advice and selling products. In the summer of 1951, as *Prevention* completed its first year in print, Rodale's claims about natural vitamins caught the attention of a German immigrant, Rudolf Weissgerber. Weissgerber had recently moved to New York from Cologne, where he had worked in the laboratories of the Madaus Company, a firm that exclusively produced natural vitamins. How Rodale and Weissgerber became acquaintances is unclear, but from their correspondence they appear to have become fast friends with a shared affinity for vitamin supplements and organic foods. On a trip to Germany in June 1951, Rodale met with the brothers who ran Madaus and made a handshake agreement on a partnership to jointly produce natural vitamin products in the United States. The brothers were enthusiastic about Rodale's "most interesting and splendid work" in the field of natural health and eager for the venture to move forward. Rodale, for his part, was ready to combine his experience running a manufacturing firm with his health ideas. Upon returning to the United States, he went so far as to have a lawyer draw up a letter of agreement for the partnership that would have created a firm "to manufacture, prepare, and distribute, both wholesale and retail, drugs and pharmaceuticals composed of matter which has not been grown with the aid of chemical fertilizers and which is non-synthetic in composition."[45]

Throughout the summer of 1951 Rodale remained excited about the venture's prospects, but grew apprehensive about how readers would respond to his financial interest in a drug firm, albeit a natural one. In a letter to Weissgerber two months after his visit, Rodale suggested the firm should go only by the Madaus name and exclude Rodale from its title. Furthermore, Rodale expressed his concern that the American Medical Association might put "obstacles" in the company's path owing to his claims in articles in both *Prevention* and *Organic Gardening*. As negotiations continued, Rodale chafed at the sense his partners might want him to "tone down" *Prevention* so as to not offend physicians. When he terminated his arrangement with Madaus at the end of the summer, Rodale suggested he might be able to help the company in other ways, but at that point he felt it was not "wise to tie up with a drug proposition," lest he give up his crusade.[46] In giving up on this partnership out of concern for his "crusade," Rodale was also being cautious about how both readers *and* regulators might view his involvement with a vitamin firm.

Aware of the boundary between selling advice and selling products, Rodale proceeded to make *Prevention* into a marketplace where those two things could come together. Over the course of the 1950s, the magazine's pages were increasingly dominated by advertisements for mail-order vitamin firms and natural health products. The earliest issues of *Prevention* contained no advertisements save for a page of classified ads for organic foods and an ad for a gift subscription.[47] In January 1951, Rodale announced to his readers that advertisements would now be accepted so long as they met the specific guidelines of the magazine's natural health philosophy. At this point the magazine was digest-sized and consisted of sixty-four pages, and the advertisements appeared only in back pages or as side columns to the text. Many of the ads in the first years were the same as those in *Organic Gardening* for products such as stone-ground flour, sunflower seeds, and books of the Rodale Press. Soon, products appeared that were aimed specifically at *Prevention* readers, such as brewer's yeast tablets, natural deodorants, and organic salt from firms like Dr. Bronner's. With each increase in its number of pages devoted to natural methods for maintaining health, *Prevention* also expanded the amount of space for ads from natural vitamin suppliers. Advertisements that had once been at the back of the magazine moved closer to the front, bringing products literally closer to Rodale's own editorials.

As the ads moved closer to Rodale's columns, the figurative distance between Rodale's interests and those of advertisers narrowed as well. Almost as soon as Rodale began running ads, readers wrote questioning his motives for offering a specific position on a supplement or other health issue. For instance, from the magazine's inception Rodale had been hailing the health benefits of bone meal tablets for their mineral content. Once advertising appeared in the magazine, ads for bone meal increased in size and frequency, eventually appearing opposite the last page of a six-page editorial extolling the tablet's benefits. Some readers wondered whether Rodale had a financial stake in firms that sold such products and whether the magazine existed to deliver editorial content or to deliver advertisements. Rodale addressed the issue head-on in 1953 in an editorial titled "What Don't You Like about Prevention?" where he republished a letter from a reader who felt advertising had compromised the validity of *Prevention*'s views. After noticing the number of ads for rose hips, desiccated liver, and bone meal appearing alongside articles touting them, the reader, whose name was not published, stated, "One can't help but wondering whether commerce wasn't being masqueraded in scientific garb."[48] Certainly, the space between Rodale's ideas and the natural products were becoming uncomfortably close— particularly when there was hardly any objective and disinterested science to show that these products worked.

Rodale defended his practice of placing ads for products opposite his editorials by describing the immense number of responses he received from readers asking where to find a product after he mentioned it in an article. When he placed an ad for desiccated liver tablets directly opposite his April 1952 article on the tablets' benefits, Rodale claimed he knew he was testing the barrier between advice and advertising. "I was sure of my ground that more people must have the equivalent of practically raw liver," he wrote, adding, "I went about seeing that they got it in a forthright fashion, breaking a few rules of the ethics of journalism and advertising in doing so. Perhaps *Prevention* is making a new kind of ethics."[49] Rodale also defended his position by explaining that what *did not* appear in the natural marketplace was more important than what did: "We will accept no product that is made synthetically, and we will accept no product for curing anything. Our magazine is devoted to prevention, and we limit our ads to that field. No liver cures or laxatives will be advertised in *Prevention*, and brother it is difficult sometimes see the easy shekels slip through our fingers, for our wives cry for mink coats and some of our typewriters need replacing. But actually, we are proud to turn such advertising down."[50]

An unspoken feature of *Prevention*'s marketplace was the fact that by selling advertising space rather than products, Rodale was free to make claims that producers of natural products could not make themselves. Indeed, for close to thirty years the largest source of advertising revenue for *Prevention* was from mail-order vitamin firms that bought large, multipage ads each month. The vitamin firms, many of them health food stores trying to grow beyond their local markets, found *Prevention* to be the ideal outlet for introducing new products and reaching new customers. Vitamins were often cheap to produce and highly profitable. However, sellers of *natural* vitamins in the 1950s had only a limited market as it was; given the regulatory barriers to the health claims their products could make, *Prevention* became essential to their business. Whereas many magazines found it necessary to keep their advertising rates low in order to stay competitive, *Prevention* found it could charge premium prices for its ad space. Furthermore, *Prevention*'s advertising standards aimed to ward off products made with synthetic chemicals and gave Rodale's seal of approval to the products and firms that joined its marketplace.

Thus, because trade regulations kept *Prevention* from selling its own health products and also restricted what natural vitamin firms could claim about their products, the magazine's ad space became a conduit for natural products. Over its first decade of publication, *Prevention* became all but a directory of ads for vitamin companies. Vitamin retailers went from buying half- and full-page ads to multipage spreads. Faulkner and May, Schif-Bio, and many other firms became a familiar sight in the pages of *Prevention*, to the point where they were more prominent than J. I. Rodale at times. Vitamin producers that had once been small, household-sized operations chronicled in their ads how their firms were growing, adding more space and distribution capacity to their operations. Far from trying to hide its relationship to advertisers, *Prevention* celebrated it. In special issues and anniversary editions the magazine thanked advertisers for being part of J. I. Rodale's crusade.

Prevention was a forum for popular critiques of modern science and medicine. It was not a scholarly journal that relied on peer-reviewed studies conducted by professionals; instead, the magazine collected and validated readers' health anxieties and their bodily experiences. *Prevention*'s goal was not to move biomedicine forward by sifting through valid and invalid findings, but rather to collect evidence that reaffirmed Rodale's preexisting theories about health, the body, and new chemical technologies. The magazine also proscribed against consuming chemically fertilized foods and labeled everything from decongestants to deodorants as unnatural. Like previous popular health reformers stretching back to nineteenth-century figures like John Harvey Kellogg and Sylvester Graham, Rodale relied on nature as the trusted source for health advice. And by enlisting the help of vitamin producers and sellers, *Prevention* offered consumers natural products as an alternative to what could be found at the modern supermarket and the drug store. While the efficacy of many natural products was unknown or certainly open to question, Rodale promoted them as vital tools for maintaining personal health. *Prevention* brought together consumers and producers of natural health products and cemented the Rodale Press as an arbiter of the growing commerce of natural health ideas and products. However, in merging health ideas and products, J. I. Rodale and his company also tested just how much freedom this natural marketplace would bear. The license to make health claims that critiqued modern medicine was one of *Prevention*'s greatest assets, but it also proved to be its Achilles' heel.

DEFENDING THE NATURAL MARKETPLACE

The commercial context within which Rodale's natural health ideas circulated was not limited to his writing or the endless ads for bone meal supplements that appeared in *Prevention*. Although Rodale did not sell his own health products to his readers, his firm did produce and sell books under the *Prevention* banner, thereby capitalizing on the marketplace the magazine created.[51] Indeed, a subscriber to *Prevention* received more from the Rodale Press each month than just a copy of the magazine: alongside the magazine came a host of flyers, circulars, and mailers for *Prevention* books and the company's other titles. These direct mailings were how the firm sold its books and how J. I. Rodale expanded his marketplace of readers and subscribers.

Rodale's direct-mail advertising operations have been largely opaque in the historical record. Indeed, the history of direct marketing as a distinct type of marketing practice has been largely unexplored.[52] The lack of historiography is compounded by the fact that direct mailings are a curious genre of primary documents. As the colloquial name "junk mail" suggests, flyers, circulars, and subscription mailers are ephemeral documents. They are cheap to produce, cheap to distribute, and easy to discard. These documents were, by design, not meant to be saved and, as such, are rarely preserved.[53] Yet these documents—and direct marketing more generally—played a central role in how natural health ideas and products circulated in the 1950s and 1960s. Indeed, direct selling was central to cultivating niche types of consumption and gave natural health consumers an avenue to contest the homogeneity of the postwar mass market. The direct market gave both Rodale and purveyors of natural products greater freedom than their name-brand competitors on supermarket shelves. However, freedom made the marketplace both prosperous and precarious. In turn, defending the marketplace created one of the greatest tests of the ideas, products, and practices at the core of the Rodale enterprise.

Direct mailings were the most common way that the broader public encountered J. I. Rodale's health ideas. In the case of the 1954 book *The Health Finder*, the Rodale Press sold over one hundred thousand copies of the actual book in the 1950s—but to sell those one hundred thousand copies it distributed over seven million pieces of direct mail.[54] Those seven million flyers and circulars reached more mailboxes than the 150,000 copies of *Prevention* that circulated each month, demonstrating the reach that direct-mail marketing gave *Prevention* as both a system of ideas and a set of products. Compiled entirely from material published in *Prevention* and stretching to more than nine hundred pages, *The Health Finder* became a model for the encyclopedia-scale volumes that the company turned out over the next several decades. With its successive waves of mailers, the Rodale Press swamped consumers with advertising materials. In contrast to the modest circulars that promoted *Prevention*, which were generally black and white and heavy on text, *Health Finder* advertisements were multipage newsletters and posters that folded out and made forthright claims about the merits of the *Prevention* system. One mid-1950s circular titled "At Last! The Truth about How to Stop Disease" outlined how readers could learn about the effects of chemicals in foods as well as the use of dietary supplements and organic foods. In addition, the ad promised readers that they could learn how to prevent and control disease with nutrition and learn the true effects of vitamins and miracle drugs.[55]

Direct-mail advertisement for *The Health Finder*. Courtesy of the Rodale Family Archives and the American Medical Association Archives.

This flyer and the untold number of others that followed in its wake marked a more aggressive set of marketing practices as well as a more direct challenge to orthodox medicine in the postwar era. The waves of direct mail raised circulation and sold books, but they also invited scrutiny from medical and commercial regulators. In his writings about health, J. I. Rodale frequently criticized expert pronouncements about diet and nutrition advice and promoted ideas that ran counter to scientific consensus. At first, Rodale's challenge to medical and scientific authorities went largely unrequited. However, by the early 1960s the company's direct mailings far outstripped the circulation of its books or magazines and became so prevalent that medical authorities could no longer ignore the little publishing house in Emmaus. Of course, Rodale diverged from mainstream medicine not only because of his ideas about health, but also because he combined those ideas with untested natural health products. Rodale's differences with mainstream medicine emerged most clearly in a set of federal trade actions taken against the company in the 1960s. Although ostensibly about advertising methods, they also unveiled how the *Prevention* marketplace—and the ideas and products that flourished within it—conflicted with established ways of understanding expertise, the body, and the health effects of new chemical technologies in postwar America. The trial revealed both the important questions that Rodale's marketplace brought to the surface, as well as the troubles Rodale created by combining his passion for reform with a search for profit.

Rodale was hardly the first (or the last) popular figure to run afoul of the medical establishment in the twentieth century. Indeed, he collided with a regulatory apparatus that was well organized and experienced with challenges to its authority. That apparatus, however, largely centered on restricting who could practice medicine and the sales of health products, not health advice. In the 1960s, medical authorities began working to shore up control over not just products such as vitamins and over-the-counter remedies, but also over ideas that countered medical consensus. At the center of these efforts was the American Medical Association. The medical profession had long policed its borders to establish its authority and diminish competing interests, and it routinely worked to restrict from making medical claims those it considered quacks, charlatans, and frauds. In 1913, the association created the Propaganda Department, which later became its Bureau of Investigation.[56] The AMA's Bureau of Investigation routinely worked with local medical societies and state and national regulatory agencies to investigate the activities of individuals and organizations considered to be on the fringe of medical science.

For medical authorities, a figure like Rodale represented a regrettable if perennial problem. Drawing from the AMA's investigations, Morris Fishbein—editor of *JAMA: The Journal of the American Medical Association* and head of the Investigation Bureau—published a monolithic book in 1932 called *Fads and Quackery in Healing: An Analysis of the Foibles of the Healing Cults, with Essays on Various Other Peculiar Notions in the Health Field*. In it, Fishbein argued that what he called medical "sects" were nothing new, but rather a predictable phenomenon. Writing in the early twentieth century after the revolution of germ theory, Fishbein was certain that all paths led toward the steady progress of scientific medicine. Both the rise and fall of unorthodox health ideas were a timeworn tradition, Fishbein claimed, and just like any fad they would pass in time. With the collapse of homeopathic and eclectic medical colleges in the early 1900s, Fishbein saw fit to declare the death of homeopathy and other unorthodox groups. In his mind, homeopathy's decline was emblematic: "Thus, in fact, pass all systems in the practice of medicine. Scientific medicine absorbs from them that which is good, if there is any good, and then they die."[57]

When the AMA created its file on Rodale in the early 1950s, the Bureau of Investigation did not see him as a particularly egregious threat to modern medicine. Just as Fishbein dismissed unorthodox medical ideas as regrettable but inevitable, the Bureau considered Rodale to be no different than any other health magazine that popularized untested or outdated health advice. Archived correspondence regarding Rodale does not begin until 1955, but Bureau of Investigation director Dr. Oliver Field suggested the AMA was aware of *Prevention* before then.[58] The Bureau's correspondence regarding Rodale greatly increased in 1956—the same year the Press expanded its direct mailings for *The Health Finder*. With each wave of direct mailings, the Bureau's files swelled with circulars featuring J. I. Rodale's portrait and a sample of his health ideas. Some of this material came to the Bureau from physicians; other material came directly from the Rodale Press. At some point the AMA itself must have subscribed to *Prevention* and then canceled its subscription, judging from the number of subscriber notices it received. The available evidence suggests that as investigations go, the AMA's was relatively benign—the Bureau collected materials and corresponded with the public and association members, but it seems to have made no concerted effort to initiate legal action.[59] Rodale's views about diet were certainly not well received, but compared to some other battles the AMA waged against alternative health figures or unapproved cancer treatments Rodale and his natural marketplace were relatively small fish to fry.[60]

The Bureau's investigation may have been mundane, but a sample of its correspondence shows that Rodale's direct mailings were the means by which millions of consumers as well as the medical authorities first encountered J. I. Rodale. Many of the letters directed to the AMA's Oliver Field are kind notes asking whether the association endorsed *Prevention* and whether Rodale's magazine was any good. Some letters came from homemakers, others from business people and health educators curious about what to make of the magazine. Letters frequently mention (and sometimes enclosed) the Press's flyers. On some occasions the flyers themselves served as stationary. More than a few letters came from doctors who reported that patients had asked about the magazine and the advertisements they received in their mailboxes. Indeed, based on the letters from local medical societies and better business bureaus inquiring with the AMA, it is clear Rodale's marketplace extended well beyond the number of *Prevention* subscribers.[61]

The AMA's response to these inquiries was always the same. With a form letter that rarely varied, the Bureau of Investigation responded, "We do not regard this magazine as a reliable source of information on nutrition and health. Many faddist preparations are advertised therein. Most of the articles which appear in it are either under the by-line of J. I. Rodale, the publisher, or carry no byline whatsoever. A few of them have been laudatory of unestablished remedies in certain disease categories." The statement went on to say—with a bit of a condescension—that J. I. Rodale had "rather unique qualifications for the authorship of some of these articles. In earlier promotional material he was described as a 'prominent and wealthy manufacturer of electrical wiring devices such as fuse plugs and switches, which are distributed nationally and internationally. . . . Ever since he was a young man, Mr. Rodale was in search of the cause of illness, but could not find it. He searched widely through the medical literature, but continued to observe increasing illness all about him without finding the remedy.'"[62]

Letters to the Bureau routinely asked what could be done to stop both Rodale's mailings and his magazine. Writers such as Harry Davis, the executive secretary of the Medical Society of St. Joseph County, Indiana, looked to the Bureau to ask if there was "anything medicine can do to help prevent misrepresentation of this type?"[63] In a letter to the association in 1961, Anne Jackson of Lohman, Missouri, worried because her parents relied so heavily on *Prevention* and Rodale's health books: "The only reason that I am concerned about Mr. Rodale and his publications, is that my father, not only reads them for gospel truth, but will not accept any further explanations."[64] For their part, AMA representatives were forthright in responding that while Rodale's ideas were a nuisance, there was little that could be done as the First

Amendment protected the magazine and its claims—medical authorities could use existing laws to limit the spread of information that was patently dangerous to health, but as there was little demonstrable harm from avoiding aluminum pans or taking bone meal.[65] In this way, Rodale's focus on preventative health gave him greater license than if he had been selling cures.

Yet tolerance for the freedom of the marketplace also had its limits. Indeed, by the early 1960s, when the Rodale Press was rolling out its tomes of advice and piles of direct mailings, medical authorities were looking for ways to shore up their control over the consumer marketplace. Even as medical science enjoyed unprecedented esteem and power, debates about national health insurance and rising medical costs brought the issue of fraudulent health advice back to the stage with some frequency. The AMA—long opposed to national health insurance and cost reforms—often pointed to "unproven" medical treatments, patent medicines, and health advice books as prime causes of soaring costs.[66] In October 1961 the AMA and the Food and Drug Administration convened the First National Congress on Medical Quackery. The conference inaugurated a joint effort to uncover health fraud and, as AMA legal director C. Joseph Stetler put it, "stamp out this evil."[67] The weekend featured prominent scientists and regulators testifying on the extent of health fraud in their field. On the subject of nutrition, Harvard's Frederick J. Stare—a national figure in popular health advice and a frequent target of Rodale's critique—claimed that "nutritional quackery" cost American consumers $500 million a year. However, according to Stare, the problem went beyond just money. "One of the evils of food faddism," he claimed, "is the doubt that it plants in minds of many on the safety of our foods, on the skill and ingenuity of food technologists, in short, on the confidence we have in our great food industry."[68] Neither Stare nor other speakers made specific mention of Rodale in their speeches, but several speakers called attention to the abundance of magazines and books with nutritional claims about natural foods and vitamins.

The fact that popular health figures like Rodale relied on the mail to circulate and sell their health ideas did not escape notice. After the first joint congress of the AMA and FDA, a Senate Special Committee on Aging held a series of hearings in January 1963 on "Frauds and

Quackery Affecting the Older Citizen," which made specific mention of J. I. Rodale and *Prevention*. The hearings covered everything from real estate scams to arthritis cures, and several speakers pointed to direct mailings as a place where regulatory structures were largely ineffective.[69] In comments made at the Second Congress on Medical Quackery in October 1963, Charles Sweeney of the Federal Trade Commission made special mention of advertising for medical books. Following a reorganization in 1961, the trade commission was embarking on a concerted effort to "establish with certainty and clarity the very basic do's and don'ts of advertising" for a range of health products.[70] After years of trailing behind, regulators were starting to catch up.

For its part, the Rodale Press had anticipated that some sort of regulatory action would eventually alter the contours of its marketplace. While J. I. Rodale knew he was wading in murky ethical waters by combining his advice with others' products in *Prevention*, by the late 1950s it became clear that advertising for his books would create legal troubles. As early as 1954, the company retained the services of the Philadelphia lawyer Morton J. Simon to offer counsel on legal issues in the publishing business. By 1959 Simon was regularly meeting and corresponding with the company's staff and offering line-by-line edits of Rodale's flyers and circulars.[71] In April 1964 the FTC issued a formal action against J. I. Rodale and the Rodale Press for *The Health Finder* and two other books. The complaint charged Rodale, as well as the publishing company, with making "false statements and representations in advertising pertaining to a book and various pamphlets concerning diet, disease, and the health of mankind."[72] Although based on advertising claims for *The Health Finder*, the FTC's action had the potential to severely restrict the business practices at the core of the Rodale enterprise.

The center of efforts to defend the company would not be J. I. Rodale, but rather his son, Robert. Robert Rodale became president of the company in 1954, and in his correspondence with staff, lawyers, regulators, and the public he appears to be a sharp, management-minded professional. Unlike his father, Robert Rodale was not given to making outlandish statements, but rather maintained a quiet, retiring demeanor. One of Robert Rodale's goals in the trial was to present the Press not as the vanguard of natural health ideas that challenged the status quo, but as a humble operation with moderate views. Introducing his father's health ideas to a member of the legal team, Robert described his father's ideas as modest and conservative: "My father planned that *Prevention*, his new health magazine, would be free of a lot of the crackpot ideas that characterized most if not all unorthodox health publications. He was not a vegetarian, did not believe that all diseases were caused by mysterious toxins that had to be fasted out of the body periodically, and he didn't believe in the medicinal power of herbs or other 'nature cures.'"[73] By suggesting that *Prevention* offered sound advice about ways of staying healthy rather than treating diseases, Robert hoped to show that there was little risk of harm in the advice the company sold. Aside from making a few recommendations on how arguments should be construed, J. I. himself had little presence in the case. The company's lawyers discussed putting J. I. on the witness stand, but in the end he only submitted a written statement on how *The Health Finder* had been compiled.[74]

To show how J. I.'s health ideas were rooted in medical literature, one of Robert's first tasks in the FTC case was to assemble the backing materials for *The Health Finder*. The book was nearly a thousand pages long and compiled entirely from *Prevention* articles, which meant that assembling the backing materials amounted to an excavation of all his father's health ideas. A team of employees combed through the book and meticulously compiled copies of the hundreds of medical articles it quoted. Many of these articles were outdated and had been selectively quoted by J. I. Rodale and his editors to support *Prevention*'s existing positions about diet and health. Nonetheless, Robert Rodale shipped off boxes of the materials to the company's lawyers so they could show that *The Health Finder*—and J. I. Rodale's ideas—were not built on one man's idiosyncratic beliefs, but rather on a foundation of scientific literature.[75]

In a sign of the gravity of the legal challenge it faced, the company did not invite its community of readers and their sentiments into the proceedings. Readers wrote to Robert and J. I. Rodale outraged at the FTC's action and offered to write letters and send money for the company's legal defense. Although the Press had built *Prevention* by involving readers in its "crusade," Robert Rodale routinely rebuffed these correspondents in a polite tone, assuring them the company's lawyers had the trial well in hand.[76] In conversation with the defense team, Robert rejected the idea of introducing reader testimonies into the record and instead pushed for a team of carefully chosen experts to defend *The Health Finder*. Readers maintained a close watch on the proceedings through 1964, but when the nationally syndicated conservative columnist James Kilpatrick wrote a piece blasting the FTC's action in August 1965, it set off a wave of reader letters addressed to the Press as well as the FTC.[77] Readers sent the Press unsolicited donations, as well as copies of their letters to the commission. Many of these letters resonate with the resurgence of political conservatism of the early 1960s, as readers expressed concern that the FTC action was symptomatic of government encroachment into the free market and personal freedom in matters of health. Robert Rodale's responses were kind and reassuring of the readers' interest, but also firm in warning that there was "always a risk in trying to stir up political action in a matter which is essentially judicial."[78] The stakes were too high for the company to take a political stance.

The genesis of the FTC's action lay in the nuances of advertising, but the hearing proved to be as much about the ideas Rodale circulated in the marketplace as the physical products of magazines, books, and advertisements. The core claims that J. I. Rodale popularized—about the merits of food supplements, the dangers of new synthetic chemicals, and the need for individuals to rely on personal experience as a form of evidence—ran counter to postwar medical and scientific consensus, and the hearing underscored those differences. As the hearing before an FTC examiner began in December 1964, the trial quickly centered not on whether the advertisements were deceptive in their representations of *The Health Finder*, but whether the health claims made in the book were accurate. The commission sought to discredit *The Health Finder* by turning to medical experts to argue the book was dangerous, not for any specific advice it gave but due to the *possibility* that a reader would rely on the book rather than a medical professional for advice. Second, FTC lawyers argued that because the book ignored clinical interventions, it could not *assure* readers of preventing certain ailments.

For their part, rather than trying to prove how effective the book's claims were, Rodale's defense team sought to argue that because the advertisements were faithful representations of the book itself, the claims of the advertising also enjoyed First Amendment protection. Rodale's attorneys maintained that the attack on the specific claims in the book was a misdirection from the larger issue of censorship of what could and could not be said in an advertisement for a book. Rodale's lead attorney was Thurman Arnold, a veteran of the Justice Department's Antitrust Division in the New Deal era who, after turning to private practice, became a prominent defender of civil liberties in the 1950 and 1960s. Arnold sought to de-emphasize the actual claims of the book and instead argued the case as a matter of rights. In Arnold's opinion, the trade commission overstepped its authority by trying to regulate speech in advertising. Quoted in an October 1965 *Advertising Age* article, Arnold asked, "Would an ad for a book by the John Birch Society be false simply because the ideas in the book are false? . . . A man's right to make a speech is protected by the First Amendment. How is he to attract listeners if he can't advertise?"[79] Right or wrong, advertising, according to Arnold, only needed to be true to what it was trying to sell.

But the rights of free speech took a back seat in the early round of hearings, which centered instead on Rodale's health ideas. Indeed, the transcripts of the hearing offer an unrivaled glimpse into how Rodale's ideas conflicted with the scientific and medical thinking in the 1950s and 1960s. Moreover, the trial highlights some of the ways that Rodale's focus on firsthand experience countered biomedical assurances of the universal safety of new chemical technologies. As the title of one of his books—*Walk, Do Not Run, to the Doctor*—would suggest, Rodale did not explicitly tell his readers to avoid modern medicine. Instead, he claimed that personal diet choices could naturally ward off disease, meaning that consumers did not need to rely solely on physicians to improve their health. His more explicit challenge came from his selective reliance on often obscure and outdated scientific findings. Likewise, Rodale foregrounded personal experience over clinical trials to support his claims about the dangers of toxics and the merits of consuming organic foods and natural supplements. While not antiscience per se, Rodale chose when to listen to scientists and when to ignore their findings. Ultimately, the trial demonstrated how Rodale's health ideas—and the marketplace more generally—were marked by an ambivalence about the advances of modern science and medicine.

That ambivalence ran through the pages of *The Health Finder* just as it did the pages of *Prevention*, leading the trade commission and its witnesses to argue that the book's greatest danger was that it *might* lead an individual *not* to see a doctor for a health problem. The commission's lawyers sought to establish this point early on by calling the cardiologist Modestino Criscitiello to the stand. Criscitiello claimed that while he agreed with some of the book's claims about the importance of diet, he routinely insisted there was a danger that patients might delay seeking "proper" treatment if they read the book.[80] According to Criscitiello, there was nothing wrong with readers choosing to learn about heart disease or any other condition from a medical textbook, "but these [textbooks] are almost uniform in their admonition that the patient or the individual undertake such advice with the supervision of his physician, or some qualified medical practitioner."[81] *The Health Finder* did not tell readers to consult their physicians, but instead told them to change their habits and trust their own experience.

Furthermore, the trade commission and its experts believed that someone like Rodale, with no professional training, had no place offering consumers health advice. Reflecting the sense that only practitioners should dispense advice, the commission made the case that a patient could not be assured that the recommendations in *The Health Finder* would be effective in preventing, relieving, or treating conditions because it ignored medical interventions. In a heated exchange with Rodale's lawyers, hearing examiner John Lewis contended that what was at issue in the case was "whether the book will assure better health and a longer life."[82] The commission's attorneys repeatedly asked witnesses if a reader could be guaranteed of preventing a handful of specific conditions. The FTC's doctors found much to disagree with in *The Health Finder*, including the fact it made no mention of available drugs for hypertension and other conditions. Prosecutors asked Dr. Donald Tschudy to run through a litany of conditions covered in the book and repeatedly inquired whether a patient would be assured of preventing things like colds, cancer, constipation, ulcers, and polio if they followed Rodale's advice. When asked about cancer, Tschudy claimed that Rodale neglected "the only acceptable means" of treating cancer by omitting surgery, chemotherapy, and radiation.[83] On polio, Tschudy called the book's discussion "passé" because the problem had been definitively solved by the Salk vaccine—which, he claimed, was the only way to prevent the disease. Over and over, prosecutors pulled apart pieces of *The Health Finder*'s recommendations about how to avoid a specific ailment and used expert witnesses to testify that the book's position was not sufficient because it ignored medical treatments administered at the hands of professionals. The book never told patients to ignore the doctor altogether, but its silence about seeking treatment ran counter to the medical profession's assumption that health advice was the domain of trained professionals.

In contrast, Rodale's legal team wanted to show that a layperson like Rodale had assembled some much-needed evidence about the long-term health effects of new chemicals that medical professionals were largely ignoring. To do so, Rodale's lawyers brought in their own set of witnesses to defend *The Health Finder* and the views of health pervasive in Rodale's magazines and books.[84] The first witness, Dr. Emmanuel Cheraskin, was an MD and dentist at the University of Alabama, who claimed that, unlike other health scientists who studied disease, he was a scientist who studied healthy people. Cheraskin began his testimony with a long discourse on what he saw as two competing views on health and disease—one view that sought to alter the environment in order to make a human body disease-free, and another that sought to improve the body's defenses against the environment. He explained that the latter view of health was what he called the "ecology and health" perspective and suggested that the benefit of *The Health Finder* was that its methods helped the body develop mechanisms that lowered susceptibility to what he called "environmental challenges."[85] Cheraskin agreed with Rodale's central premise that the body had a natural ability to ward off disease and chronic illnesses and saw techniques such as those Rodale promoted as a way to fortify the body's defenses against the environment.

Rodale's defense team hoped to show that Rodale had assembled valid evidence about the health effects of chronic exposure to chemicals even if his methods were unorthodox. That claim took center stage with the testimony of clinical ecologist Theron Randolph, a Chicago physician who in the mid-1940s began experimenting with ways of isolating allergic reactions to low-level exposures of chemical compounds. In the 1950s Randolph and a handful of other allergists developed a new field of medicine, clinical ecology, that would evolve in the 1980s into the discipline of environmental medicine.[86] Appearing before the FTC on behalf of Rodale, Randolph described himself as an expert in allergies and applied toxicology and offered his experiences of studying patients' personal histories and creating controlled experiments to determine the sources of allergic reactions. Randolph was specifically interested in individual susceptibility to household chemicals and insecticides that had come into use since the end of World War II. When he pointed out that *The Health Finder* was first published in 1954, Randolph claimed the book was prescient in highlighting the growing yet largely unacknowledged dangers of synthetic chemicals in everyday life. Furthermore, *The Health Finder*, "in contrast to most books on health, is written not from the standpoint of treatment, but from the standpoint of the prevention of disease."[87] In his testimony, Randolph ran through dozens of entries in the book where he agreed with Rodale's claims about the hazards of a certain substance and how proper nutrition might prevent certain chronic conditions.

Throughout his testimony, Randolph emphasized how the book highlighted areas where the "demonstration of cause and effect is exceedingly difficult" and complimented Rodale's ability to maneuver in parts of medicine that were "not completely black or white."[88] Indeed, many of Rodale's positions on the role of diet and exposure to chemicals echoed what Randolph outlined in his own 1962 book, *Human Ecology and Susceptibility to the Chemical Environment*.[89] Whereas J. I. Rodale had assembled his ideas from a hodgepodge of published sources combined with his experiences and those of his readers, the experiments Randolph detailed in his book aimed to provide clinical evidence of the hazards of synthetic chemical compounds. Clinical ecologists studied what the historian Michelle Murphy has called "the ordinary built environment of late capitalism" and focused their attention on subjective experience of the body with its surrounding environment.[90] Unlike toxicologists, who focused on the observable effects of a specific dose of a chemical and reasoned toward a general relationship between the human body and that substance, Randolph and his group of clinical ecologists aimed to isolate the subclinical and idiosyncratic effects that chemical compounds *could* have on an individual body.

The notion that synthetic chemical compounds or foods affected different bodies in different ways ran counter to one of the central organizing principles of modern medicine. Suggesting there were multiple causes, and multiple methods, to prevent disease was entirely counterintuitive to what Allen Brandt and Martha Gardner call the "biomedical paradigm of specific cause and cure."[91] In this paradigm, all bodies were the same regardless of the environment they inhabited or the substances they encountered. By contrast, Rodale and researchers like Randolph held that individual bodily experiences could differ with the environment, and that those individual experiences undermined biomedicine's assurances of both certainty as well as safety. Moreover, in calling for behavioral change—often in the form of diet guidelines or food supplements to limit personal exposure—Rodale's publications placed the onus for health not on doctors and laboratory results, but on individual consumers and their choices. Emphasizing the individual experience of the body's health, and its reactions to foods, chemicals, and other substances in the surrounding environment, Rodale's and *Prevention*'s view of health in many ways echoed older ideas about the body that predated the rise of laboratory medicine.[92] Just as the body was once understood to be open to the air, water, and soil that surrounded it, Rodale argued that even in the heyday of postwar biomedical achievements the health of the body remained susceptible to its surrounding environment.

Although neither Rodale nor his readers were experts, for years they assembled evidence of their subjective experience with the modern environment of daily life—its pollutants, detergents, synthetic building materials, mass-produced foods, nasal decongestants, pesticides, and fluoridated water. They asked much-needed questions about the health effects of these new substances, despite the fact that it would take many years for authorities to take such concerns seriously. Undoubtedly, a key reason why scientists overlooked these questions was because they came from magazines like *Prevention* and figures like Rodale. Rodale prized evidence that supported his theories and assembled firsthand experience in place of clinical evidence. Moreover, Rodale packaged his natural health theories with an untold number of poorly tested and often dubious health products. Rodale and his readers were farsighted in calling attention to how many new chemicals might be affecting human health, but they also rushed headlong to embrace food supplements and natural health remedies that strained credulity. In this way, the FTC action reveals how Rodale's marketplace created a necessary forum for consumer health concerns about diet and the environment. At the same time, the marketplace proved better at giving consumers products than generating valid evidence. Rodale and his natural health consumers learned to rely on intuition and experience, and picked and chose which scientific conclusions—as well as which products—to adopt and which to ignore.

The tension that emerged between Rodale's natural health consumers and scientific authorities would only grow with the changing environmental values of the late 1960s and early 1970s. Whether it questioned fallout from atomic testing, the need for new mega-dams in the American West, or the protection of endangered species, environmentalism championed a skeptical and critical outlook on scientific advances and expertise. Indeed, one of the environmental movement's great legacies was its push for consideration of the unintended consequences of new scientific and technological advances. But another defining feature of environmentalism was that it held some scientific conclusions close and rejected others. Like J. I. Rodale and his consumers, environmentalists learned to question experts in white lab coats and the certainty of their conclusions while also elevating the insights of fields like ecology. Many environmentalists would also be quick to embrace products and practices that validated their preexisting opinions, regardless of whether those products or practices aligned with scientific consensus. Rodale's battle with authorities over the marketplace proved to be prescient— not because time would ultimately prove that J. I. Rodale was right, but because that battle was the first of many more to come.

• • •

After an initial hearing in December 1964, which pitted the opinions of medical experts for and against Rodale's publications, the original complaint against Rodale was sustained by an FTC examiner. On appeal before the full commission, Rodale's defense team doubled down on its strategy of de-emphasizing the books' health claims and foregrounding the case's First Amendment issues. The fact that the Press continued to fight the FTC action several years after discontinuing advertising for the books in question gives some indication of how important its advertising practices had become to the overall operation. Indeed, the Rodale Press continued the battle in a federal appeals court in 1967 after a divided trade commission upheld the original decision.[93] While other publishers might have simply stopped the ads for a specific publication under such circumstances, the Rodale company's entire operation hinged on the profitability of its natural health claims. In newspaper coverage of the case, Thurman Arnold stated that if necessary he was prepared to take the case to the Supreme Court. In their federal appeal, Rodale's lawyers argued that advertisements were an extension of the book itself, and thus to censor Rodale's ads was to silence his ideas. Indeed, the millions of flyers, mailers, and circulars the company circulated along with its books and magazines were inseparable from Rodale's health ideas, which posited individuals' freedom to consume and adopt health ideas as they saw fit. A consumer's freedom to imbibe advice and products—with or without the approval of experts and authorities—would become a defining feature of marketplace environmentalism in the 1960s and beyond. The marketplace gave consumers the ability to pick and choose which brand of heath advice to subscribe to and which type of experts and evidence to follow. The marketplace also provided consumers with ways to challenge the biomedical consensus about the safety and efficacy of new chemical compounds. At the same time, it also provided an ever-growing array of products—many with little if any scientific evidence to back up their claims—with which consumers could pursue their chosen health philosophy.

Rodale's battle with the FTC did not end until December 1968 when a federal court of appeals ruled not that the company had a First Amendment right to freely advertise its ideas, but that the commission had violated due process when it ruled on a different premise from the original complaint. Although the Rodale Press failed in establishing a precedent for distributing unorthodox health ideas under the First Amendment, it secured the niche market for natural health ideas.

At a time when medical research aimed to uncover the specific etiologies of disease in a universalized body, J. I. Rodale and *Prevention* suggested that sources of disease were not singular but multifaceted. Likewise, the magazine argued that the source of good health could be found not in a doctor's prescription, but in the relationship between a body and its surrounding environment—a dynamic that doctors were largely ignoring in the postwar years. Rodale demonstrated that relationship by combining his personal bodily experience with those his readers eagerly shared. Combining those experiences with evidence clipped from scientific sources, Rodale argued there was much that remained uncertain about science, medicine, and technology in the postwar era.

Prevention offers a window into not only Rodale's critique of science and medicine, but also a broader set of "health-seeking behaviors" that consumers—with the help of firms like the Rodale Press—adopted in postwar America. Such behaviors, as Nancy Tomes has argued, reflect health concerns that have often expressed themselves not in hospitals and health care policy but in the marketplace.[94] Taking into account these "health-seeking behaviors" of Rodale and his readers reveals a lively commercial culture that grew in response to concerns about the risks of new chemical technologies in food and medicine as well as the built environment of daily life. It can be tempting to see these buying habits of natural health consumers as a soporific that made these individuals feel better but accomplished very little in the world. That type of thinking largely echoes older analyses of consumption that saw it as a distraction from the "real" work of industrial and political organizing.[95] Yet, by viewing consumption less as a black box that was either "good" or "bad" but instead as a critical and dynamic process, *Prevention* demonstrates an emerging set of tools and practices that consumers grasped to enact their concerns about health and the environment in daily life.

At the same time, Rodale and *Prevention* demonstrate an often-unacknowledged ambivalence about science that was woven into postwar environmentalism. Environmentalists challenged the power of experts and sought to transform the management of risk and uncertainty in the 1960s and 1970s. At the same time, environmentalism continued to rely on the insights and methods of science to set normative standards. However, like Rodale's readers, environmentalists also relied on their firsthand experience and turned to the marketplace to ratify their concerns when scientific consensus could not. *Prevention* provided a popular forum that validated personal anxieties with direct evidence and carefully selected science to back up Rodale's preexisting natural health theories. And although his forum gave voice to emerging health concerns about toxics that were largely overlooked by scientific authorities, it also responded with a plethora of poorly tested food supplements and an ever-growing pile of natural health paraphernalia. With *Prevention* Rodale showed how the virtue of the marketplace—its ability to foster personal choice and its openness to diverging ideas—was also its vice.

THREE

OUR POISONED EARTH AND SKY

Organic Citizens and Consumers

IN A 1959 PAMPHLET TITLED *THE WORLD'S HAPPIEST GARDENERS*,
the Rodale Press profiled a number of enthusiasts of the organic
method. The pamphlet began with the first-person story of Lois Hebble,
an organic enthusiast who, along with her husband, Speck, bought a
twenty-acre farm outside Decatur, Indiana, in 1949. With help from
family, the Hebbles built a ranch home on the property and moved there
in 1955. The couple raised livestock and maintained five small fields
where they rotated corn, oats, and hay. Mrs. Hebble described her husband, a machinist at the nearby General Electric plant, as a "part-time
farmer," the one responsible for building and maintaining the fences
and outbuildings, and the "chief user of farm equipment." Mrs. Hebble
was the "head gardener, in charge of starting all flowers and vegetable
plants; cleaning stables; caretaker of milk, butter-maker; fruit preserver;
vegetable canner and freezer, plus all the rest that goes with a family of
four children."

Like many farm families, the Hebbles' household budget was tight.
To help buy school clothes and books, and to save money for college,
thirteen-year-old Iris and twelve-year-old Ben sold berries and raised
rabbits. After detailing the fruits and vegetables she grew in her garden,
Mrs. Hebble discussed the costs of putting in her garden. She could not
say exactly how much her garden saved her, but she figured she only
needed to spend ten to fifteen dollars a week at the grocery store as a
result of all that she grew and preserved. Mrs. Hebble knew families of

a similar size and "moderate means" who spent nearly twice that on their weekly groceries and "they don't get nearly as good food as we have." As for the farm, "there won't be any money spent on expensive chemical fertilizers or sprays, you can bet." To stretch their budget, the Hebbles collected organic matter from many sources to enrich their soil—accepting tons of free leaves from the city, gathering sawdust from local mills, and taking spoiled hay from other farms. Reflecting on the value of "organic living," Mrs. Hebble closed her essay by commenting, "I think this way of living is wonderful. I know we could never afford to be paying for our new house with our present income if we did not save money on our food this way and if we had medical and dental bills to pay all the time. And, as you can see, it really is a wonderful way to raise a family!"[1]

Five years later, in 1964, the Rodale Press published a seven-hundred-page volume on the ubiquitous threat of toxic chemicals called *Our Poisoned Earth and Sky*. The book, like others published by the company, was largely drawn from material already published by J. I. Rodale and his staff. But whereas *The World's Happiest Gardeners* featured images of smiling couples, healthy families, and robust retirees, the cover of *Our Poisoned Earth and Sky* showed a man in a spray suit with a breathing mask and an airplane casting chemicals from high above a forest. Beyond just the cover images, the book's tone about the dangers of chemicals and toxic exposure departed from the Rodale Press's earlier publications. The jacket asked how much readers knew about the food and pollution laws protecting citizens, and whether their own state was "authorized to douse you, your children, and your garden with poison from the air?" Instead of tips for keeping soils rich in humus, the book detailed the chemicals in foods, cosmetics, drinking water, air, and countless other substances of daily life.[2] In addition to describing the ubiquity of toxic chemicals, the book was forthright about writing to local legislators and taking action against polluters. Enlisting readers in a common cause against chemicals, the book declared, "Even if you have nothing to sue about, you can write letters. You can write letters to the legislators, and you can also write letters to the papers. Some of them may be printed, and every one that is, helps."[3]

How did the happy gardeners of the 1950s become the activists fighting against the intrusion of chemicals in the environment in the next

Direct-mail advertisement for *Our Poisoned Earth and Sky*, 1966.
Courtesy of the Rodale Family Archives and the American Medical
Association Archives.

decade, and what role did the Rodale Press play in facilitating that transition? J. I. Rodale had long described himself as the founder of the organic
"movement" in the United States, but it was not until the late 1950s that
"organic" signified something more than a method for fertilizing soils.
In the 1940s and for much of the 1950s, to be an organic gardener meant
to choose to make composts rather than purchasing fertilizers that were
manufactured by synthesizing nitrogen and other soil nutrients. But
beginning in the late 1950s, organic enthusiasts began to reject the use

of chemicals in their own backyards, in the environment, and in daily life. Like many other Americans, organic enthusiasts were learning more about the threats to their health that were raining down from the atmosphere, building up in their soils, and flowing through the food and drink they consumed. As they learned more about these new threats, being an organic gardener was no longer just about making compost—it came to stand for something more.

In his classic history of postwar environmentalism, Samuel Hays describes the emergence of what he calls a "toxic perception" in the postwar world. Hays locates the origins of concerns about pesticides with wildlife biologists, food and drug regulators, and public health officials that tallied the growing effects of pesticides on both people and the environment.[4] In the pages of Rodale's *Organic Gardening and Farming* the work of scientists played a prominent role, but it was in the experience of readers where such a "toxic perception" took hold. Because they collected the experiences of readers, the Rodale Press publications serve a site where we can watch the formation of shared identity and a common cause among organic gardeners.

Rodale's *Organic Gardening and Farming* brought together the efforts of gardeners as both consumers and citizens. While this aspect of his history was largely overlooked at the time because of *Prevention* and the questionable advice and products it peddled, J. I. Rodale is increasingly viewed as a prescient voice in questioning the use of pesticides such as DDT many years before the issue reached headlines in 1962 with the publication of Rachel Carson's *Silent Spring*. Less appreciated is the role that Rodale's publications, rather than just J. I. himself, played in tying together a nascent movement aimed at ending the indiscriminate use of chemicals. Because *Organic Gardening and Farming* responded to and included readers in the production of the magazine, it created a place where information could be shared and action could be coordinated. Transforming the prosaic concerns of gardeners about soils and foods into action started with a bustling group of organic gardening clubs that came to life through the pages of *OG&F*. At the same time, a group of editors and writers at the Rodale Press, particularly J. I.'s son, Robert, articulated the importance of environmental protection on the scale of the home, the garden, and the body. Since launching *Organic Gardening and Farming* in 1942, the company's publications knitted organic gardeners together with a shared set of ideas, practices, and products. In the late 1950s and throughout the 1960s, however, the company also helped move gardeners beyond their compost heaps.

A PRACTICAL REVOLUTION

When the cultural critic Raymond Williams explored the complex etymologies that shaped "keywords" of our cultural vocabulary in 1976, the word "organic" did not escape his purview. In its earliest incarnation it implied an instrument or tool, much like church "organ" or a part of the body. Starting with the Romantic movement of the mid-nineteenth century, it came to stand in contrast to a word with which it had once been synonymous, "mechanical." By the early twentieth century, Williams claimed, the word had taken a primarily conservative cast in social thought, where "organic" described a society that preexisted the rise of the modern state and industry, a notion exploited for darker purposes during the rise of totalitarian regimes in the interwar years. Writing in the mid-1970s, Williams found that in his own time it had become a description of a specific relationship to society, such as an ecological relationship. Additionally, Williams noted, it now referred to a "specialized use of farming and foods, with a stress on *natural* rather than *artificial* fertilizers or growing and breeding methods." This use of "organic," Williams claimed, was "linked with general criticism of *industrial* society."[5]

Twenty-five years before Williams laid out his definition, the word meant something far simpler for those who identified themselves as organic gardeners. At its most basic, "organic" described a method for increasing the biological content of soils through composting techniques rather than chemical fertilizers and controlling insects without resorting to chemical sprays. These practices surely ran counter to the general trend of agricultural science—which had been busy synthesizing fertilizers and new pesticides for decades—yet those who chose organic methods in the 1950s often did so not to challenge modern life, but because they found it to be more healthful, practical, and, in some ways, *more* modern than available alternatives. In this way, *organic* was not an out-of-hand rejection of industrial society and modern life, but a search for what the sociologist Ulrich Beck has called a "new modernity."[6]

J. I. Rodale was outspoken about the benefits of the organic method for the health of soils and humans; however, aside from his editorials, *Organic Gardening and Farming* was hardly a polemical space. J. I. Rodale continued to produce these monthly editorials for *OG&F* even after his son Robert took over day-to-day operations of the magazine in the early fifties. These pieces often highlighted how the use of chemical fertilizers harmed the biological life of soils and contributed to drought and the erosion of farmland. Yet those critiques did not extend to pushing for a radical change in the political, social, and economic forces that underlay the production and consumption of chemicals in agriculture. Both J. I. and Robert Rodale frequently impugned the "chemical interests" they felt controlled agricultural science and kept the organic method from being scientifically researched. In a 1955 series called "Organic Economics" J. I. claimed that synthetic insecticides and fertilizers meant "the farmer is really left holding the bag for the chemical companies and equipment manufacturers. They [chemical companies] are like the 'house' in gambling places, getting their share, win or lose." The magazine frequently called into question why the USDA and state agricultural colleges and experiment stations were not investigating the organic method, and often pointed to the political and economic influence of chemical companies as an explanation. In Rodale's estimation, farming journals and magazines, which benefited from extensive advertising for chemicals and machinery, also carried water for chemical companies: "They heap nothing but scorn on the organic method for if that system of farming should ever become widespread in its practice, they fear there would be far less advertising income for them." As an alternative, Rodale told his readers that when the organic method "takes over," there would be just as many "organic products to manufacture and advertise," and that a whole new consumer market would be created.[7]

In his most strident critiques of food production, Rodale aimed to show how organic ideas would lead to broader changes in the farm economy. Rodale claimed in a 1956 piece titled "The Organic Creed" that the organic method was "a vigorous and growing movement, one that is destined to alter our conceptions of the farm and the garden and to revolutionize our methods of operating them in order to secure for ourselves and others more abundant and more perfect food." Pointing out the growing scale of farms that new machinery and chemical technologies made possible, he suggested that organic growers "were against the operation of hundred thousand acre farm-factories." However, the growers opposed such farms because they violated what he called the Law of Return—the dictum to return farm wastes to productive purposes—not because they consolidated land or capital. Rodale suggested that unlike other farmers, organic farmers could not focus only on producing one commodity crop: "The organiculturist must not practice one-crop monoculture but must engage in a balanced agriculture with cattle as part of the general program. He must be smart in the ways of soils and crops, observing the reaction of the land to the actions of man."[8]

In other editorials, Rodale suggested the need to form cooperatives as a way of supporting organic food production at larger scales. Rodale was never an advocate for radically restructuring the political economy of agriculture, and given the political climate at the height of the McCarthy era it seems unlikely he would have critiqued capitalism too strenuously. In May 1956 he told readers, "I am a capitalist and I believe in capitalism, but the capitalist principle is murder as far as food is concerned."[9] He pointed to cooperative farming models in Europe as a potential solution and suggested that readers might need to form cooperative relationships with farmers on their own. But Rodale spent more of his editorial columns describing how conventionally produced foods affected human health than he did weighing in on questions of politics. He might just as easily switch from a series on farm economics to a travelogue about farming in Central America to a series on using electricity to stimulate growth and vitality in plants. Rodale's personal politics rarely entered into either of his magazines or any of his other activities.

Even if there was some strident language about chemical companies found in Rodale's editorials, the remaining pages were full of practical and prosaic advice for gardeners. Indeed, Rodale's core audience was middle- and upper-class homeowners who chose to garden with compost. Between 1949 and 1954 Rodale had tried to connect with farmers by operating a separate magazine called *The Organic Farmer*. When that magazine failed, Rodale created *Organic Gardening and Farming*, which, despite the title, focused primarily on gardening. Through their stories of garden successes and failures and their reviews of recommended procedures, OG&F's writers wove together a short course in organic methods, which aside from avoiding chemical inputs would not have been all that different from the practical advice found in most popular gardening magazines and books of the day. In a 1961 manual drawn from the magazine's columns, *How to Grow Fruits and Vegetables by the Organic Method*, Rodale's staff included sections on every possible step of the home-gardening process, from drawing plans for the garden in winter, to testing and preparing the soil, to planting and transplanting, to harvesting and storing surplus.[10] With descriptive instructions for the organic cultivation of fruit, nuts, and herbs, the book offered little invective against modern agriculture or modern life, but a great deal of practical advice for the home gardener.

One of the ways the magazine underscored practicality was by telling readers that organic methods were a frugal choice. Just as Lois Hebble in *The World's Happiest Gardeners* found avoiding chemical fertilizers and sprays to be the best way to afford her family's homestead in Decatur, perhaps the greatest value associated with the organic method was pecuniary. In articles written by Rodale's staff and in contributions from readers, there was a clear sense that as a system for saving and reusing garden wastes, the organic method could also be a matter of thrift. Articles such as "How to Spend Your Garden Dollar" and many others argued the method not only saved money otherwise spent on insecticides and fertilizers, but could become a source of income as well. In addition to advocating canning and preservation of homegrown foods, the magazine encouraged home gardeners to sell their extra produce to local markets and at roadside stands.[11] The magazine promoted home food preservation as the best way for organic gardeners to preserve their harvests and have access to organic foods year-round. While not explicitly anti-consumerist, this type of advice about frugality and doing more work yourself stood out from other consumer magazines in the 1950s that highlighted the ease and convenience of packaged and prepared food products. Most consumer magazines depicted the work of food production and preparation as a thing of the past and were chock-full of advertising for the latest frozen foods

April, 1959   35 Cents

ORGANIC
Gardening and Farming

Organic Homesteading
In Florida   ...p. 31
Planting Secrets of the
Experts   ...p. 38

Cover of *Organic
Gardening and
Farming*, April
1959. Courtesy
of the Rodale
Family Archives.

and time-saving kitchen devices. By contrast, *OG&F* embraced home food production and offered readers patient and practical advice to make it a reality.

For readers, it was the practical articles in *OG&F* that had the most appeal. Each issue of the magazine in the 1950s featured a "With the Editor" column written by J. I. Rodale, which later in the decade would be taken over by his son Robert. However, in a 1955 reader survey, when asked to name the articles they found most helpful, readers named very few written by J. I. and instead chose articles on topics such as pruning, insect-control tips, earthworms, tree planting, tilling, quick compost methods, and treating plant disease without chemicals.[12] Respondents to the survey also told the editors which departments of the magazine they enjoyed the most, and many reported that the "Letters" section was what they turned to first. Just as letters printed were a source of evidence and camaraderie for natural health enthusiasts in *Prevention*, learning and sharing practical advice with other enthusiasts kept readers eagerly returning to *OG&F* each month.

The avid gardeners who read Rodale's magazine proved more than willing to share their own experiences along with their practical solutions and gardening knowledge. For all the systematic rigor J. I. Rodale claimed to apply to organic experiments on his own farm, in the hands of Rodale readers the method proved to be far more malleable. In a 1956 "Fall Fertilizer Round-Up" the magazine highlighted readers from a variety of growing regions and their methods for fertilizing soils. Robert Sharp of Ira, Vermont, created a layered compost heap consisting of plant waste, chicken manure mixed with sawdust, sheep manure, ground limestone, ground rock phosphate, soil, and a "soil activator" known as Activo. Elsie Picot of Florida started her compost off in garbage cans and then turned it into potting soil by adding peat moss, sand, dried sheep manure, charcoal, parakeet droppings, and bone meal. Mrs. Picot's neighbors, the Underwoods, chose not to build compost piles, but used a compost grinder to shred leaves and cuttings to be used as mulch. Mrs. E. A. Turlington of Venice, California, described how she put "buckets" of her compost mixture around the base of her fruit trees in the fall and then let winter rains and snow "filter its goodness down to the tree roots."[13] While they could not vouch for a reader's piece of practical advice, the magazine's editors frequently reminded readers that the organic method could be as much an art as a science.

The magazine also highlighted the practicality of the organic method by repurposing timeworn methods from a generation of gardeners who had come of age before pesticides and fertilizers were common. One of *OG&F*'s most prominent and prolific contributors in the late 1950s and 1960s was Ruth Stout, a Connecticut garden writer in her seventies who developed a method of keeping her garden covered entirely in a mat of hay, paper, weeds, and garden waste. This method,

Stout claimed in *OG&F* articles and books, reduced the labor involved in gardening and produced remarkable results. Stout had devised her method decades earlier, but it was only once she was featured in *OG&F* that her garden became a site of interest for organic enthusiasts. Stout was bemused by the number of people who toured her garden after it was featured in a July 1956 piece listing fifty places for organic gardeners to visit.[14] Stout had developed a practical if somewhat idiosyncratic solution to a problem gardeners and farmers shared—how to get the most out of soils with the smallest amount of labor. Furthermore, Stout's gardening practices were emblematic of a type of gardening knowledge and practice that had once been common before the widespread adoption of chemical fertilizers and sprays. A resourceful use of garden and kitchen wastes had, in the not-too-distant past, been an everyday occurrence and an essential household skill. However, by the mid-1950s new chemical technologies made relying on biological matter something that stood out. To a certain extent, Stout's garden could only become "organic" once a chemical alternative came into existence.

Even when organic gardeners adopted advice rooted in the past, the magazine's editors promised that a new generation of power tools made those methods more modern and practical than ever. Since the 1930s, when Sir Albert Howard began publishing the composting ideas he had developed in the context of plantation agriculture in colonial India, organic advocates in England and the United States continually ran up against the problem of the labor, time, and cost that producing compost required. Even at the scale of a farmstead or a large backyard garden, the amount of labor needed to produce composts could be a hurdle. With a new array of farming tools—such as lawn tractors, rototillers, shredders, and mowers—being scaled down for home use in the years after World War II, organic gardeners had new implements to help reduce labor. *Organic Gardening and Farming*'s editors raved about the new "power gardening machines," which eliminated the labor of pushing mowers, hoeing weeds, cutting with scythes, and dragging wheelbarrows.[15] Many of the stories in the magazine showed editors and writers using these devices and offering the pros and cons of the newest models and attachments. Likewise, in the same way that *Prevention* was filled with food supplement ads, the pages of *OG&F* in the 1950s were filled with advertisements for the latest power tools.[16]

Machinery helped bolster the argument that the organic method could be applied at scales larger than the backyard garden. Compost piles in suburban vegetable patches and flowerbeds were one thing, but making and applying composts at the scale of a farm was a different story. In a 1959 profile of a two-hundred-acre farm in upstate New York, editor Jerome Olds detailed how a mechanized system of compost production had allowed the Carsten family to rebuild their soils and increase their yields. Each year the Carstens composted over four hundred tons of manure with the help of an automatic barn cleaner and spreading equipment. In addition to handling waste on their own farm, they gathered over fifty tons of leaves from a nearby town, as well as sawmill wastes and roadside plant trimmings. All this work of piling, moving, turning, and spreading organic composts would have been prohibitively time- and labor-intensive, Olds claimed, without the use of machinery.[17]

Just as a new generation of power tools were essential for making composts, so, too, were they essential for operating a homestead. The magazine did not think its readers were giving up on modern life in order to eke out a living in nature; rather, it addressed them as modern consumers who would adopt tools and technologies to make their lives easier and more convenient. The magazine in the 1950s was eager to appeal to the growing ranks of "sundowners," farmers who owned twenty acres or fewer and worked their land as the sun went down after work. Machinery would be essential for achieving the ideal suburban lives and landscapes of what one Rodale writer called these "country dwellers–city workers" who were escaping the confines of the city and seeking the health and peace of the country. In a 1954 OG&F piece hailing "The New Exodus," writer Thomas Powell claimed, "It is dawning upon many of us that the problems of city life far outweigh its advantages. Hemmed in by steel and concrete, in huge concentrations that breed slums, crime and discontent, the city dweller's lot is an unhappy one. He daily faces smog, traffic hazards, fear of the A-bomb . . . housing shortages and an insidious, terrifying loss of individuality." Yet, in order to accomplish the practical tasks of running a farm and enjoying life, an escape from the city was hardly an escape from technology: "But send the people back to the land, armed with modern technology and the science of organics, and prosperity and good living will be their heritage."[18] Producing food with the organic method may have required more work, but new technologies made that work easier than ever before.

Much like his views on agricultural production, J. I. Rodale's views on homesteading were built around practical concerns more than politics. In an April 1957 issue devoted to the "modern homestead," J. I. Rodale specifically laid out what he saw as the relationship between the organic method and homesteading. As always, health remained at the core of J. I. Rodale's enthusiasm: "To have a small piece of land and to work it on a part-time basis would be an ideal way of assuring sufficient daily healthful activity and, at the same time giving a family the healthiest kind of food." Rodale went on to prescribe how to select the proper size and location for a homestead.[19] When he encouraged readers to be "pioneers" in leading a back-to-the-land movement in the 1950s, he was emphatically *not* arguing for radical decentralization of economic production. Instead, he argued that living in the country and having a small farmstead promoted improved health. Rodale also routinely described the purchasing of land as a sound and stable investment, and he took his own advice by slowly accumulating parcels in and around the Lehigh Valley.

Moreover, the vision of an "organic homestead" did not mean rejecting modern tools, but rather using them differently. In a May 1961 editorial titled "Every Man a Homesteader," Robert Rodale mused about what it meant to create an "organic homestead" in the postwar world. When the magazine first introduced the phrase in April 1957, Robert and the other writers were not entirely sure what they were trying to suggest by it. "To some," Robert noted, "the word homestead connotes the wild pioneer days when people lived in sod houses or log cabins and struggled for years to make the land yield its blessings. People today don't want to work that hard, some say, and therefore the word homestead is not attractive." Robert Rodale was convinced, however, the phrase continued to hold important meaning for organic enthusiasts. For the original homesteaders, "the land was their life, for better or for worse. Organic gardeners today are just as concerned about the land as any homesteader of old, even more so." Echoing Frederick Jackson Turner's theory of history, he felt that homesteading made organic gardeners part of a modern vanguard: "We are trying to carry the stewardship of the land to a higher order of perfection, to a point where the fruits of that land will produce not just life, but a better life."[20] Yet even these moments of idealism were couched in practical reasons that appealed to organic enthusiasts. The reason to embrace "modern homesteading," according to Robert Rodale, was to provide a family with a year-round supply of healthy, organic foods. Homesteaders, he argued, were not satisfied with only having organic food for their families during the months their garden produced; instead, they wanted to have "an all-year-round supply of fruits, vegetables, grain, eggs, some kind of meat and even milk from cows or goats." What would drive people back to the land in the United States, Robert Rodale suggested, would not be wars or economic depressions like in the past, but instead a search for healthy foods that were unavailable in the sleek new supermarkets of the 1950s. Predicting that it would be "a long time before you can walk into any supermarket and buy organically grown, unsprayed food," Robert Rodale told gardeners they would have to rely on their own land for the foreseeable future.[21]

While certainly dissenting from some aspects of consumer society in the 1950s, the Rodales and their cadre of gardeners pushed back against some elements and embraced others. Indeed, the "organic revolution" the Rodales promoted on the pages of OG&F was practical more than political. They found older gardening methods and ideas to still be practical and frugal choices while at the same time embracing modern tools and gardening machines. They rejected the convenience of synthetic pesticides and fertilizers while encouraging the use of fossil-fueled machines that made it easier to produce compost. They elevated the ideal of an organic homestead as a contrast to the suburban tract home but subscribed to a shared vision of an idealized life of health, comfort, and prosperity. Even when it challenged the consensus of agricultural scientists and food producers in the 1950s and 1960s, OG&F maintained a moderate tone and instructed readers in the pleasures of making their backyards into organic oases. Rodale's organic enthusiasts were committed gardeners who wanted to produce as much of their food as possible using their own compost-enriched soils, but they did not seek to turn back the clock on modern life. Aside from their compost heaps, their organic oases would likely not have stood out from other houses in the postwar suburbs. However, when those oases became threatened by chemical intrusions, organic gardeners proved to be less inclined to keep to themselves—the practical and personal choices of gardeners could also become political.

THE RESPONSIBILITY OF BEING ORGANIC

Although it is difficult to exactly identify who was subscribing to OG&F in the 1950s and 1960s, from the profiles that appeared in the magazine it is clear the audience was gardeners with both the time and the resources to lavish care on their soils. These devoted gardeners were primarily older Americans who owned their own homes and had a passion for their gardens. Some focused on their fruit trees, others on specific flowers like roses, while still others treasured their herbs and vegetables. Yet those gardeners also ran the risk that their efforts could amount to nothing. When an airplane dropped pesticides onto a nearby farm, or the state highway commission sprayed roadside weeds, these gardeners felt as if the hours they had spent turning compost piles and building soils rich in organic matter had been for naught. Moreover, they perceived more than just their gardens to be under assault from chemicals. As a result of the expanding array of new technologies in the 1950s, these gardeners felt the choices they made about their soils had consequences beyond their own backyards. Describing the increasing ubiquity of chemicals in daily life, J. I. Rodale suggested in a 1958 editorial titled "What Does Organic Mean" that there was a new sense of responsibility among organic gardeners:

> We must become active articulate churchgoers and citizens. We must not sit in fear of the self-appointed authorities who are, dog-in-the-manger fashion, standing in the way of improvement of the world's conception of nutrition. We must speak up to our ministers, to our teachers, congressman, judges, businessman, scientists and statesman. We must be organic on the soil, in our homes, in our offices, on the streets, in our churches, in the schools, in the voting booths, and in the vegetable and meat markets. We must be vocally and actively organic. We must live it day and night, making no exceptions, tolerating no loopholes or subterfuges.[22]

Rodale's message demonstrates the fact that organic gardeners expanded their horizons in the late 1950s and early 1960s. Even as the magazine filled its pages each month with seemingly mundane advice about perennials and ads for rototillers, OG&F played a central role in helping organic enthusiasts counter new chemical technologies outside their garden gates. In the same way that the magazine acted as a gathering place for different compost methods, so, too, did it become a place where readers could connect with one another's experiences of chemicals. These experiences, like much of the evidence Rodale relied on in *Prevention*, were often anecdotal and deeply personal, but they nonetheless established shared understandings and strategies. Readers in the 1950s told stories about what happened when a neighbor or a friend used DDT, or they sent in clippings from their local papers about the effects of roadside spraying on flowers, bushes, and wildlife. Such stories emerged from different places across the country, and through the pages of Rodale's magazine they could be recast as a shared experience and a shared responsibility across disparate locales. Rodale's magazine worked to help readers connect their own backyards with those of other organic enthusiasts. In addition to creating a shared set of gardening practices around the organic method, the magazine gave readers the power to organize themselves into a nascent but active network of organic gardeners, consumers, and concerned citizens. And it was this network that demonstrated marketplace environmentalism's potential as a political force.

The work of organizing organic gardeners began first with gardening clubs. Within a few years of publishing his magazine, J. I. Rodale mentioned the letters he received from readers describing their interest in forming gardening clubs devoted to organic methods. Like any other set of groups, garden clubs in the mid-twentieth century had their various divisions—some were organized around an affinity for a specific set of plants, such as roses or orchids, while others might be more general, focusing on perennials or vegetables. Gardening clubs referring to themselves as "organic" did not appear until the late 1940s, when a small set of clubs chose to define themselves by their preferred fertilizing method. By the mid-1950s clubs were a regular feature in OG&F, and the magazine announced the formation of state and local groups and publicized their activities. Beginning in 1954 the magazine compiled a yearly directory that listed seventy-eight clubs in twenty-four states.[23] In many ways, it was these gatherings in home basements and public libraries that sowed the inauspicious seeds of the organic movement, where J. I. Rodale's ideas were transformed into action.

These early clubs were certainly small—perhaps led by one devoted gardener with a spouse and a few friends—but through the pages of *OG&F* they located their activities in a larger context. Just as they used the magazine to share composting tips, enthusiasts used Rodale publications to share information and strategies on forming clubs and taking active roles in their communities. In the January 1956 issue of *OG&F* the magazine's editors announced that 1956 would be a banner year for organically grown food and organic gardening clubs. The magazine claimed that clubs could be a "potent force for community betterment," and that they were the best way to introduce others to the organic method. To that end, writer Audrey Stephan suggested clubs should make a goal of having each member bring three new people to meetings over the course of the year. Likewise, program chairpersons should plan to discuss a different principle of the organic method at each meeting to get new members up to speed. To increase visibility, Stephan suggested that clubs use local papers to announce meetings and activities.[24] Connecting with other organic clubs was another important goal. The magazine frequently told clubs to model their efforts on those of a particularly active set of clubs in Michigan. Formed by ten clubs around the state and comprising close to five hundred members, the Federated Organic Clubs of Michigan was the earliest and largest organization centered on organic practices. Their 1956 Fall Round-Up (held at the Delhi Township Hall in Holt, Michigan) drew over four hundred people for two days of farm tours, symposiums, lectures, and potlucks. Thanks to coverage in local and state newspapers as well as *OG&F*, the weekend became an annual event marked with great fervor among organic enthusiasts.[25] In the years to come, similar club events would be held in California, New York, Florida, and Colorado.

Clubs not only exchanged ideas and camaraderie, they brought together gardeners to buy and sell organically grown foods. A feature of events such as the Fall Round-Up was often a produce auction or swap meet where enthusiasts bought and sold their organic goods. This marketplace was also replicated in the classified pages of both *Prevention* and *OG&F*. Such marketplaces reflected a central problem that organic enthusiasts faced in the 1950s—namely, that there existed only a very small consumer market to meet their demands. *Organic Gardening and Farming* tried to increase the availability of organic produce by educating small-scale producers on how to sell their organic produce and how to find buyers. The magazine offered advice on how to advertise and display produce at roadside stands and even printed cards that sellers could use to explain the organic method and its health benefits.[26] The magazine also frequently ran stories about how clubs could extend their activities from swap meets to cooperative buying and eventually into small-scale stores.[27]

Health food stores, like organic garden clubs, were another place organic enthusiasts came together as both consumers and citizens. For many years health food stores had existed as independent islands scattered across the landscape. Some stores had begun for particular religious or social purposes, while others had been created out of interest in better health. These organic enthusiasts and health food consumers who subscribed to Rodale's magazines in the 1950s and 1960s have generally been overlooked in favor of their much younger and hipper counterparts who became the focus of media attention in the late 1960s. The food historian Warren Belasco concludes that older health "nuts" in the 1950s saw organic foods as a means for treating their specific ailments and living longer, while younger consumers a decade later were drawn to these stores by the underground vibe and a desire to subvert industrial food production.[28] In this sense, health foodists of the 1950s—to use Michael Ackerman's kinder term—saw their involvement in health food stores in a limited scope.[29] However, a closer reading of Rodale's magazines reveals that there was much more going on in health food circles in this period. These foodists were not as media savvy and memorable as the radical "Diggers" of San Francisco in the late 1960s, but through their activities in both the garden and the marketplace these enthusiasts rooted their activities in a context larger than their own backyards.

One of the key ways *OG&F* aided organic consumers was by serving as the vital source for shared information and interpersonal connection. To that end, in the late 1950s the Rodale Press created an "active" space for organic gardeners with a monthly feature called "Organic World." Before 1954 "Organic World" had been an occasional column, but with the start of Robert Rodale's tenure as editor it became the frontispiece of the magazine, providing bulleted news items from around the country. Although much of the magazine's content remained decidedly practical and apolitical, in the "Organic World" section the magazine directly told readers how to confront the wider world of chemicals. Like much of what the Rodales published, the items covered in the column could be a mixed bag—a blurb about the world's largest brush chipper might sit next to a plea to readers to write Congress in support of the Delaney Bill regulating food additives.[30] But the section also publicized matters such as gatherings of gardening clubs and meetings of state and regional natural health groups like the Natural Food Associates. It was also the space where Robert Rodale, in particular, developed his editorial point of view and made some of his most overt statements against the chemical industry and its influence on government and agricultural research.

As was common in Rodale publications, the "Organic World" section read like a digest that gathered together small pieces from academic, scientific, and popular news sources. An August 1955 edition, for instance, reported on an address to the American Academy of Nutrition by Dr. William Coda Martin on the inferior nourishment of Americans and the poorly understood effects of sprays, dyes, and antibiotics on the quality of food. The next item, drawn from the *Chicago Tribune*, reported on a ton of tomatoes produced in Australia by using thick layers of compost in a greenhouse. Two items drew from Britain's leading organic magazine, *Mother Earth*, while another came from New Zealand's *Compost Magazine*. Another item mentioned a finding of the United States Public Health Service that up to thirty-five disease-carrying insects were found to have developed resistance to certain pesticides. On this point the magazine editorialized, "It is becoming increasingly clear that an endless circle of more toxic chemicals is not the solution to either pest or disease control." A final item in this grab bag of stories reminded farm operators to apply for the expanded Social Security coverage that began in 1955.[31] "Organic World" also reported on local- and state-level developments of interest to organic enthusiasts. Updating readers on a bill in the Wisconsin legislature in 1957 that would have allowed the use of sulfites to prevent "potato darkening," the magazine stated, "The moral here is that state legislatures must be watched carefully, for they seem to be much more subject to industry pressures than Congress and they also appear to be taking on work which should rightly be the province of the Food and Drug Administration."[32] Insect outbreaks, droughts, and other seasonal events were frequently mentioned as well, and every so often the column offered a bit of "news of the weird" for organic gardeners, such as a 250,000-ton compost heap or a gigantic pumpkin grown without chemicals.[33] In 1963 Robert Rodale would borrow this format of "Organic World" and create a new stand-alone weekly publication, *The Health Bulletin*, which provided a bulleted list of current events and political talking points on natural health issues in the United States.

The "Organic World" column was also where the editors addressed readers most directly about getting involved with the magazine and with issues affecting organic enthusiasts. "All of us on the editorial staff here in Emmaus are in reality working for you" the column declared in 1955.[34] The editors frequently reminded readers that their involvement in the magazine was a barometer of the strength of organic enthusiasm in the country. In 1958 Robert Rodale summarized the state of interest in organic methods and the magazine's role:

> In America, interest in organic methods is at an all-time high (if the readership of this magazine can be used as an index of such interest). The subscriber list of Organic Gardening and Farming now totals 175,000, more than ever before. Just 18 months ago the circulation was half that amount. We feel that one of the most important reasons for this growth is the fact that more people are waking up to the dangers of eating foods treated with liberal amounts of spray poisons and grown on soil lacking natural fertility but puffed up with chemical fertilizers. People are reading about organic gardening in the hope of growing their own food that they can rely on to be unchemicalized.[35]

Much like helping readers form garden clubs and publishing indexes of natural food suppliers, "Organic World" was a site where editors, along with its readers, used the magazine as a place to create a network of mutual concern about pesticides and chemicals. The creation of such a network would be foundational to recognizing that chemical exposures were not just a concern in one locale but rather across the entire country. American consumers had long relied on networks of print to link their local, personal actions to broader social and political movements. As Lawrence Glickman argues in his history of consumer activism, networks of "long-distance solidarity" were foundational to creating shared group identity across geographic and political distance. In the pages of OG&F in the 1950s and 1960s, readers' disparate concerns about health and chemical exposure—which they expressed in their own backyards—could be woven together to reflect a broader set of concerns—and increasingly a broader set of actions.[36]

What it meant to be an organic gardener took on new meaning when synthetic chemicals intruded into yards and homes. For centuries, food growers had relied on biological methods like birds and cultural methods such as companion plants to outwit insects. Likewise, the use of chemicals in farm production was also common prior to 1945. Growers had long applied various preparations and compounds to protect their plants, and substances derived from arsenic became common in battles against pests in the second half of the nineteenth century.[37] Gardeners, for the most part, had little use for these industrial-grade chemicals, which were often expensive, dangerous, and complicated to use at home. That would change in the decade after 1945, as a new class of chemical pesticides made their way to market. As the historian Edmund Russell recounts in his work on the links between pesticides and war technology, chemical manufacturers eagerly sought to scale down chemicals that had been developed during the war for use in the home.[38] Like the rototillers, lawn tractors, and the bounty of other products that consumers purchased, powerful pesticides became common household goods in the 1950s. These synthetic chemicals provided a tool for creating tidy, manicured, and pest-free landscapes—orderly natural spaces that complemented the orderliness of the postwar suburban home.

Stories about gardeners taking action moved from the back pages as the application of insecticides on public and private lands became a rallying cry for organic gardeners to unite in direct political activity. In May 1954 the magazine reported on the story of six-year-old Michael

Ogden from Hood River, Oregon, who died earlier in the year after coming in contact with the powerful insecticide tetraethyl pyrophosphate, known as TEPP. The story had circulated in newspapers around the country, and *OG&F* claimed that "thousands" of readers sent clippings from their local papers that reported the boy's death. In a piece titled "Needless Death versus Organics," the magazine's editors wrote that they were saddened that it took the death of a child to bring national attention to the dangers of such a substance.[39] Several months later, in October 1954, the magazine made brief mention of a group of organic gardeners who succeeded in stopping aerial spraying near Bridgewater, Connecticut. Frank and Helen Hadley, who were members of the Organic Soil-Builders Club of Litchfield County, had agitated through the local press to stop the spraying of DDT to prevent gypsy moths.[40] Such news items, about local groups battling local- and state-level spraying programs, appeared with increased frequency in *OG&F* in the late 1950s and point to the fact that organic enthusiasts were becoming less and less content to take care of only their own backyards.

As was common in Rodale publications, evidence of the dangers of pesticides and other chemicals often began with anecdotes gleaned from news articles. Stories of acute poisoning incidents on farms proved to be a rich source. A single paragraph in the "Organic World" for February 1956 mentioned a farmer in Missouri who noticed paralyzed quail after a neighboring farm sprayed Aldrin for grasshopper control, another farmer who saw fish die after cattle sprayed with toxaphene wandered into the water, and a farmer whose neighbor's cat was poisoned from eating birds in a garden sprayed with Aldrin.[41] In the hands of the Rodale editors, a 1956 story about Canadian fisheries scientists who were doing tests to determine the amount of DDT in streams that was lethal to fish translated into a news item titled "DDT Kills Canadian Salmon."[42] As would become common, the acute dangers of pesticide toxicity easily translated into clear evidence of the dangers for those who used them in the home and garden.

The fact that pesticides applied from aerial sprayers could intrude onto nearby homes and fields proved to be of particular concern to organic gardeners. When the United States Department of Agriculture's gypsy moth eradication program began in the spring of 1957 in the Northeast, aerial spraying reached a densely populated and rapidly suburbanizing region where new residents lived in close proximity to areas of agricultural production.[43] *Organic Gardening and Farming* reported in August of that year that "the gypsy moth campaign in the East is waking up Yankees to a problem that has been bothering residents of other states for years. Airplanes have taken over spraying chores in many areas on a wide variety of crops, and have created numerous problems. . . . Aerial spraying is cheap, but it is almost impossible to control the area of application accurately."[44] In his article in the same issue, "The Gypsy Moth Tragedy!" Robert Rodale described the terrifying site of airplanes spraying lands indiscriminately: "Many organic farmers had the horrifying experience of seeing converted World War II twin-engine bombers roar across their fields dropping acrid clouds of DDT that killed insects, birds, and fish alike. Fields that had been cared for organically for years were covered without warning with a dose of poison that even the U.S. Department of Agriculture warns should be used carefully and should not be allowed to get into livestock feed and human food."[45] As they fell from the sky or drifted from one field to the next, pesticides might miss their target and organic gardens could become collateral damage.

Rodale Press had been sharing anecdotes on the hazards of insecticides for years, but in 1957 the aerial spraying for gypsy moths sparked a call to arms for organic gardeners. In a November 1957 editorial titled "The Spray Gun against Man," J. I. Rodale suggested that gardeners organize themselves as both consumers and citizens to take action against aerial spraying. Departing from an approach that had often been apolitical, Rodale editorialized that the first thing the concerned public could explore was lawsuits to halt spraying. The next step would be for the public to "exert a form of boycott; that is, it can go back to growing its own vegetables. It can form groups of voters that will favor candidates possessed of political consciences. It can write letters to newspapers and people in public office." More important, Rodale claimed, readers could target grocers with their concerns about pesticides.[46] Voicing a theme that would be repeated by the Press for the next three decades, he suggested that by speaking to a manager and asking for unsprayed fruits and vegetables, organic enthusiasts could register their concerns about pesticides in an arena that was often responsive to consumers.

A month after that editorial appeared, in December 1957, *Organic Gardening and Farming* declared in an article headline that "The Battle to Halt Mass Poisoning Is On." The article with that title centered on a group of Long Island residents who filed for an injunction in the spring of that year to stop the spraying of DDT. The group was led by the well-known ecologist and curator of the American Museum of Natural History Robert Cushman Murphy, along with Mary Richards and Marjorie Spock. The article described Spock, the sister of Dr. Benjamin Spock, and Murphy as dedicated organic gardeners, and the other plaintiffs as residents interested in conservation, human health, and the protection of natural resources. Although unsuccessful in stopping the spraying that year, the group asked the judge to halt New York State's planned five-year program of spraying in the area. The case, the plaintiffs hoped, would set a legal precedent against aerial spraying. Quoting Marjorie Spock, the magazine declared the Long Island case to be the front line in the battle against aerial spraying: "This is important: we are not just fighting for ourselves—we are fighting for the health and well-being of everyone in the country. If we win this case, it will serve as a precedent for similar actions all over the United States."[47]

Readers of *Organic Gardening and Farming* took an active role in generating publicity and support for the Long Island case. In "Organic World," editors kept readers apprised of the latest developments and encouraged their involvement. The Long Island plaintiffs asked the magazine to help establish a fund for legal expenses, and by February 1958 readers had sent $550 in donations for the case to Emmaus.[48] When the magazine published a letter from Marjorie Spock thanking *OG&F* readers for their support, she claimed that in the year ahead "brand-new important evidence on the dangers of DDT and such will be brought out, making this a scientific as well as legal event."[49] No longer relying simply on anecdotal evidence from backyards and bodily experience, organic gardeners hoped to establish a precedent to stand in court.

The Long Island plaintiffs lost, but the case succeeded in collecting a great deal of scientific evidence on the impacts of DDT that had been scattered across academic journals. As the historian Christopher Sellers has demonstrated, the case became well-known for the research it gathered on DDT and the foundation it gave Rachel Carson for her book on the subject. Furthermore, Sellers argues that few other legal battles in the postwar era "propelled the emergence of an environmentalist imaginary as directly or importantly" as the Long Island case.[50] Such an imaginary, which entwined the ecological effects of chemicals on wildlife with the health impacts on humans, was certainly not limited to organic enthusiasts. Nonetheless, Rodale's organic gardeners were rapidly forming themselves into a network that shared not just gardening tips, but also strategies for turning their local battles into a national movement.

Even though the magazine still offered helpful tips and practical gardening advice along with plenty of ads for health food stores and soil activators, the controversy over aerial spraying brought a more politically charged tone to its pages. Following the 1957 gypsy moth eradication program in the Northeast, the summer of 1958 witnessed a widespread campaign in the South against the fire ant.[51] Just as it had the year before, OG&F kept readers apprised of the latest developments and encouraged action to stop the spraying. Describing how the fire ant program would apply chlordane, dieldrin, and Aldrin to millions of acres, writer Marilyn Sibley exclaimed, "Other voices must speak up against the mass use of insecticides. The time to prevent a repetition of the gypsy moth tragedy is now!"[52] In the "Organic World" for September 1958, the magazine urged readers to "stop now and think what *you* have done and *you* can do to stop this aerial spraying of private property. Write to *all* your elected officials."[53] Even if they lived outside an area targeted by eradication programs, the magazine encouraged readers to take a stand.

At the same time, the magazine began a more concerted effort to link organic gardening to conservation. J. I. Rodale had certainly advocated soil conservation practices in many of his writings about farming and gardening since the early 1940s. However, by the 1950s he spent the majority of his time writing in *Prevention* about the effects of synthetic substances on the health of the human body. In OG&F the emerging concern over aerial spraying gave Robert Rodale and his team of writers an opportunity to link organic gardening more directly to conservation. In a special issue devoted to "Conservation Today" in 1958, the magazine's writers made this connection explicit. Thomas Powell, in an article titled "Conservation Is Your Business," claimed emphatically, "*Every activity of an organic gardener or farmer is a conservation activity, for it aims to preserve and increase the basic resources that nourish and sustain us.*"[54] Jerome Olds argued that building soils organically was an act of what he called "positive conservation," and Audrey Stephan claimed that an organic garden was a sanctuary from DDT for birds.[55] In the monthly column on gardening clubs, the magazine suggested partnering with local chapters of the Audubon Society and the Wildlife Association. Rather than dwelling on conservation problems, an organic gardening club could "get things rolling" and become a "center of *conservation* doing."[56]

Organic Gardening and Farming also counseled readers that their gardening practices could produce a line of defense against chemicals, including those chemicals associated with atomic fallout. Strontium-90, a radioactive isotope, rained over vast swaths of the globe in the 1950s as a result of atomic testing. Fallout from these tests made national headlines when it was discovered that the isotope, when it settled onto grasses consumed by cows, attached itself to calcium and accumulated in milk.[57] Because the isotope mimicked calcium, Rodale's magazine counseled that a calcium-rich garden could reduce how much of the substance a plant took up. In August 1958 a headline in the magazine told readers "You Can Prevent Strontium Poisoning" by applying heavy doses of lime to garden soils.[58] Similarly, in keeping with J. I. Rodale's nutritional philosophy, the magazine counseled that a diet rich in foods produced from organic soils would likewise build up the body's defenses to strontium. In addition to writing to Congress, editor M. C. Goldman told readers in 1959 that "starting with your own garden and diet, there *is* something you can do about the mushrooming menace of radioactive fallout."[59] Just as an organic garden could be a sanctuary from DDT for birds, so, too, could it be a respite from other chemicals that seeped into daily life.

Whereas aerial spraying and conservation were points the Rodale Press could use to rally its subscribers around the "responsibilities" of being organic, the issue of radioactive fallout produced mixed results. For all the worthwhile questions the company asked and the assistance it offered readers, it was still in the business of promoting often-questionable health products, particularly in the pages of *Prevention*. For the better part of a decade, both *Prevention* and *OG&F* had been unabashed champions of the food supplement bone meal and declared that the supplement was essential to building up the body's strength and resistance to disease. These calcium-rich tablets, naturally derived from animal bones, were a centerpiece of *Prevention*'s natural health system well before concerns about strontium-90 arose. Indeed, the number of advertisements and articles touting the many benefits of bone meal supplements at times bordered on the comical. In the wake of concerns about atomic testing, American consumers purchased similar supplements in the late 1950s in hopes of preventing the effects of strontium-90 building up in the body. However, when a 1961 *Consumer Reports* piece tested the amount of strontium present in supplements themselves, including bone meal, it found drastically higher amounts of the isotope in the natural supplement. In a lengthy 1961 *Prevention* article titled "Is the Strontium 90 (Fall Out) in Bone Meal Dangerous?" J. I. Rodale criticized both the methods and conclusions of the *Consumer Reports* tests. Writing in the same issue, Robert Rodale presented evidence from tests the Press itself commissioned that countered the *Consumer Reports* findings.[60]

Critics seized on the company's continued recommendation of bone meal tablets as evidence that Rodale cared more about profits than about human health. Natural vitamin and food supplement firms were the major advertisers in *Prevention*, and despite the increased circulation of *OG&F* in the 1960s the Press continued to rely primarily on advertising revenue from its health magazine. Stephen Barrett, an Allentown-area psychiatrist who battled with the Rodale Press over its opposition to fluoridated water, charged that the Press recommended the tablets despite the demonstrated hazards. Ruth Adams, J. I. Rodale's longtime editorial partner at *Prevention*, left the magazine in 1962 over differences with Rodale on the subject of strontium and bone meal. While Barrett asserted that Rodale fired Adams to conceal the dangers, Adams recalled the scenario differently. In a letter to the Rodale biographer Carlton Jackson, Adams claimed that Rodale firmly and sincerely believed in the safety and efficacy of bone meal, and that her departure was amicable.[61] Regardless of why she left, the strontium issue is a reminder that the company's marketplace could bring readers together but also inadvertently drive them away.

But if the issue of strontium-90 was complicated, aerial spraying remained something around which readers could rally. As more and more experts began to connect aerial spraying to damages to wildlife and the environment more generally, Rodale's organic enthusiasts had more company than ever before. In July 1959 *Organic Gardening and Farming* featured a cover story titled "The Case against Poison Spray" that solidified the subject as a central part of the magazine's mission. Describing the image of a plane dousing a field that would later be echoed by Rachel Carson in *Silent Spring*, the magazine stated, "This was once a scene of lovely rural tranquility. However, it is now commonplace to note the almost daily appearance of spraying planes over our countryside. Our protest is not based on esthetics but rather on sober, realistic observation of what spraying is doing to the country and our wildlife." By highlighting the effects on wildlife OG&F could show it was not alone. As evidence of how prevalent the issue had become in recent years, the magazine excerpted stories about spraying from a variety of organizations and publications, including the *Farm Journal*, the National Audubon Society, *Sports Afield*, *Harper's Magazine*, the *American Journal of Digestive Diseases*, the American Medical Association Committee on Pesticides, the *Providence Journal*, the New York Zoological Park, *Conservation News*, the US Fish and Wildlife Service, *Nature* magazine, and *Gleanings in Bee Culture*. The issue also featured an interview and profile of Mary Richards, Marjorie Spock, and Robert Cushman Murphy, who had initiated the Long Island case two years earlier. Predicting more legal challenges would be in the offing in years to come, the editors offered a list of lawsuits from around the country regarding "spray damage" that might be used as a reference for future cases.[62]

After years of sending in their gardening tips to OG&F, Rodale's readers were now sending letters about their own local experiences with aerial spraying and looking for advice on what to do next. Mrs. Salome Stark responded by sending a dollar for ten reprints of "The Case against Poison Spraying," which the Press reproduced from its July 1959 story. Mrs. Stark claimed the reprints would "make excellent ammunition to add to my protests against the horrible poisoning campaign we are subjected to here in Lakeland, Florida." Another reader, Ella Robinson, echoing traditional gender roles of wives and mothers as protectors of domestic spaces, suggested that the reprints should be distributed to women's clubs across the country. As everyone knew, "once the woman of the house is awakened to the danger from poison sprays, she will

Cover of *Organic Gardening and Farming*, July 1959. Courtesy of the Rodale Family Archives.

do something about it." Earl Browand of Panama City reported, "One noticeable result of the recent spraying for fire ants is the absence of a familiar note from birds of any kind. It is a pathetic situation." Evoking a scene similar to the one with which Carson would open *Silent Spring* with three years later, Browand claimed, "At this rate it is not hard to visualize the day when our grandchildren will ask 'What is a bird?' and 'Where did they all go?' Not a pleasant thing to think about, is it?" Browand claimed he was eager to send copies of *OG&F*'s articles to his local paper and encouraged other readers to do the same: "It is my earnest hope that people everywhere will not only read your story, but will talk to their neighbors and to their newspapers and keep talking of it. The powers that be do not heed one voice, but they will listen to an aroused people. Let us form societies and band them together into a mighty voice and control the mass extermination of our wildlife."[63]

As enthusiasts widened their scope, they also extended the responsibilities of the Rodale Press into issues well beyond composting. After hearing from readers and clubs about their local battles against aerial spraying, the company took an even more active role in late 1959 by declaring its intention to be a national "clearinghouse" to help battle aerial spraying. When a state bill was introduced in Pennsylvania in 1959 that would have authorized spraying on public as well as private lands, the company directly contacted both *Prevention* and *OG&F* subscribers across the state and asked them to write their representatives. At the same time, editors contacted organic food growers and asked them to tell their customers. From this experience with its own "spray emergency," the magazine advised readers to create a community plan for when the spray issue might arise in their own area. Offering the services of its editorial staff to anyone in the country "wanting to prevent passage of spray legislation or mass spray campaigns," editor Jerome Goldstein claimed, "Whenever such a situation arises, write us at once and we'll do what we can to be of some help."[64] In gathering readers' experiences and sharing those experience with others, the Rodale Press made idiosyncratic and personal experiences—and its magazine—into a common denominator for the organic movement. And although that movement and J. I. Rodale had been on the margins for almost two decades, by the early 1960s more Americans than just organic gardeners would start wondering about those airplanes, the stuff they dispersed from high above, and what it might mean for the future.

By early 1960, J. I. Rodale and the editors of *Organic Gardening and Farming* declared they could feel the lid was about to come off the long-simmering threat of chemicals in food and the environment. Although aerial spraying of DDT and other pesticides was fast becoming a defining issue for organic gardeners, it would be the residue of a pesticide that lingered inside cranberries that Rodale believed would awaken many Americans to the threat of chemicals in everyday life. The "cranberry scare" occurred in November 1959 when the Department of

Health, Education, and Welfare secretary Arthur Flemming announced that some cranberry products on the market were tainted with the residue of aminotriazole, a powerful herbicide that the FDA listed as a carcinogen. While Flemming could not say how many cranberries contained the residues, he famously warned American consumers just before Thanksgiving to double-check the product's safety prior to purchasing. As sales plummeted by two-thirds in the holiday season of late 1959, the USDA, the FDA, and agricultural and food lobbies aimed to convince the public that cranberry products were safe.[65] Writing in March 1960 J. I. Rodale claimed that hundreds of letters and telegrams had flooded the company's office "suggesting that we jump into the fray and make as much capital out of this incident as possible." Likening the cranberry scare to pulling a thread on a garment, Rodale was certain more "explosive incidents" lay ahead that would arouse even more interest. As he had since the early 1940s, Rodale repeated his hope that a novelist might step in and write a modern version of Upton Sinclair's *The Jungle*, sparking a call for reform on par with the landmark food and drug laws of the early twentieth century.[66]

However, the book that changed how Americans understood chemicals would be Rachel Carson's *Silent Spring*.[67] Portions of the book first appeared in the *New Yorker* in the summer of 1962, and editors at the Rodale Press eagerly awaited the impact its full publication would have later that fall. Robert Rodale had noted in the "Organic World" as early as February 1960 that Carson was at work on how chemicals "upset nature's balance," and reported the book would be titled *Man against Earth*.[68] By September 1962 the magazine was alerting readers to the fact that Carson's title would be a Book of the Month Club selection in October and sang the praises of her "masterpiece."[69] Over the next several months, the magazine kept readers informed on the number of letters reaching the Food and Drug Administration, the formation of a presidential committee on the topic, and the reactions of the chemical industry. Recounting the sales of the book, the number of editorials it had sparked, and a soon-to-be-aired *CBS Reports*, editor Jerome Olds claimed, "It's as if a lid that kept down criticism and resentment against poison sprays had been suddenly blown off."[70]

Of course, by the fall of 1962 J. I. Rodale had been using his magazines to call attention to the dangers of pesticides for some time. But like many of his claims, Rodale relied foremost on evidence from his own experience and that of his readers, mixed with a broad spectrum of scientific and medical opinion culled from sometimes-questionable sources. For a substance such as DDT, Rodale certainly uncovered some scientific literature to support his claims, but just as common could be pieces like "Adventures in Self-Analysis toward Health," in which Rodale deduced the cause of his dizzy spells by avoiding the cherries he was fond of eating and reasoning that pesticide residues on the fruit caused his ailment.[71] *Prevention*'s stories about pesticides came sandwiched between testimonials about food supplements and dietary regimens. Rodale on occasion dismissed fire ant eradication programs as a government "hoax."[72] *Organic Gardening and Farming* also carried a great deal of advertising for questionable nutritional supplements and soil treatments, and its grab bag of readers' experiences could easily slide toward quackery. Even as his magazines helped bring together concerned organic gardeners in the late 1950s and early 1960s, outlandish ideas about health and nutrition made both Rodale and his readers personae non grata in the world of science.

While Robert Rodale and other writers at the Press expressed enthusiasm about *Silent Spring*, J. I. Rodale's response was more ambivalent. By 1962 Rodale had largely retired from day-to-day operations of his company and had engrossed himself in various fiction and playwriting projects. With Carson's book published on the heels of OG&F's twentieth anniversary in June 1962, he felt compelled to argue that Carson was repeating what he had been saying all along. In the handwritten notes for his autobiography from 1964, Rodale writes, "The whole organic gardening and farming movement in the United States owes its existence to me. I am its acknowledged leader and have made many radio [and] television appearances."[73] Speaking to a group in 1966, Rodale remarked, "Insofar as Rachel Carson and her book 'Silent Spring' is concerned, I began to write about this subject 15 years before she did, and continued in every issue to hammer away at the dangers of the chemical method for controlling insects and disease."[74] Rodale claimed his issues with the book were more substantial than sour grapes. Referencing Sir Albert Howard, he wrote in 1963 that "one failing of Rachel Carson's book is her neglect of discussing modern changes in soil management as a factor [in] increasing insect and disease infestation. . . . Rachel Carson in *Silent Spring* did a good job as far as she went, but she completely overlooked the destruction of the soil fertility of our lands due to the use [of] commercial fertilizers, and the fact that this imbalance in soil brings on insects. . . . Rachel Carson here is your next book—an analysis of what commercial fertilizers are doing as far as insect and disease infestations are concerned."[75] In a 1973 interview with biographer Carlton Jackson, Robert Rodale claimed his father fully supported what Rachel Carson was doing but "felt a little hurt that she didn't mention his work in any way."

Carson did not cite Rodale or mention chemical fertilizers in her book for good reason. By many accounts she sought to avoid being associated with organic gardeners, who were often characterized, as Carson was by her critics, as unreasonable women with little grasp of science. Anticipating an attack from many in the chemical industry, Carson needed to avoid being dismissed as a food "cultist," as organic gardeners and alternative health practitioners were frequently called in the early 1960s. Frank Graham Jr. of the Audubon Society told Carlton Jackson that Carson, like some other scientists, had sympathy for the organic cause but was "a little suspicious of the organic farmers' nostrums." Although the Press later turned up evidence that Carson had once been a subscriber to *OG&F* and *The Health Bulletin*, J. I. Rodale tried and failed on at least one occasion to get Carson to share a speaking bill with him.[76] Robert Rodale, for his part, understood that if Carson had cited J. I. she risked her credibility in an already contentious debate: "You see, if you used him, right away you'd be labeled as a crackpot, if she had used him as a reference. [So I] can understand her point of view." Even beyond J. I. Rodale personally, Carson may have found the ideas of organic enthusiasts to be too inflexible for her nuanced, scientifically astute analysis of the costs and benefits of using pesticides. Robert Rodale claimed that for a scientist, "even though something is bad that means you can still use a small amount of it and it [won't] hurt you. [Whereas] we said avoid it entirely on philosophical grounds. [And] r.c. didn't."[77]

Carson's wariness speaks volumes about how the environmentalism developing in Rodale's publication in the 1960s emerged in tension with an environmentalism focused on field studies and laboratory results. The do-it-yourself results of *OG&F* would hardly have stood up to norms of scientific credibility, but it was more the fact that the Rodale

Press also paired its environmental activism with questionable advice and products that made it anathema to most scientists. Nonetheless, Rodale and his company helped popularize a view of the body as open and vulnerable to environmental influences, and laid crucial groundwork for Carson in pushing these issues toward mainstream attention. But even as she critiqued assumptions about the safety and efficacy of pesticides and relied on citizens to gather scientific observations, Carson needed to be wary of the unscientific slide that Rodale and his readers often made toward pseudoscience.

Regardless of the shared ambivalence between Rodale about Carson, the notoriety of her book and the national attention it drew to the issue of pesticides galvanized organic gardeners. Each month in the mid-1960s *OG&F* carried more and more stories of local and state groups organizing to stop aerial spraying and appealing to their fellow gardeners for help. Organic gardening clubs that once reported on their round-ups and produce swaps now reported their organizing strategies and updates on their local battles. The magazine further attempted to be a clearinghouse by listing names and addresses of groups and committees formed around the country. The magazine's editors claimed, "Many of the nation's largest publications when writing about insecticides, give the impression that organic gardeners, bird watchers, some sportsmen and ardent conservationists, etc., are the only ones calling attention to the problem of over-poisoning." Instead, the magazine suggested, battles against pesticides and aerial spraying were bringing more and more groups together.[78]

With a larger audience paying attention, the Press saw the years after *Silent Spring*'s publication as a turning point for the organic movement. Robert Rodale declared 1963 to be "A Year of Action" for organic gardeners. Not only did Rodale want gardeners to help with their local battles against aerial sprayings, he wanted them to increase their support for organic growers and research into biological methods of insect controls. Linking the marketplace with environmental action, Rodale mentioned that some citizens in New York and Chicago had banded together into buying clubs in order to purchase unsprayed foods.[79] Robert also made some concerted efforts to publicize the acute danger farm workers faced by coming into the most direct contact with pesticides. In a November 1963 editorial he decried the country's "shabby" treatment of migrant workers and detailed the deaths from parathion exposure among workers in peach-growing states. Noting that picking a crop and being exposed daily to heavy doses of chemicals was more hazardous than ingesting the trace amounts of residue as a consumer, Rodale pointed out that many of the workers were likely unable to read the warnings and instructions about proper handling of pesticides and therefore frequently suffered the most dire consequences.[80] This crucial point came up on occasion in OG&F but was largely obscured by its focus on the risks of pesticides for consumers and the health of their bodies and their lands.

As the impact of Silent Spring widened, the Rodale Press aimed to show it had been a part of this conversation from the start. In 1964 the company produced an encyclopedic tome called Our Poisoned Earth and Sky. Over seven hundred pages long, it mined the last decade of Rodale publications for stories about chemicals in food, cosmetics, medicines, drinking water, and air pollution. Advertisements claimed the book "shows why today's poisons *may be more devastating than an atomic holocaust*. As you read page after page, it will open your eyes to the dangers faced by you and your family, and by unborn generations. This book shows that *there will be no escape from this poison for any of us—unless we wake up and do something about it!*"[81]

Although clearly aimed at capitalizing on the success of Silent Spring, Our Poisoned Earth and Sky nonetheless demonstrates that Carson and her critique did not emerge from a vacuum. It is surely valuable to note that J. I. Rodale said some things first, but it is more important to see how his magazines threaded together the organic movement before there was much scientific or political attention to environmental issues. Organic Gardening and Farming gathered disparate experiences with chemicals and allowed readers to connect changes in their own local environment with changes happening elsewhere. It helped make the personal choices of a consumer—at the scale of the home, the body, and the garden—stand for something larger. It also certainly helps explain why Rachel Carson found such a receptive audience for Silent Spring. And while they would hardly receive as much credit as Carson for launching the environmental movement, by the end of the 1960s more Americans than ever would wonder if maybe J. I. Rodale and those little old ladies in tennis shoes were maybe on to something after all.

In May 1967 *Organic Gardening and Farming* celebrated its twenty-fifth year of publication. Assessing the organic movement's progress since the magazine's inception, Robert Rodale was proud of how many people the magazine had inspired to change their growing methods; however, he reminded readers that in many ways very little had changed:

> The conditions which caused my father, J. I. Rodale, to start *Organic Gardening and Farming* back in 1942 all still exist today. The humus in farm soil is being depleted by shortsighted farming methods. Much of the organic matter produced on our farms is still being wasted, through the destruction or burying of garbage. Too many chemicals are still being used in the production and processing of food crops. The health quality of our food is still not as high as it should be. People are still too far separated, both physically and spiritually, from the land which supports them.[82]

At the same time, Rodale could not help but consider the important changes that had occurred in that time. Environmental pollution, which Rodale claimed had once been limited to "small areas of filth in a few localities," was now a matter of "worldwide contamination." He pointed to the small particles of DDT building up in the tissues of almost every living creature, the residues of atomic fallout spreading around the globe, and the air pollution making many cities unlivable. "Clearly," he claimed, "pollution has come of age as a problem since 1942."[83]

The emergence of air and water pollution as national issues along with the budding environmental movement of the late 1960s changed what it meant to be organic. Whereas gardeners once turned to organic methods because they believed it was a more practical method or that it produced healthier food for themselves and their family, by the late 1960s enthusiasts increasingly argued the method was also better for the planet. In the pages of Rodale's magazine, saving farm and garden wastes to create composts became a means of conserving natural resources. Avoiding sprays in the garden not only produced healthier tomatoes for the home, enthusiasts argued, but also sent fewer pesticides washing into streams. Combining citizen action and consumerism, organic gardening became an act of environmentalism. In this way, even though J. I. Rodale was far from an ecologist, his company and its publications cemented a link between health and ecological protection in the late 1960s.

The Rodale Press did not drastically change its approach with the rise of greater public attention to issues of pollution. Even as pollution grabbed more headlines, the magazine remained largely focused on prosaic matters of the home and garden. Its June 1968 issue featured a cover story about the homestead of Bruce and Margilee Rozell of Tyler, Texas, and their method of maintaining soil fertility by using a cover-cropping method. The issue also featured stories about using sawdust, the virtues of summer squash, and a new section on "home handicrafts."[84] Yet tucked inside of the issue were updates on the amount of DDT washing into Lake Michigan (and its effects on fish) as well as efforts to preserve endangered species. A brief article by Jerome Olds argued, "If we really want pollution control, we as citizens have to begin acting like we mean it. We've got to get the message across to the officials we elect to office."[85] This combination of the practical and the political defined Rodale's magazines in the years to come.

As many historians have noted, support for environmental protection efforts frequently enjoyed bipartisan support in the late 1960s. At both the state and federal level, laws regulating pollution were popular with voters on both sides of the aisle.[86] Nonetheless, the editors of OG&F walked a fine line in their use of the magazine as a platform for political advocacy. In a March 1968 editorial profiling the efforts of the Environmental Defense Fund, Robert Rodale recognized that readers likely would have different political opinions about the Constitution, but he thought all would agree "that Americans have a constitutional right to the cleanest possible environment consistent with the general welfare." Arguing that environmental protection was neither a radical reinterpretation of the Constitution nor a barrier to progress, Rodale stated, "To my way of thinking, trying to find conservation in the constitution lies somewhere between the two political poles of constitutional interpretation—property protection versus social change."[87] Although readers could disagree over the means, he felt that finding ways to protect the environment was surely a goal all could share.

Robert Rodale's attempt to find a middle-of-the-road view reflected the fact that while much of the support for environmental protection in the 1960s came from left-leaning young people, *OG&F*'s readership remained predominantly older. Urging his readers to "vote organically" in November 1968, Robert recognized that readers had little in common with, and likely little patience for, "those bearded, unwashed demonstrators." At the same time, he stated that even if *OG&F* readers were not "out on the streets parading and painting signs on posters," many surely understood the discontent about the country's direction.[88] However, in suggesting that readers "vote organically" Rodale did not tell readers for whom to vote. Politicians and political parties, he felt, had yet to address the growing uncertainty with technology that organic enthusiasts shared. Voting organically, he claimed, meant to "live and eat as naturally as possible, and hope by our example that we can show others that even greater happiness and satisfaction can be achieved if we work together for a more natural society."[89] The organic movement, as Robert Rodale construed it, was an ecumenical big tent, with room enough for anyone interested to join.

To recast the concerns of organic gardeners as issues of environmental protection, the Rodale Press in the late 1960s increasingly turned to the science of ecology to support its claims. The biologist Barry Commoner became a leading public figure in the late 1960s with his books about the ecological effects of the modern economy, *The Science of Survival* (1966) and *The Closing Circle* (1971). When Commoner declared in 1968 at a meeting of the American Association for the Advancement of Science that chemical fertilizers were "massively intruding" on freshwater lakes around the country, *OG&F* seized on it as evidence of the importance of organic cultivation practices in maintaining ecological quality. The writer Maurice Franz quoted Commoner at length in an article titled "Inorganic Nitrates Threaten Health and Cause Widespread Pollution." Although Commoner was particularly interested in the danger to public health created by nitrates from agricultural runoff in drinking water, the *OG&F* staff read his work as supporting the claims about soils and health they had been making for decades. Linking Commoner's work to the history of organic agriculture, Franz claimed that Commoner's insight was similar to the "distrust of

Cover of *Organic Gardening and Farming*, August 1969. Courtesy of the Rodale Family Archives.

artificial fertilizers in the mind of Sir Albert Howard" so long ago. Moreover, the ecologist's work seemed to demonstrate that organic enthusiasts had been right all along. Robert Rodale argued in past decades organic gardeners "were thought odd for even suggesting that fertilizer could have an effect beyond the field on which it was applied." Extrapolating from Commoner's concerns about fertilizers, Rodale stated, "Now the tragedies of technology have rudely shocked many scientists into taking a questioning attitude towards all new chemical substances."[90] In ecologists like Commoner the Press found scientists who shared some, though not all, of its critique of the indiscriminate application of chemicals.

Commoner, like Rachel Carson, appears to have admired the spirit of Rodale publications but was hesitant to endorse the organic philosophy too fully. Although he never met J. I. Rodale, Commoner visited with Robert and the staff of *Organic Gardening and Farming* in the early 1970s and frequently read the magazine. In a 1972 letter Commoner claimed that because organic gardeners could glean a basic scientific understanding of biology from their own experience and "access to a moderately good public library," there was no reason "a priori to denigrate non-professional views about gardening—when they are clearly based on actual observations properly recorded." Commoner, who placed great value on public access to scientific information, supported the use of organic matter in maintaining soil fertility and recognized the value of the skepticism the Press promoted: "This idea [organic matter] and general skepticism about the scientific views resulting from modern agronomic research, which emphasizes chemical intervention in the natural cycles is a sound aspect of Rodale's work." Yet Commoner was less comfortable with how Rodale's magazines expressed skepticism of other types of scientific knowledge. With respect to some of the other claims that the company circulated and the products it sold, however, Commoner was more cautious. He stated emphatically that he did not read *Prevention* and that the value of self-taught science did not extend from the garden to the biology of the body. Although "amateurs can contribute a great deal to the field" with respect to biology, he claimed that matters of health were another matter entirely.[91] Even as *OG&F* helped bring together matters of health and ecology, the excesses of the marketplace made overcoming Rodale's reputation a challenge.

In addition to ecologists, organic enthusiasts latched onto the work of philosophers and critics to advance the argument that gardening was an act of resistance in an overly technological and polluted world. As early as 1965, Robert Rodale was referencing the French philosopher Jacques Ellul in his editorials, which he would do repeatedly in his writing in the next ten years. Introducing readers to the argument of Ellul's book *The Technological Society* (1964), Robert writes, "His central view is that while technological advancements may benefit us in the short run, they will eventually entrap us because a technological development is not moving forward according to a plan over which man has control." Rodale pointed to the unintended consequences of science in the development of synthetic detergents that did not break down in waterways, automobile exhaust that polluted the air, and the life-extending medical advances that aided overpopulation.[92] Robert Rodale claimed in June 1966 that he had started reading and rereading *The Technological Society* a year earlier, and that the book had "haunted" his thoughts ever since. Ellul's ideas allowed Robert Rodale to link organic practices not just to a critique of agricultural science and medicine, but to a more general critique of the modern world.

Yet even in moments where he sketched a bleak vision of the future, Robert Rodale invariably returned to the garden as a point of hope: "Movements of reform and technical revolution—such as the organic gardening and farming movement—reflect the disenchantment of a segment of the public with a portion of 'the system.' You and I are building a shelter against technique on our own homesteads, where we strive to use natural methods to the greatest extent."[93] In the coming years, the Press incorporated more and more environmental messages into its publications, adopted the science of ecology as evidence of how an organic garden could be an "island" free from chemicals, and produced an array of articles and books telling readers how to build their organic homesteads. Yet even as he instructed readers on how to create their own islands, Robert Rodale encouraged those same readers to see those islands not as disconnected from one another, but as part of a unified movement against chemicals: "Instead of seeing ourselves as isolated protestors against the folly and injustice of synthetic living, we should think and act like the leaders that we are. The more the world becomes chemicalized and polluted, the more valuable and meaningful [is] even the partial purity of life that many of us can create for ourselves. Our gardens are like Noah's Ark—a way to preserve what is good today so that it can be put to use on a larger scale by people of the future."[94] The significance of an organic garden was no longer limited to the food it provided.

Even as presidential commissions, foundations, and respected scientists in the late 1960s took an interest in matters of environmental protection, Robert Rodale told readers not to lose sight of the importance of their gardens. In 1969 he told readers their gardens were part of a "chain of influence" that led first to state capitals and then on to Washington, DC: "It's time for all of us to use our gardens as [a] means to tell everyone that a pure environment is something that we all can have, especially around our homes. *Your* garden is on the front line."[95] By March 1970 *Organic Gardening and Farming* was reaching half a million readers each month, up nearly one hundred thousand in just two years. This rapid growth in circulation, certainly due to the growing national interest in environmental protection and ecology, made the Rodale Press an increasingly visible site of environmental activism. "With a half-million active people getting *Organic Gardening* each month plus all the others reading each issue," editor Jerome Olds claimed, "we have the nucleus of a most effective force to get something done."[96]

The Rodale Press both contributed to and capitalized on the popular enthusiasm for environmental activism in the early 1970s. On the heels of Earth Day in April 1970, the Press rechristened its *Health Bulletin* as *Rodale's Environmental Action Bulletin*, a weekly newsletter aimed at the growing ranks of environmental activists. No longer working to be a resource just for gardeners battling against aerial spraying, the *Bulletin* created an information exchange for the ecology action groups that were organizing around the country. Functioning like an expanded version of the "Organic World" column that started each issue of *OG&F*, the *Environmental Action Bulletin* covered a potpourri of environmental issues in the early 1970s. But the scope of the pollution issues the *Bulletin* addressed far exceeded what was found in the magazine. A single eight-page issue of the *Bulletin* in June 1970 covered topics like the exploitation of shale oil lands, the dangers of antibiotics in animal feed, thermal pollution from power plants, sulfur dioxide, the problems with Standard Oil's claims about its emission-cutting gasoline, glass recycling efforts in Ann Arbor, congressional hearings on pollution of Long Island Sound, the amount of phosphate going down the drain per load of laundry (broken down by detergent brand), and a list of contact information for state agencies.[97] In the same way that *OG&F* once profiled organic gardening clubs, the *Bulletin* profiled leading ecology groups around the country and offered tips on how readers could create one in their local community. A key element to organizing such groups and widespread environmental action was information. A 1970 profile of a Santa Barbara ecology center described the "reference library of books, periodicals and pamphlets ranging from farming to city planning. The center also houses a film library, a book store, a large up-to-the-minute calendar on local and regional activities in the ecology field—and desk space for interested individuals and organizations that don't have a work space of their own."[98] Eager to be the publication that threaded together these hotspots of ecology and action, Rodale's *Bulletin* published the names and addresses of organizations and encouraged readers to contact one another.[99]

The *Bulletin* also sought to cultivate a link between the marketplace for organic food and environmental activism. On May 23, 1970, the Rodale Press convened a one-day Organic Food Marketing Symposium in Allentown to address the problems of organic production standards. The *Bulletin* described how organic food retailers believed the organic food movement had been created by older people "out of need," but it was now being taken over by younger people "out of conviction" and concern about environmental pollution. The *Bulletin* also made the case that environmental activists should not discount organic gardeners. Referencing the relationship between food production and the pollution crisis, the newsletter's editors claimed, "Oddly though it may appear to many who think of *Organic Gardening* only as it relates to a little old lady in tennis shoes tending her backyard compost heap, the greatest number of people asking those questions and doing something to solve them are subscribers to J. I. Rodale's magazines."[100] Just because Rodale's readers had not come from campus protests and teach-ins did not mean they should be excluded from the ecology movement.

Indeed, the Press argued that popular awareness about pollution validated ideas it had been circulating for over twenty years. More important, it validated J. I. Rodale. Writing on "The Social Significance of Organic Foods" in June 1970, the *Environmental Action Bulletin* made a direct link between organic foods and environmental concerns: "When J. I. Rodale started a small magazine with a handful of subscribers back in 1942, neither he nor anyone else could predict its role in 1970. In fact, even in 1970, only a handful are still aware of how his Organic Gardening ideas relate to the very core of many environmental problems today."[101] The Press attempted to turn the fact that J. I. Rodale had been disregarded for so long—even among conservationists—into cultural capital. In March 1971 Robert Rodale claimed, "The fact that the organic method has been regarded as fanatic and faddist in the past (and still is in some quarters) is a guarantee of the present imperative usefulness of the organic idea." The attention of scientists and the public to issues of pollution signaled that J. I. Rodale had been right all along. In a hagiographic piece about his father that Robert published upon the twentieth anniversary of *Prevention* in 1970, he argued many of his father's claims had been "hard to accept years ago, but they are now being echoed by experts of the highest academic repute."[102]

No one asserted that the newfound attention to pollution validated J. I. Rodale more than J. I. himself did. Although he had felt slighted by the attention given to *Silent Spring*, by the end of the 1960s he felt as if he was receiving a measure of due respect. In his articles and speeches Rodale frequently repeated a favorite quote from John Stuart Mill about new ideas going through phases of ridicule, discussion, and finally adoption. By 1966 Rodale felt "we are half out of the ridicule stage, and one-quarter into the discussion stage."[103] Four years later he felt confident enough to state, "No longer are we called crackpot cultists . . . we are advancing into the adoption stage by leaps and bounds." As evidence of this progress J. I. pointed to the fact that he had recently been interviewed "in a friendly way" by a correspondent from CBS and that *Time* magazine had recently visited his farm for a story on the growth of the organic movement.[104]

Attention to J. I. Rodale and his company certainly had increased with the growing public awareness of environmental issues. While Rodale received some national press over its legal battle with the Federal Trade Commission in the mid-1960s, a greater number of stories focused on J. I. as the founder of a movement to grow food without using chemicals. One of the earliest positive profiles of Rodale appeared in 1966 in the *Saturday Evening Post*. The author, Eleanor Perényi, described J. I. as quirky and quixotic, playfully calling him part of the "great race of fanatics." Perényi, a well-known figure of postwar garden writing, was sympathetic to say the least. An early adopter of organic methods of fertilization, she claimed that for all the idiosyncrasies of Rodale's claims, he was essentially "right" in his pursuits. She recalled that 1940s composters like her "threw out the poisons we had been using in our Victory Gardens, sent for earthworms, praying mantises and ladybugs to kill our aphids, all to choruses of laughter . . . but we knew in our hearts that Mr. Rodale was right." In the title of her piece, Perényi called Rodale the "apostle of the compost heap" who had his moment of revelation when he encountered Sir Albert Howard so many years ago.[105]

Perényi would later write in her 1981 memoir, *Green Thoughts*, that the commission she received to interview Rodale gave her the excuse she needed to meet the man and visit the farm she had read about for so long: "I had long wanted to set eyes on him and the farm, which I took to be a latter-day offshoot of those nineteenth-century experiments of living off the land, something like Bronson Alcott's Fruitlands, all unbolted bread and water and vegetarianism but without the metaphysics." On the surface J. I. Rodale appeared as if he "belonged in another century," but upon closer inspection Perényi recalls that with his formal three-piece suit and overcoat Rodale was "an incongruously formal figure against the backdrop of rich Pennsylvania farmland." Marveling at the quality of the compost heaps and the livestock on the farm, Perényi recognized that Rodale had a deep knowledge of "how things worked" despite some of his more unconventional ideas.[106]

Perényi's characterization of Rodale as the "apostle of the compost heap" echoed that of James Kilpatrick, who in a syndicated editorial on the company's legal battles in 1965 had called Rodale a "small apostle of nonconformity."[107] In profiles that appeared in newspapers and magazines in the coming years, the town of Emmaus was commonly called a Mecca for organic believers and followers of J. I's "philosophy."[108] The Rodale Press hardly shied away from the notion of J. I. as an "apostle" or a "prophet" of organic foods and natural health. Writing in the anniversary issue of *Prevention* in 1970, Robert Rodale claimed that the best way to describe his father "is to say that he is a prophet. That one word sums up his life better than any other." His prophecies extended from knowing that one-way streets could solve traffic problems in New York in the 1920s, to his ideas about urban renewal, to his warnings about food additives, sugar, pesticides, and synthetic chemicals.[109]

Taking stock of how concerns about pollution had become a national issue in the early 1970s, J. I. Rodale could not help but agree that his "prophecies" were coming true. In an extensive interview with *Penthouse* magazine, Rodale was emphatic that the increased interest of young people in organic farming was validating his ideas. "The young are going to save us," he told interviewer Gay Bryant. "Suddenly these hippies and dropouts, who had been making a lot of noise, read my writings and found something real. There is so much truth in what we say that, if you are not prejudiced, you must become convinced." Asked if he thought he would have had more success if he had been a politician rather than a publisher, Rodale, always one for a good quip, claimed his ideas upset too many people and he would likely have "been shot in no time." He also emphasized that he identified himself as a writer more than anything: "Now that there is a growing number of people working on health food along my lines, I can sit back with some satisfaction. It would be foolish for me to step out and try to be a senator. I am better off in this corner, thinking, writing, and spreading the printed word. I can talk to literally millions through my magazines."[110] The marketplace had given Rodale the tools to make a name for himself, and broader public recognition seemed to have vindicated at least some of his prophecies.

The characterization of Rodale as a farsighted prophet was cemented by his best-known treatment in the popular press. A June 1971 *New York Times Magazine* cover story proclaimed him the "Guru of the Organic Food Cult." Wade Greene profiled organic food as an idea that came to Rodale thirty years ago, and one the Press had "nourished to its current popularity." Greene claimed that the signs of the organic movement's moment were everywhere—"in women's pages, smart conversation, in the sprouting of scores of little stores with barrels and bins and quaint names like 'Ounce of Prevention' and 'The Good Seed' and 'Mother Earth and Sons.'" In addition to a flourishing of organic gardening courses in colleges, organic farms were becoming "almost commonplace" in certain regions. Greene claimed at the center of this "loosely clustered" movement was J. I. Rodale, whose Emmaus home was the "movement's Mecca," and J. I. its "foremost prophet." Greene picked up on J. I.'s interesting blend of idealism and capitalism, calling him, at the very least, "a very popular health freak."[111]

Greene described Rodale as a "walking testimonial to his health theories." Although he was seventy-two and retired, Rodale remained full of vigor and showed little sign of slowing down. Giving Greene a tour of his home and farm, Rodale showed off a machine that emitted short-wave radio waves that he claimed to sit under for twenty minutes a day. He also showed off his pantry and the seventy different food supplements he took each day, as well as the fields and greenhouses that provided him with organic food. Rodale was clearly basking in the attention he and his ideas were finally enjoying. Yet Greene, as with more than a few who profiled Rodale, struggled to discern if Rodale was not putting him on just a little bit. Even a fan like Eleanor Perényi could claim that Rodale's humor bore a distinct resemblance to Baron Münchausen, a stock comedy character who made fantastic and dubious claims of his exploits. Greene claimed at times J. I. seemed to be "practicing comedy at times as well as writing it." Despite sensing that Rodale took more than a little enjoyment in being known as a "crackpot," Greene could not ignore the growing support Rodale's ideas had in popular circles and the fact that at least some scientists were paying attention as well. After many years fighting for acceptance, the Rodale Press was now winning some "important cases in the courts of public opinion, and of some reputable scientific opinion, too." Quoting a statement of Barry Commoner's on the role of organic gardeners and birders in recognizing the effects of pesticides on ecosystems, Greene reminded readers the Press had pointed to the dangers of DDT as early as 1949.[112] The Press and its organic enthusiasts had raised valid critiques, even if the medium it used had more in common with the *Ladies' Home Journal* than it did with *Science*.

It was in this context that J. I. Rodale made his appearance before a national television audience in 1971 as the "guru" of organic food. Riding a wave of publicity, J. I. accepted an invitation to appear on the *Dick Cavett Show* in the days after the publication of the *New York Times Magazine* story. Rodale was eager to introduce himself to a television audience and to cement himself as the quirky, but serious, leader of a movement to change how Americans farmed, gardened, and understood their own health. After a lifetime of waiting in the wings—having his ideas dismissed by experts and authorities despite the support of his readers, having his plays produced but derided, having seen others given credit for popularizing concerns about health and the environment—Rodale's first major television appearance would be his chance, at last, to be a celebrity.

Rodale was understandably nervous. His wife, Anna, recalled needing to calm him down before he went on stage. But when it was time for the taping to begin, Rodale's gift for showmanship overcame his nerves. He was, as usual, both self-deprecating and full of facts, making fun of himself but also showing passion for his beliefs. He brought along organic vegetables for Cavett as props and described how organic foods helped people live longer and enjoy greater health. With good comic timing, Rodale employed some of the campy punch lines he had worked out over the decades, telling Cavett about how he had fallen down a flight of stairs a few years ago, but because he knew his body was protected—thanks to bone meal—he laughed all the way down. At one point Rodale repeated an oft-used quip that he was going to live until one hundred and two, unless he was run down by a sugar-crazed cab driver on the streets of New York.[113]

That line became one of J. I. Rodale's best known, because in a moment of much crueler comic timing it would also be one of his last. Dick Cavett recalls that Rodale was extremely funny for half an hour and reminded him of Leon Trotsky as he talked about health foods. As Cavett welcomed the show's second guest, Rodale moved to another couch and soon started making a loud snoring sound that the host and his guest initially mistook as part of Rodale's shtick. Soon Cavett noticed that J. I. was ghostly pale. Under the glare of stage lights and with television cameras rolling, medical interns attended to Rodale, who was unresponsive. By the time he reached a local hospital, Rodale was pronounced dead, by way of a massive heart attack. Although the show never aired, Cavett recalls that J. I.'s death was headline news the next day and the story of his passing became part of late-night television folklore.[114]

Some critics saw Rodale's death at the age of seventy-two as evidence that organic foods and natural health methods did little to help Americans live longer, disease-free lives. For his readers, the remarkable life Rodale lived and his extensive output of books and plays—not to mention how long he had lived with a diagnosed heart condition and that he had outlived others in his family—was proof that a diet of organic foods and natural supplements could enrich life, even if it could not extend the years indefinitely. Ultimately Rodale's moment as a "guru"

demonstrates how the marketplace could provide a measure of valida-
tion when science and medicine could not.

• • •

J. I. Rodale's high-profile passing in 1971 came at the end of a decade of
remarkable growth for his company and the organic movement in the
United States. Starting with the quiet toil of gardeners in their backyards, concerns about chemicals used on soils and in food production
had reached national headlines, and more Americans every day wondered about the long-term effects of pesticides on their own health and
the natural world. While certainly not the only source of activism in
support of environmental protection, the Rodale Press helped bring
together concerns regarding health and ecology in the 1960s and
enlisted its readers as consumers and citizens in the process. With the
help of the Rodale Press, the practical, and at times provincial, concerns
of organic gardeners became the issues of environmental protection.

Organic gardeners in the 1950s had consumed Rodale's practical
advice and learned to build their own soils without fertilizers and to
avoid pesticides around the home and garden. But as chemicals rained
down from planes and evidence mounted that they could build up in
soils and bodies over time, being an organic gardener took on a new
valence in the 1960s. Just as the Rodale Press had once collected readers' evidence to create its own vernacular science around organic practices, the pages of its magazines—and its marketplace—served as a
collection point for readers' varied experiences with pesticides. Taking
local experiences and local battles and merging them into a national
network, Rodale Press publications were thus foundational to the creation of a network of organic consumers and environmental citizens
in the postwar United States.

Despite all the complexities and contingencies of history, we often
still rely on the simple tool of the timeline to explain historical developments. Certainly, if one were to create a timeline of the landmark
moments of postwar environmentalism, events like the publication of
Silent Spring in 1962, the Santa Barbara oil spill in 1969, and the first
Earth Day in 1970 would need to be marked in large, bold letters. However, less easy to fit on that timeline would be the moment when one

gardener started worrying about what the township was using to control roadside weeds and so asked other local gardeners what they thought. It would be hard to know exactly when someone purchased a subscription to *Organic Gardening and Farming* and started buying different tools to grow his or her favorite fruits and vegetables. Even more difficult to find would be when a gardener clipped a piece of news from a magazine about an aerial spraying incident in another state and put it in his or her files, just in case such an issue came up locally. It would be all but impossible to find room on such a timeline for the millions of piles of compost that dotted backyards as gardeners and citizens rethought the use of synthetic chemicals. While all those moments are in many ways lost, we do know J. I. Rodale and his magazine helped make them happen.

While J. I. Rodale was far from an ecologist and his methods could easily slide toward quackery, both he and his brand of environmentalism have a place in environmentalism's history. By the end of the 1960s, popular attention to ecology and environmental issues drew more readers than ever to Rodale publications. In the decade to come the Press would move the organic idea further beyond the compost pile. In *Organic Gardening and Farming* and a proliferating array of commercial publications in the 1970s, Rodale's marketplace environmentalism grew beyond bringing gardeners together to protect their bodies and their organic tomatoes. The Rodale Press adapted the organic idea for the growing ranks of environmentally minded Americans in the 1970s and developed marketplace environmentalism into a way consumers could improve themselves along with the natural world. Indeed, the company made organic into a style of living.

FOUR

ORGANIC LIVING

Marketplace Environmentalism in Organic America

IN 1972 THE RODALE PRESS'S WEST COAST EDITOR, FLOYD ALLEN, began a monthly series in *Organic Gardening and Farming* called "Looking for Organic America." The series profiled farmers, gardeners, and homesteaders who had adopted organic practices, visiting the farms and gardens they called home. That same year, a newly created Rodale Press Film Division produced a short documentary called *Looking for Organic America* that juxtaposed the practices of agribusiness and rural decline with the promise of emerging markets in organic production. While the farms, homesteads, and natural foods markets featured were modest, they served as evidence that "Organic America" was growing. In turn, the Rodale Press sought to become the arbiter between the producers and consumers who were calling Organic America home. In the early 1970s the Press organized the first national symposiums that brought together organic producers and agricultural officials, and at the same time launched one of the first farm certification programs in California. Using its status as the national clearinghouse on all things organic, the Rodale Press sought to build some structures into a marketplace that was still in its formative stages.

But the Rodale Press also recognized that Organic America represented a marketplace for more than just fruits and vegetables grown without chemicals. It was also a marketplace ripe for the ideas and advice the Rodale Press produced and sold. The late 1960s and early 1970s are rightly recalled for producing modern environmental laws and being the moment when environmental protection became a matter of national political debate. But it also produced millions who were paying attention to environmental issues and interested in both products and ideas that were hard to find in the mass marketplace of the day. The Rodale Press expanded the definition of "organic" and leveraged its information-gathering skills to identify and market to this emerging group of environmentally minded consumers. Whereas in the 1950s and 1960s the Rodale Press publications offered a site for critiquing scientific and medical expertise and brought readers together around natural health concerns and consumption habits, in the 1970s the company more fully established marketplace environmentalism as a means of selling "organic" as a personal style of living that reflected and enacted environmental values. By understanding a segment of consumers and developing a relationship with them over time, the Rodale company carved a niche for itself and its type of environmentalism in the crowded marketplace of the late twentieth century.

By the end of the 1970s the Rodale company had expanded its notion of an organic lifestyle to include everything from making natural Christmas presents to designing homes to use energy efficiently. The company sold a consuming style out of anti-consumption. Indeed, over the course of the decade the company made "organic" into a capacious and flexible set of lifestyle ideas and consumption practices that could adapt marketplace environmentalism to the shifting winds of consumer interests. Yet the very adaptability that allowed the company to increase its number of readers also made marketplace environmentalism ephemeral. Making your own yogurt or heating with a woodstove were easy to sell as a lifestyle choice that saved money, brought personal satisfaction, and helped improve the planet. The harder task was showing that those individual choices made much difference in terms of natural resource use and ecological protection. The Rodale company's remarkable growth in the 1970s underscores a critical question that continues to bedevil today's green marketplace: did changing consumer lifestyles actually change the world?

A SANE LIVING SYSTEM

The explosion of popular interest in environmental issues in the early 1970s proved to be both a boon and a burden for the Rodale Press and its brand of marketplace environmentalism. The monthly circulation of *Organic Gardening and Farming* nearly doubled between 1966 and 1972 to 750,000, and *Prevention* began reaching well over a million readers.[1] Additionally, the company's books found new outlets in the aisles of health food stores and co-ops opening around the country. As a 1969 profile of natural health food stores in Northern California described the reading selection at San Francisco's Hip Health Foods, "Rock albums are stacked next to spiritual tracts, papers and books on Yoga. One entire section contains practically all of the titles published by Rodale Press, along with classics like Euell Gibbons' fascinating 'Stalking' series."[2] Unlike many publishing houses who were new to environmental topics, the Rodale Press had close to thirty years of publishing experience by the early 1970s. The company's books, magazines, and pamphlets had long served as guides for those interested in natural health and producing food without chemicals, and in the early 1970s there were millions of new consumers who were eager for this type of guidance.

The challenge for the company was how to distinguish itself in an increasingly crowded marketplace. While a plethora of magazines were devoted to homes and gardens in the 1950s and 1960s, there had ostensibly been only one devoted to gardening and farming without pesticides. Similarly, vitamin and health product advertising was ubiquitous in postwar mass media, but there had been only one national outlet for natural vitamin and health products. With the explosion of popular interest in health, ecology, and environmental issues in the early 1970s, that was no longer the case. Magazines like *Mother Earth News* and the *Utne Reader* now sat alongside books like Alicia Bay Laurel's *Living on Earth* (1971) and titles from Shambhala Publications like *The Tassajara Bread Book* (1970) and a seemingly endless variety of imitators. As the sociologist Sam Binkley argues, much of the boom in book publishing in the 1970s was fueled by publishers searching for the next *Whole Earth Catalog*, which had originally been published only in the Bay Area but became a national best seller when it was picked up by Random House.[3] The success of such titles meant the Rodale Press was no longer alone on the co-op bookshelf.

The company responded to this challenge by expanding its concept of "organic" and forging marketplace environmentalism as a do-it-yourself response to both the ecological and economic uncertainties of the 1970s. The Rodale Press recast "organic living" as a signifier for a whole set of practices—and consumer choices—that integrated personal health, environmental concerns, and self-improvement. Although the Press never lost sight of teaching readers how to grow the most flavorful tomatoes, in the 1970s it sought to broaden its readership by teaching readers how to cultivate an organic lifestyle.

Front and center in this effort was J. I. Rodale's son, Robert Rodale. Robert had been writing and editing *Organic Gardening and Farming* since his early twenties when, at his father's insistence, he dropped out of a journalism program at Lehigh University and joined the publishing company full-time. He became president at the age of twenty-eight, and J. I.'s death in 1971 left the company in Robert's hands. At a time when more and more Americans were discovering organic ideas he became the face and the voice of the Rodale Press. By many accounts Robert, who generally went by Bob, was retiring and studious. Like his father he was not a specialist in a discipline but had the patient habits of a scholar and writer. Born in 1930, Bob was in his forties in the 1970s and so was a generation removed from those young idealists decamping to communes at the time. Bob, married with five children, lived in a modest home that had been built on the original *Organic Gardening* farm in the 1950s. Even as he wrote about organic living, he presented himself as a pragmatic family man with austere personal habits rather than an idealistic crusader. In the 1971 profile of the Press published just before J. I. Rodale's death, the *New York Times Magazine* writer Wade Greene claimed Robert Rodale was the "increasingly respectable look of the organic movement. . . . Where J. I. is a tilter at windmills, a denouncer of denouncers, Robert tends to be quietly earnest, and to talk and write in moderate tones."[4] Over the course of the 1970s Bob used his own lifestyle as proof of how to create a happy life.

One of the clearest signals of how the company pushed to expand the organic idea beyond the garden in the early 1970s was that Bob Rodale's writing began appearing in places other than *OG&F*. For several years he produced a syndicated weekly column called "Organic Living" that appeared in dozens of newspapers around the country. In these columns he offered a primer for those new to the world of natural foods about what to eat, as well as a glimpse of what an expanded vision of "organic" could look like. Writing about how to deal with stress and

Robert Rodale (1930–1990). Courtesy of the Rodale Family Archives.

the anxiety of modern living, he urged readers to improve their lives with tidbits of advice like "Don't let the telephone, radio, and television dominate you. Take the radio out of your car and see how your life becomes more peaceful. Learn to stay away from the telephone for part of the day. . . . Invest in a pair of sturdy shoes instead of another bottle of aspirin or tranquilizers." These were small steps toward creating a personal system to "fight tension organically by making your life more natural."[5] Bob wrote about his own diet as well as his own personal health habits, and at the same time he shared insights gleaned from scientific research. His columns described natural foods and natural health practices as part of a systematic approach to improving the body and living more naturally.

Like the *Prevention* system of the 1950s, the "organic living" system Bob outlined was rooted in routine behaviors and daily practices of diet and personal health. However, in the context of the environmental concerns of the early 1970s, Bob Rodale suggested that these personal choices took on new meanings. In a March 1972 column titled "An Ecology Test," Rodale explicitly tied personal choices of health and fitness to an overall awareness of environmental problems. Following ten questions about "household ecology" relating to the use of detergents, energy, and insecticides in the home, Rodale offered a "Natural Foods Pantry Test" and a "Personal Fitness" test as well: "The shape your body is in tells a lot about how you are coping with your environment. . . . People who get good scores are helping themselves, and are making the world a cleaner place too."[6] Using personal health as a baseline, Rodale argued that air and water pollution had considerable effects on the body's overall health. A "personal health-building program" was an important step to fight the effects of pollution: "If you live with polluted air, your whole body is being affected. Therefore you need a complete and effective approach to health far more than people living in clean air regions."[7] Rodale often had less to say about taking political action, but he occasionally used the syndicated columns to nudge readers toward activism on environmental issues. In addition to suggesting that readers join local environmental action groups and write letters to both companies and government regulators, he routinely suggested talking to a local supermarket manager about health and environmental concerns. "In a world that's becoming increasingly chemicalized, degraded and needlessly unnatural, you can stop taking it on the chin, and start dishing it out," he counseled.[8]

Bob Rodale's often-sanguine suggestions about how to live organically nonetheless echoed some of the dire predictions that dominated early 1970s popular discourse about the environment. Pollution and the preservation of natural areas had long been animating causes of environmental concern, but by the early 1970s energy use, population growth, and global resource scarcity—as evidenced by Paul Ehrlich's 1968 best seller *The Population Bomb* and the Club of Rome's 1972 report *Limits to Growth*—made environmental protection seem a matter of survival. Bob Rodale's vision of organic living drew freely from prominent ecologists and critics of technology of the time while reiterating his company's practical advice about how to grow one's own food and improve personal health. In 1972 Rodale collected his monthly editorials from *OG&F* of recent years into a book titled *Sane Living in a Mad World: A Guide to the Organic Way of Life*. The book's tone reflected a sense of crisis that went well beyond soils and backyard gardens. Referencing the computer models of resource use and exhaustion that informed *Limits to Growth*, he argued, "Our way of life has been shown to be wrongly conceived and planned, and extreme methods in making America more natural, more reasonable in its burden on the ecosphere, are called for." Rodale made the case that the organic idea remained an effective personal response to this ecological crisis. As he described it, the organic idea was no longer limited to composting methods, but encompassed broader changes in both the economy and society:

> There is one method that fills the bill, and that's the organic method. If everyone became organically minded and backed up that way of thinking with organic actions, the dire predictions for America's future surely could be thwarted. In an organic America, the sales of chemical pollutants would end. There would be no problem with additives in food and no drugged meat to worry about. Garbage would be less of a problem because organic wastes would be composted. Sewage would enrich farm fields, not pollute rivers, lakes and harbors. Automobile smog would be minimized, because more people would be living on small homesteads and raising much of their own food, not commuting to jobs in large cities. Any type of pollution you can name would dwindle in an organic world.[9]

Wade Greene noted in his 1971 article that Robert Rodale kept multiple copies in his office of the microbiologist and humanist Rene Dubos's Pulitzer Prize–winning book *So Human an Animal* (1968) and the philosopher Jacques Ellul's *The Technological Society* (1964) to distribute to visitors.[10] In *Sane Living* Bob mentions having read and reread Ellul's manifesto on the dehumanizing effects of technology. What Rodale took away from Ellul and others was that complex technology was at the root of many environmental and social problems, and that technology alone was unlikely to solve them. The scary prospect for Rodale was that no one individual or group was guiding these complex systems. "The big worry," he claimed, "about this inexorable march of progress is that it lacks guidance or purpose." Describing a world of polluted rivers, decaying cities, and dwindling prospects for the future, Rodale painted a grim picture of a world dominated by technology and its unintended consequences.[11]

Against this backdrop, Rodale suggested that a carefully considered system of personal choices could help readers protect themselves, improve their lives, and help the natural world. If an impending crisis brought about by technology and pollution was the consequence of contemporary life in the United States, then his proscriptions for organic living offered another path. What Rodale called his "sane living system" involved several aspects, but he assured readers they were all "variants of gardening, better eating, and physical improvement." Even in moments when he sketched out a dire situation, he told readers they were not helpless and that solutions were within their reach. Describing the benefits readers would gain from adopting his system, Rodale suggested, "Most important of all, though, you will find how these seemingly varied ideas combine to show you a way out of the frustrations of life in a modern, overdeveloped society. You will see, by opening your eyes to the ways of life that rely more on human efforts and less on machines . . . that sane living is possible, even in a world where everyone else is being lured toward madness by the promise of continued technological miracles."[12] The world may have felt as if it was spinning out of control in the 1970s, but Rodale claimed that individuals had the power to change the choices they made in their daily lives—and in doing so confront the personal, social, and environmental challenges of their time.

Rodale sought to back up these ideas with evidence of what organic living looked like. In the same way that his father had built experimental plots for composting to demonstrate the organic method in the 1940s, Bob sought to create firsthand evidence for how to make such a broader system of "organic living" a reality in the 1970s. Aided by profits from rising circulation, the company opened a series of research units in the 1970s for testing out the ideas, tools, and projects of organic living. These research units put their focus on the domestic sphere. In October 1973 *Organic Gardening and Farming* announced the arrival of a new monthly feature in the magazine called "Organic Living." Echoing many of the themes that appeared in Bob's syndicated columns, the magazine told readers the new selection of articles would "make sure that you get the information to make your homes and kitchens just as organic as your garden."[13] Its first issue, edited by the company's own Nancy Albright, featured articles on a new nutrition rating guide from the public interest group Center for Science in the Public Interest, herbal remedies, the market for organic buckwheat, the role of vitamins in composting, and tips on how to preserve foods. Albright was also the author of the recently published *Rodale Cookbook* (1973), which she described in the magazine as "stuffed with natural gourmet recipes and garnished with a liberal sprinkling of organic living ideas."[14] Spanning more than four hundred pages, the book contained recipes for soups, salads, entrees, and desserts prepared with natural foods. In addition, the book offered lessons in nutrition, instructions for growing sprouts, ways to use soybeans as substitutes, tips for incorporating wheat germ into recipes, the merits of making bread with young children, and a guide to natural food stores across the nation. The book, like many Rodale publications, offered patient and detailed advice and spent more words describing how to cook vegetables to preserve nutrients than it did indicting modern food production. Still, Albright closed her introduction to the book by stating, "We are in the forefront of a cultural food revolution. Our traditional American eating habits are being looked at with new eyes. I believe the direction this revolution takes in the future largely depends on each one of us."[15]

To demonstrate what organic living looked like in practice, the Rodale Press created its own domestic laboratory as well. Albright's recipes drew from her experience as the head cook at the Press's "Fitness House." To fulfill the needs of the company's growing operations, Bob Rodale had purchased a house near the Press's headquarters in 1970 to locate the staff of the short-lived *Fitness for Living* magazine. In the coming years, the building became home to an employee cafeteria that doubled as a natural foods test kitchen for Albright and her staff. In articles and books, the "Fitness House Kitchen" was a place where the company's health claims and philosophies were transformed from ideas into practical applications. Photos in the company's books and magazines showed employees, including Bob Rodale, gathered over dishes of vegetable quiche and piles of organic grains. Moreover, the kitchen was a place where readers could see how it was done and learn for themselves how to make their own domestic spaces organic: "You will get to know Nancy Albright as you read her descriptions of how things are done in the Fitness House Kitchen." Editor M. C. Goldman claimed, "When she explains how to make soup stock or how to bake a loaf of bread, you know *you* can do it just by following her explicit instructions."[16] With the right guidance, the Press told its readers, anyone could meet the challenges of creating a personal system and enjoy the rewards of learning to live organically.

The domestic sphere also figured prominently in *Stocking Up*, a guide to home canning and food preservation that became one of the company's best-known titles in the 1970s. Editor Carol Hupping Stoner filled the book (published in 1973 and again in 1977) with ideas that went well beyond the garden. Like many of the company's titles, *Stocking Up* relied on well-worn kitchen and garden advice with a contemporary sheen of environmental awareness and organic concerns. In her introduction to the book Stoner described the need for a new text on home preservation that combined the insights of the last thirty years of food safety without relying on the last thirty years of chemicals. Reminding readers that there was a time "when raising and preserving one's own food without the aid of chemical fertilizers, sprays, hormones, medications, and additives were a real part of life for millions of American families," she aimed to show how it could be done again.[17] With over half a million copies sold in the first edition, the book would become the go-to text for homesteaders and those seeking to learn how to preserve the foods they grew. *Stocking Up* and a number of other successful titles demonstrated that "organic living" was something about which many consumers wanted to know more. As the company created more do-it-yourself texts like *Stocking Up* in the 1970s, it was aided by a newly created Rodale Research and Design Group that tested wares and constructed demonstration projects for the organic home and garden. To accompany articles and books on home food production, the research group tested products like electric food dryers and ice cream makers and experimented with designs for homemade smoke houses and root cellars. The research group, according to Bob Rodale, was created "to speed the development of better techniques that you can use" to grow food and to "live organically."[18]

The transformation of the Rodale Press into a laboratory for organic living became even more evident with the purchase of a new farm to house the company's research operations. The Press had long tested gardening methods and tools on its farm in Emmaus, but in June 1972 Bob Rodale announced that the company had purchased a three-hundred-acre farm to test commercial-scale organic growing and to create "an organic educational center." Like the Fitness House, the research center would be a site where ideas and projects could be tested and demonstrated for readers. "We are not out to produce papers for scientific journals," Bob Rodale told readers, "and we're not basically trying to prove that the organic method is superior to conventional farming and gardening. We're simply looking for better ways to do the things that we think you want to do."[19] The original farm on the edge of Emmaus that J. I. Rodale had purchased in 1941 was relatively small, and by the early 1970s housing developments encroached on the property. The area surrounding what would be known as the "New Farm" was still predominantly rural and could handle the thousands who would visit the site each year. Describing the New Farm a few years after it was acquired, Robert Rodale claimed, "Our goal was to a create a more complete demonstration of organic techniques in use—not just attractive vegetable gardens and ornamentals, but also other features in organic living and homesteading. We intended to show visitors alternate energy systems, fish-farming by organic methods, homestead-size poultry and animal husbandry methods, beekeeping, tree farming, and similar activities."[20] To complement these educational efforts, the company restored a one-room schoolhouse on the property for a "Primitive Man Center," which Rodale described as a "constantly-changing museum showing how the life of primitive peoples can offer useful ideas and techniques relevant to our life today."[21] The New Farm mixed old and new technologies to create a test site for what organic living could look like in the 1970s.

At the same time, the company used its skill of collecting and disseminating information to create educational resources for ecology centers and environmental groups. Through a newly created educational services division, the company produced film strips, worksheets, and reference books that provided the materials for what it called the "classrooms for organic living" emerging across the country in the 1970s.[22] The materials focused on subjects like composting, gardening, recycling, and basic ecology, and targeted every level of education from elementary schools through college and community groups and senior centers. "Organic people," according to one instructional text, were those who knew better about the dangers of chemicals and understood that humans are happier when they "partner with the earth." Organic people resisted junk food and "body pollution" and rethought their sedentary ways of living. The organic state of mind was "an alternative state of mind," one where people were "latching on to a new life style, *organic living*."[23]

These educational materials and the flurry of other publications that came out of Rodale's research operations suggested that organic now meant something more than just a composting method, or even simply a rejection of chemical pesticides. It now defined a way of living and personal choices in the home and the garden, as well as a way of thinking about economic relationships and their impact on both people and the natural world. In an introductory chapter to *The New Food Chain: An Organic Link between Farm and City* (1973), the editor of Rodale's *Environmental Action Bulletin*, Jerome Goldstein, asserted that the impact of the organic idea was rapidly outgrowing the compost heap: "And as more and more people see it, the organic idea provides a model route from where we are now to where we would like to be in the future. . . . The word organic is becoming a linking symbol upon which a consumer can relate to a producer. It is a substitute for national brand advertising via television, newspapers or magazine; the word organic when truly defined cannot have a national brand because its essence is localization and personalization." Emphasizing that personal choices could be a source of hope in a troubled time, Goldstein added that the organic idea "offers us a game plan—a personal action plan—that takes us beyond wringing our hands, preaching and so forth. This organic force may very well be our best reason to be optimistic at this time."[24]

The Rodale Press still taught readers how to make compost and grow the best tomatoes, but it also told them how to *be* organic.

Whether in syndicated columns about organic living or in the bustling hive of the company's research operations, the Rodale Press aimed to capture the zeitgeist of popular enthusiasm for ecology and environmental action in the 1970s by redefining organic as a style of living. To that end, many of the company's endeavors and its publications aimed to show how personal consumption habits could be a means of responding to the era's environmental crises. This turn toward describing organic as more than just a method of growing food came at a time when "lifestyle" itself was an increasingly popular way to explain the changes occurring in American culture and society. The social transformations of the 1960s—brought about by the baby boom, the women's movement, the antiwar movement, as well as the civil rights struggles of racial, ethnic, and sexual minorities—left many Americans searching for their own identity in the 1970s. "Lifestyle" was a term that captured alternative modes of identity and became a common means for describing how the counterculture departed from the mainstream. For the Rodale Press, lifestyle provided a lens for critiquing American consumption habits as well as a means for prescribing how to construct a more benign and environmentally conscious alternative.[25]

As a concept, lifestyle also bears the distinct marks of late-capitalist consumer societies, where consumers define themselves with the choices they make about what to wear, what foods to eat, and what media they consume. A style of life allows both individuals and groups to define themselves with consumption choices. Furthermore, inherent in the notion of lifestyle is that it is a flexible mode of self-expression and therefore built on flexible modes of personal consumption.[26] Indeed, it was the very flexibility of lifestyle as a concept that allowed the Rodale Press to apply "organic living" to an expanding array of personal choices in the 1970s. Once the term "organic" was no longer limited to soils, it could also mean switching from refined to whole grains, or giving up wingtips for Earth Shoes, or adopting natural cosmetics, or maybe learning a new skill like woodworking or home canning. Indeed, being organic could mean many things, all at once. As a lifestyle, organic also meant developing a particular relationship to nature, one that was reflected in personal habits. The Rodale Press rarely suggested that choosing a lifestyle was a replacement for or superior to political action, but instead characterized the organic way as a comfy and cozy alternative to mainstream consumerism.

Yet flexibility had its downsides. The notion of lifestyle also bears the marks of a consumer society where fashions change from season to season and year to year. As easily as a consumer could pick up the style of organic living with the help of a Rodale article or book, they might just as easily adopt another a few months later. More important, it was difficult to know if personal changes in lifestyle had any appreciable impact on how a modern consumer economy utilized and discarded natural resources. With its focus on an organic lifestyle, the Rodale Press followed a larger trend in environmental politics in the 1970s that turned away from protest and toward personal choices. The Press became a leader in marketing an organic lifestyle with its endless stream of how-to books and carefully tested advice. The company would also apply less effort to uniting readers to combat the use of synthetic chemicals, for instance, and more toward studying and developing a market based on selling books to environmentally minded consumers. In this way the system of "organic living" that Bob Rodale wrote about and the company displayed in its test kitchens and research centers in the early 1970s certainly gave environmentally minded consumers a sense of agency and the hope that their personal choices amounted to something more. Yet the question of how consumer choices led to more fundamental reforms or simply generated more profits was one that both marketplace environmentalism and the Rodale Press would struggle to answer for decades to come.

FINDING SPACE IN A CROWDED MARKETPLACE

The Rodale Press popularized the notion that organic could define a distinct style of living that a consumer could choose as a response to the ecological crises in the 1970s. Yet this attention to lifestyle also reflected new realities of the American economy. Indeed, the company's embrace of organic as a lifestyle cannot be fully understood without consideration of the decade's changing media and consumer marketplace. Companies that produced goods and the professionals hired to sell them found they were faced with an increasingly saturated marketplace in the late 1960s and early 1970s. Moreover, marketers struggled to understand the uncharted consumption habits of emerging social groups who did not fit the mold of white, suburban, middle-class consumers. In response to these challenges, marketers ultimately turned to the concept of lifestyle to reframe consumption as offering consumers something more than just material acquisition. For the Rodale Press, focusing on the organic lifestyle became a means of honing in on the habits and desires of a segment of American consumers and carving out a niche for itself in the saturated marketplace.

Publishers and marketers alike struggled with new competition and changing consumer habits in the 1970s. Magazine publishers in particular needed to find new methods of appealing to readers' interests because periodicals faced fierce competition for advertising dollars from television. At the same time, magazine circulation and production costs were growing. The rule of thumb in the publishing industry for much of the twentieth century had been that advertising rates increased with circulation, so in the 1960s mass-market magazines focused on growing their total number of readers and, in turn, raising their advertising rates. Increasing circulation, however, also incurred new costs in production and distribution and created a spiral of rising expenses, such that even a growing magazine with millions of readers could become steadily less profitable over time. These troubles became abundantly clear when perennially popular magazines that had once been common in many American homes folded. The *Saturday Evening Post* ended in 1969, *Look* ended in 1971, and *Life* ended its publication as a weekly magazine in December 1972.[27]

In many ways, a smaller audience provided special-interest publishers with an advantage. A magazine like *Organic Gardening and Farming* may not have reached tens of millions of readers each month, but as a special-interest periodical it did not need to appeal to the broad tastes of American consumers. One advantage that special-interest magazines had over their mass-market counterparts was that smaller titles could focus their editorial voice—and, importantly, their advertising content—to the interests of their specific audiences.[28] Rodale's *Prevention* maintained a firm grasp on the natural vitamin and food supplement market throughout the 1970s, and *OG&F* swelled from 160 pages each month in 1971 to 240 by 1976. Those increased pages were certainly filled with stories about homesteading, home food production, and many aspects of "organic living," but they were also full of ads for all manner of tools, books, and supplies that a consumer would need to pursue an organic style of life. The ability of special-interest magazines to carefully target their advertising became an asset for the Rodale Press.

Publishers also faced the challenge of selling to consumers in a marketplace saturated with options. This was an issue faced not only by publishers but also by producers, marketers, and advertisers more generally. As the historian Lizabeth Cohen has argued, the unprece-dented economic growth of the postwar years had been predicated on economic policies and cultural mores that brought more and more people into the consuming ways of the middle class. The success of this expansion, however, did not come without anxiety. Since the late 1950s manufacturers and marketers had worried that consumers in an age of abundance would eventually reach the apex of their ability to consume and that steady growth would give way to contracting markets. Whereas economic downturns in the past spawned new efforts to study problems of production, maintaining a robust consumer economy created new impetus to study and solve the problems of consumption.[29] Adapting concepts from academic disciplines such as sociology and behavioral psychology to better understand consumer motivation, marketers in the 1960s began to focus on differences *within* segments of the mass marketplace. Marketers had long focused on American consumers through various groupings such as race, class, ethnicity, and gender. However, some marketing professionals began to argue that such group-ings were no longer accurate enough to capture the increasingly indi-vidualized interests of consumers and the consumption patterns of emerging groups.[30]

Adding to these challenges was the fact that the social upheavals of the 1960s and concerns about pollution and resource use made adver-tisers and marketers uncertain about the future of their professions. In the wake of Vance Packard's best-selling books that critiqued advertising and consumption—*The Hidden Persuaders* (1957) and *The Waste Makers* (1963)—marketers debated what role their own profession had in the excesses of resource use and abuse in the consumer economy. Writing in the *Journal of Marketing* in 1971, marketing professor Laurence Feld-man likened his profession to a real estate agent who had sold a home with a lovely view on top of a cliff but whose base was being constantly eroded. Marketers had succeeded in creating "endless opportunities for choice," he claimed, but they also promoted material consumption over the needs of society. Feldman argued that in order to slow the growth in material consumption, marketers would need to rethink the purpose of their profession. The marketing profession could change, he claimed, by "expanding the emphasis on nonmaterial consumption" and "stressing societal criteria in consumption."[31] In a 1969 piece in *Business Horizons*, marketing scholar Leslie Dawson had similarly suggested that businesses in the future would need to become more responsive to the changing "human and social demands" of the time, and that the marketing concept remained ill-equipped to respond to demands beyond those of a particular good or service.[32] A new approach to marketing, Dawson argued, would bring business to a new level in its relationship to society. Rather than a market of goods, Dawson hoped businesses would create markets for "human fulfillment."[33]

Searching for a concept that facilitated segmentation and recast the social purpose of their profession, marketers centered their attention on understanding the particular "consuming style" of a group of consumers. Rather than simply counting numbers to add up into mass-market sales, researchers aimed to create more nuanced pictures of consumers and their interests. As early as 1962 the American Marketing Association formed a "Task Force on Life Styles," which laid the foundation for applying the concept of lifestyle to describe how various groups within the mass market developed their consuming practices and associations with various products.[34] The "lifestyle" concept according to one of its early marketing theorists, William Lazer, referred "to the distinctive or characteristic mode of living . . . of a whole society or segment thereof. It is concerned with those unique ingredients or qualities which describe the style of life of some culture or group, and distinguish it from others. It embodies the patterns that develop and emerge from the dynamics of living in society."[35] In this way, "lifestyle" offered a means of parsing the mass market as well as a hopeful and progressive vision of the role of business in society. Looking forward at the end of a turbulent decade, Lazer claimed in 1969, "One of the next marketing frontiers may well be related to markets that extend beyond mere profit considerations to intrinsic values—markets based on social concern, markets of the mind, and markets concerned with the development of people to the fullest extent of their capabilities."[36] What this detour into the history of marketing shows is that by the 1970s businesses shifted from marketing products to marketing styles of living that could be achieved with the help of their products. A business could sell a product and at the same time sell something more.

Editors and executives at the Rodale Press may not have been reading marketing theorists, but they clearly understood that the organic lifestyle could be used to develop markets based on the consumption habits of environmentally conscious consumers. In 1971 Jerome Goldstein produced a book titled *How to Manage Your Company Ecologically*, which sought to convince business executives that environmental consciousness could be both profitable and help protect and improve natural resources. The first step, according to Goldstein, was to recognize the development of a new range of consumer niches that needed to be segmented. Quoting from business executive Marion Harper, Goldstein argued for business to "respond to the increasing variety of life-styles, Mr. Harper stresses the need for 'segmentation. The affluent market is made up not of masses but of highly segmented groups that have to be served, appealed to, with very special forms of innovation in information. . . . Companies have to search for a narrower and narrower product-people base for marketing growth.'"[37] Goldstein was bullish on demonstrating that it was in the best interests of businesses to pay attention to the emerging segment of environmentally conscious consumers. He claimed that the publicity that surrounded environmental issues in the early 1970s "has made a sizable percentage of Americans understand that a relationship exists between what they buy on the supermarket shelf and what they deplore in the waterway." As a result, these consumers would be seeking alternatives, and so he asked businesses to consider, "What do you make, what service do you perform, what buying power do you bring that lead to an alternative to environmentally-degrading product or service?"[38]

The Press also devoted its resources to advocating on behalf of this emerging segment of consumers. Writing in a 1972 piece about the need for a reliable national market for organic foods, Goldstein claimed the

Press was contacting supermarket chains about creating areas devoted to organic foods. Directly linking environmental awareness to consumer markets, Goldstein asked readers to contact their own grocery stores and express their interest in starting a "special section offering organically-grown and natural foods," and encouraged readers to write for free printed material titled "Help the Environment, Eat Organic Foods."[39] The company also used the growing size of its readership as evidence that organic consumers were a market segment worth serving. As part of its efforts to develop the market for organic foods, Rodale Press editors lobbied the United States Department of Agriculture to appoint someone inside that department to address the needs of the small but growing cadre of organic farmers. In 1973 Jerome Goldstein related how he had told a department official that OG&F now had eight hundred thousand readers and that thought it would be "fair to assume that in that number there were between 10,000 and 50,000 farmers who could benefit from USDA recognition of their existence." The official did not appoint someone to serve organic farmers, but he was apparently quite impressed by the strength of the organic market despite the magazine's modest circulation numbers. Goldstein writes that the official asked, "How could *Organic Gardening* magazine have 800,000 subscribers and be thriving, and *Look* magazine be out of business?" Goldstein's answer was that the organic movement relied on direct connections between producers and consumers. Despite the fact he had "no predictions about the future of mass marketing," Goldstein felt certain that this small segment of consumers demonstrated "that one-to-one personalized and specialized marketing . . . holds the key to jobs and profits for a great many Americans in the future."[40] In a crowded marketplace, identifying the specific interests that defined the lifestyle of a group of consumers—even their environmental interests—could be the key to marketing to them. Over the course of the 1970s the Rodale Press worked to make "organic" not just a gardening method or a set of concerns about pesticides and pollution but also a style of consumption it marketed to its segment of consumers.

The irony of course was that the company sold this style of consumption as a form of anti-consumption. The organic lifestyle the Rodale Press promoted in the 1970s eschewed store-bought tomatoes for those grown and canned at home and emphasized how living simply could be both a source of pleasure and a way to improve the natural world. If the company had been selling vegetables or any other material goods it would have been self-defeating to instruct consumers how to get by with less. But what the Rodale company actually produced and sold was information. It sold a different style of living and the information consumers needed to make that style a reality. This helped the company skip over some of the thornier questions about its own environmental impact. Publishing books and magazines relied on the production of paper, which often came from some of the same companies environmentalists were battling in places like the Pacific Northwest. Moreover, the segment of affluent consumers the company targeted were those whose very lifestyles placed the greatest burden on natural systems. As the historian and nature writer Jennifer Price has suggested with respect to nature shops at malls in the 1990s, the deeper and more troubling irony of the organic lifestyle was that the very "naturalness" it ascribed to products and practices helped conceal the very real material effects of an organic lifestyle.[41] In addition, the type of marketing practices the company adopted, particularly its direct-mail operations, relied on exploiting some of the most wasteful consumer habits. The company targeted its segment of consumers with millions of mailings and advertisements, many of which were rapidly discarded in household trash and ultimately landfills. The process of creating a lifestyle—even an organic one—was never complete. Those wasteful practices were central to how the company marketed the organic lifestyle, and crucially they were how the company studied environmentally minded consumers and which direction their consumption habits might be heading next.

HARVESTING THE MAILING LIST

Over the course of the 1970s the Rodale Press found more avenues for growth within its segment of the marketplace. In May 1977 an Associated Press story stated that in 1976 the Rodale company had turned out 2.5 million books, up over a million from the year before. In the same period, advertising revenue for *Prevention* and *Organic Gardening and Farming* jumped 25 percent.[42] In 1977 the firm acquired another magazine for the first time, *Bicycling!* and turned Rodale's research division into a commercial side project called Rodale Resources Inc.[43] Despite the company's growth and its expanding reach, Bob Rodale presented his own lifestyle—and the company itself—as the embodiment of what a modest, healthful, and organic lifestyle looked like. Whenever stories about the company appeared in media, writers could not avoid describing Robert's comfortable and sensible attire and how the pleasant, pastoral surroundings of the company's rural campus contrasted to the hustle of the New York publishing world. Similarly, observers noted the dedicated employees of the Press who enjoyed low-cost organic lunches at the Fitness House and the workday exercise breaks they took at the company's facilities. Adding another showcase, the Press's main building christened a new library in 1977 that was constructed with the type of passive solar design its publications promoted. In the late 1970s Robert Rodale linked all the company's various elements—from its research in organic farming techniques, to its test kitchens, to its advertising policies, to its publications, to his personal approach to health and nutrition—to a central mission focused on giving people the information they needed to improve their lives and the world around them: "We feel the average person has been underrated. . . . Our mission is to show people that they have within their own hands a much larger portion of their destiny than other organizations care for them to know about."[44]

To a certain extent, the fact that millions bought Rodale Press titles in the 1970s is evidence of the growing ranks of environmentally minded consumers. But there is another story, harder to see in numbers alone. Obscured by the company's sales figures is the story of how the company closely studied its readers to adapt the organic lifestyle—and the publications that sold it—to keep up with changing consumer tastes. Over the course of the 1970s the Rodale Press developed a set of marketing practices that helped the company directly identify environmentally minded consumers and create books carefully crafted to their interests. By adopting a capacious and evolving definition of the organic lifestyle, the company wedded timeworn appeals of self-improvement with modern techniques for studying consumer interests. What the company's marketing techniques reveal is how it developed a sophisticated system for producing and selling its books to an audience of environmentally minded consumers. And in the endless and often ephemeral iterations of organic living that rolled out of Emmaus, the limits of this approach

Cover of *Organic Gardening and Farming*, August 1975. Courtesy of the Rodale Family Archives.

came into focus—Rodale's marketplace environmentalism was better equipped to change the style of modern consumer culture than it was at questioning the fundamentals of that culture.

In January 1971 the Rodale Press advertised what it called "an exciting new service for men and women who read Rodale publications." "The Organic Gardening Book Club" would help readers create "a treasury of helpful guidance in hard-to-find books" on subjects like natural health, pollution, and gardening. The company knew there was a demand for such a service, it claimed, because it knew its readers: "These people, we know, are alert to the danger of pesticides and pollution. They understand the benefits of organic living. They want brighter health and longer lives. *And they recognize the crucial importance of getting as much information as possible. Quickly. Authoritatively.*" The firm was uniquely equipped to help its readers because, in its own estimation, "Probably no one in the world sees as much useful information about organic living as our Rodale editors. Regularly, they sift though mounds of manuscripts, evaluate hundreds of books, study works that are not even available in better bookstores."[45] With this book club and many similar offers, the Press promised readers exclusive access to the detailed knowledge its editors assembled as well as an unceasing flow of new materials.

Just a few years later the company promised its readers it was becoming a clearinghouse for information on more than just gardening without chemicals. Fusing several of its new publications with its older ones, the company launched the "Self-Sufficiency Book Club," which brought together low-energy design, home handicrafts, natural health, and a new activity, bicycling, under one rubric. One promotional mailer for the club claimed, "People want to get back to basics and put human values ahead of material ones . . . to live in closer harmony with their environment . . . to be healthy and fit . . . to use the resources the world gives us for rich, full and peaceful lives." The mailer featured the smiling countenances of five Rodale Press editors as they went about gardening, woodworking, and preparing healthy foods. The values of the book club, the ad suggested, reflected the values of the editors and the Press itself: "The SELF-SUFFICIENCY BOOK CLUB is a lifestyle 'support network' too. Because through our books, we hope to share ideas, inspiration and practical information with people who share our—and your—way of life."[46]

This appeal was emblematic of how the company promoted itself as an information resource for those looking to craft an environmentally conscious lifestyle in the 1970s. Although it is tough to generalize about the company's subscribers, it is clear that in the 1970s it aimed to reach those ecologically minded consumers as they settled in as homeowners and breadwinners. The company was not aiming for those on communes and college campuses, but those who were starting families and buying land of their own. The company viewed its audience as over-whelming white, and even if they chose to preserve their own food and build a solar greenhouse, it still looked like the idealized image of the American family in the mid-twentieth century. More than anything, the company's readers were hobbyists. They were gardeners, bakers, woodworkers, bicyclists, and home handymen—and those who aspired to learn those types of hobbies as part of their lifestyle. Yet, while hob-bies might sound like something quaint, they were a powerful tool for identifying a group of consumers and studying their consumption habits. With something like its Self-Sufficiency Book Club, the Rodale Press did not simply aim to sell a single title about woodworking or herbs, but to identify those readers who were interested in such topics and figure out what topics they might be interested in next.

The company reached out to consumers by marrying enduring con-cerns about personal improvement with contemporary anxieties about energy and the environment. Self-sufficiency took on a new valence after the oil embargo of 1973 and the subsequent economic downturns of the next decade. The company produced well-researched and detailed manu-als about subjects like solar greenhouses that told readers how building one could save them money in a time of rising food and energy costs. Yet the company also sold these types of books by telling readers that learning to build a greenhouse would provide the perennial promises of consumer satisfaction like improved health and happiness. The same could be said for any number of the how-to books that the company produced in the 1970s—whether those titles were about cooking with herbs or manuals for bicycle repair. This aspect of the company's mar-keting strategy emerges most clearly in a memoir written by a pioneer of the mail-order industry named Walter Weintz, who worked with firms such as *Reader's Digest*, the Book of the Month Club, Time-Life Books, and the Rodale Press. In *The Solid Gold Mailbox* Weintz asserts that the first rule of success in marketing through the mail was having "an *idea* for an appealing product that can be marketed at a profit." Yet that simple rule was complicated by the fact that in order to be appeal-ing, "a product must satisfy a need or a desire that is harbored in the breasts of men and/or women in commercial numbers." Such basic human needs and wants, Weintz suggested, were things like "the need for love, security, wealth, success, health, religious faith, amusement and entertainment, popularity, and whatever else brings happiness. The wants include ambition for self and children, desire for self-improvement (win friends, broaden your education, overcome self-doubts and fears); personal accomplishment (do-it-yourself); the need for respect and praise of your family and friends."[47] Styles might come and go, but these were the basic desires of consumers, year in and year out.

Weintz's list of consumers' aspirations neatly matches those that the Rodale Press used to create a reliable marketplace for its organic living and self-sufficiency books in the 1970s. Doing more for yourself, gaining greater security, improving personal health, saving money, gaining the respect of friends or family—these were the promises the company used to market to environmentally minded consumers. Moreover, with the help of Walter Weintz and other direct-marketing professionals, Robert Rodale and his company made those themes central to how the company promoted and sold its publications. Weintz and his son Todd began working as consultants for the company in the 1960s, after circulation manager Bob Teufel approached Weintz at a Direct Mail Advertising Association convention. The company's success in the 1970s, according to Weintz, relied on Robert Rodale's adherence to the basic principles of mail-order marketing after his father's passing in 1971. Weintz credited Teufel's business acumen and his "drive" with increasing sales, but "the other reason was Bob Rodale's firm belief in the basic *mail-order* tenets on which Rodale was founded: *helpful* do-it-yourself advice, and information that satisfied basic human needs for health, happiness, and a sense of accomplishment."[48] Relying on a core set of themes allowed the company to identify consumers who were interested in subjects like organic gardening, low-energy design, woodworking, and natural health, and to market books directly to those consumers over and over again.

Although the finer points of mail-order marketing might seem removed from compost pits and aquaculture ponds, they answer the important question of *how* the Rodale Press developed a market and popularized this type of do-it-yourself advice for environmentally minded consumers. The marketing model the company relied on identified a group of consumers and continually marketed books to that group. Such an approach had distinct advantages. Marketing directly to consumers by mail was a means for a special interest publisher like Rodale to gauge both the type and, critically, the *number* of books consumers would buy. As most production and distribution costs were tied up in an unsold book, predicting how many books might be sold *before* printing was a core challenge for publishers who sold in traditional bookstores. Selling books directly reduced the risk of having books returned from stores and at the same time helped lay the groundwork for selling future titles.

Rather than selling a huge quantity of a single book, a predictable audience meant publishers could profit more by selling a similar genre of books to a defined segment of consumers. The Rodale Press did not produce tens of thousands of copies of a title about how to heat a modern home with wood and then try to convince the public at large to buy that book. Instead, it used its mailing lists to identify readers who would likely buy that book and marketed directly to them. A book club devoted to a theme or a hobby created what Janice Radway calls an "open channel of communication" between a publishing house and its consumers. Once opened, a publisher aimed to keep that channel filled by giving readers a constant source of products.[49] As *Publishers Weekly*'s William Goldstein claimed in 1982, the fact that the Rodale Press focused its book titles around a single message like self-sufficiency likely surprised "those weaned on the tactics of commercially oriented New York houses that often issue books to satisfy an unknown audience." Rodale Book Division vice president and publisher Richard Huttner told Goldstein, "In New York trade publishing it's a new ball game with every book. At Rodale there's a predefined market."[50] Unlike a mass-market publisher, the Rodale Press did not need blockbuster titles—it knew its audience and the subjects they were interested in, and created books that met its audience's tastes.

What makes this an important part of the story of marketplace environmentalism is that many parts of the Rodale Press's operations that reflected the company's environmental commitment—its aquaculture ponds, employee garden plots, jogging paths, and handyman workshops—also played a central role in how the company researched, developed, and tested the market for its publications. With *Prevention*'s circulation above two million and *Organic Gardening* over one million, combined with lists of former subscribers, by the end of the 1970s the Press had house lists of more than four million book buyers. Of the company's $29.8 million in books sales in fiscal year 1981, 85 percent came from direct-mail sales. The remainder came from the various book clubs associated with the Press's magazines, with only 5 percent attributed to in-store sales.[51] Mailing lists were also vital to how the company created the very content it sold. The Rodale Press carefully managed the development of books and test-marketed ideas using names culled from its lists. Thirty in-house editors produced nearly 50 percent of its output by the early 1980s, which ranged between thirty and thirty-five books a year. Marketing director Eller Rama told *Publishers Weekly* that the company used monthly surveys to identify the subjects of greatest interest to readers. Those subjects were then ranked and tested in focus group interviews four times a year. The firm then combined this type of "qualitative" approach with quantitative evidence from test mailings. While a big hardcover book was still in development, the company sent pamphlet-scale versions and other promotional materials for the title to targeted portions of its lists. In this second round of testing, "instead of counting responses as an indication the book's potential," Rama claimed, "you're counting orders." In the event of insufficient orders, a book project could be stopped or changed with minimal losses.[52] Even if a book never saw the light of day, the materials could be recycled into a future project, thereby minimizing the risk of losses in the creative process and helping the editors craft a better-targeted product the next time around.

By test marketing various iterations of a basic theme, the Press capitalized on the fact that those who bought one book about a particular subject would likely buy another. The results of this process are best illustrated in the success of *Prevention* editor Mark Bricklin's *Practical Encyclopedia of Natural Healing*. The company first published the book in October 1976 and over the next several years sold more than 1.2 million copies, with only one hundred thousand of those sold through traditional bookstores.[53] Rather than rushing to produce a sequel to the book, the firm spent five years testing various incarnations of the "natural healing" theme in articles for *Prevention*, *Organic Gardening and Farming*, as well as countless mailers and small pamphlets sent to subscribers. Some of these publications were substantial, such as the seventy-page *Healing With Nature* (1978); other items were more mundane, such as *Food Guide* (1979) or a single-page introduction to first aid, *Prevention Magazine's Quick and Natural Kitchen Medicine*.[54] These materials and countless others found their way into the mailboxes of customers on various lists, and the response rates gleaned from each of these mailings helped the company shape its next product. In 1981 when the press published Bricklin's sequel, *The Natural Healing Cookbook*, it sold over three hundred thousand copies in its first year. A year after that the Press unveiled *The Encyclopedia of Natural Home Remedies*, which before it was even ready to be shipped had already sold ninety thousand copies.[55]

The fact that the company sold millions of books about food preservation, natural healing, organic gardening, and home improvement in this manner surely demonstrates that more Americans were interested in the anti-consumer and environmentally conscious lifestyle the Rodale Press promulgated in the 1970s. But it also demonstrates the increasingly sophisticated marketing tactics the company used to identify a niche of consumers—those drawn to anti-consumerist and environmental messages—and how it produced and sold books that targeted them over and over. By identifying a consumer's interest in a hobby or set of books, the Press could learn about broader consumption habits as well. Indeed, by the end of the 1970s the company studied its lists for further insights about its niche of consumers and sought to harvest its mailing lists for clues about how environmentally minded and health-conscious consumers could be valuable to other businesses. Beginning in the early 1980s, Rodale's marketing research department began producing and distributing studies such as *Diet as a Lifestyle: A Profile of American Women*, which demonstrated demographically that those who consciously controlled their weight were on average higher earners, more educated, and more apt to purchase cosmetics, apparel, and appliances. In a similar study, *Health Food Store Shoppers: A Lifestyle and Product Usage Profile*, the research department claimed that despite the small size of this demographic segment, health food shoppers distinguished themselves from the general population "in lifestyle, in buying style, and in product usage." With reams of computer-generated data analysis, the study argued that there would be "big rewards" for advertisers who learned to target this audience and "big trouble" for those who did not.[56] And with its lists of millions of names and addresses, the company had the tools to make such targeted marketing a reality.

What emerges from the company's success at identifying a niche of consumers in the 1970s is the tension between how the Rodale Press used the tools of consumer culture and the anti-consumer lifestyle it sold. In marketing do-it-yourself books with careful instructions for growing your own food or making your home use energy more efficiently or treating everyday ailments with natural remedies, the company sought out those consumers who were looking for alternatives to the high-consumption lifestyles of average Americans. Yet the company relied on some key strategies of consumer culture to bring its readers back to the well. Not only did it blend contemporary environmental and energy concerns with well-worn promises of health and satisfaction, it developed and applied sophisticated techniques for studying and parsing consumer habits and preferences. The company demarcated a segment of Americans who were interested in matters of natural health and the environment, and then marketed aggressively to that segment. The success of the Rodale Press rested not only on adding more names to its mailing lists, but also on selling to those names time and again.

In addition to the ideas and techniques the company applied to the marketplace, its growth rested on some of the same wasteful and environmentally destructive practices of the twentieth-century consumer economy its customers presumably wanted to avoid. The direct marketing of books required printing and shipping tens of millions of mailings to American homes, the majority of which ended up in the trash. Likewise, the type of glossy envelopes and multipiece mailers the company generated required high-quality paper that in the 1970s could not be made with recycled fibers. Those mailings often included plastic and other objects as part of the package, which made it difficult, perhaps even impossible, for consumers to recycle them. While the Rodale Press produced information about how to live simply, garden organically, and conserve resources, it was still very much engaged in the material process of transforming natural resources and producing wastes with effects on both humans and the natural world.

Moreover, the very flexibility of the "lifestyle" notion encouraged consumers to pick up one new habit as they discarded another in the iterative and ephemeral process of what Anthony Giddens referred to as late modernity's "project of the self."[57] That process relied on consumers endlessly trying out different styles—for instance, changing the foods they ate, the clothes they wore, and the types of hobbies and interests they pursued. For a media company like the Rodale Press, the organic lifestyle involved teaching consumers about how to garden, how to heat the home, even how to "Have a Natural Christmas" (as one pamphlet title promised).[58] No longer simply about whether to compost, the organic lifestyle encompassed a whole range of consumer choices, each of which required accumulating more knowledge, more skills, and often more books and gadgets in order to achieve it. What made this process ephemeral was that with each new goal or ideal added to a lifestyle, the goalposts could move farther away. The process of creating a lifestyle—even an anti-consumer, environmentally conscious one—was never complete.

Not only were lifestyle changes ephemeral, they often bypassed the work of environmental protection that was achieved through political organization. Lifestyle changes often looked attractive and rewarding on promotional materials and book covers but changed very little about how modern consumer societies protected and managed natural resources. In the 1960s the Rodale Press had been actively engaged in bringing its readers together to battle aerial spraying and to share information across disparate locales. By the end of the 1970s the company taught readers how to remake their homes and hobbies and learned how to sell books to its audience over and over again. Rather than mobilizing citizens, the company harvested its computerized mailing lists of millions of names to market new book titles and develop new lifestyle variations. Marketplace environmentalism was better at growing the number of subscribers than sustaining and enacting a more fundamental critique of the modern consumer economy and its toll on the environment.

• • •

A key debate for historians of consumer culture is whether consumers adopted certain practices, styles, and products because they were "duped" by advertisers and marketers, or whether those consumers made active choices as "agents" who then shaped the market and effected change with their interests and demands. An earlier generation of scholars tended to describe consumers as being deluded by producers and the popular culture that sold them on certain habits and products. In contrast, a later generation of scholars found unexpected avenues within consumer culture where consumers made their own meanings. These scholars interrogated how audiences themselves used the artifacts of popular culture—paperback books, recorded music, television shows, even advertising itself—to actively fashion identities that were unintended by the authors and commercial entities that produced and distributed those artifacts.

Yet for the crowded marketplaces of consumer societies in the late twentieth century, such simple frameworks as "dupes" and "agents" fail to explain the complexities and ambiguities of the back-and-forth relationship with its consumers that a company like the Rodale Press cultivated to sell an organic lifestyle. The Rodale Press enlisted readers in creating that lifestyle, and it became successful in the 1970s by selling the information consumers needed in order to adopt the habits of anticonsumerism. As the economist Juliet Schor claims, in recent decades the companies that have thrived are those "who figure out how to successfully sell agency to consumers." Whether they were seeking a gardening book in order to learn how to grow food on an organic homestead or a bottle of bee pollen at the natural foods store to avoid the doctor's office, even when consumers sought alternatives to high-consumption lifestyles they could not escape a marketplace where their evolving desires and identities became commodities themselves.[59]

Viewed in this light, the Rodale company thrived in the 1970s by creating and selling an organic identity and agency to consumers—an identity that required consumers to enlist firms like Rodale to help them achieve. Under the guidance of Robert Rodale, the company combined its patient and detailed advice about how to make the home, the garden, and the body more natural with perennial promises of self-improvement. It identified the names and addresses of consumers interested in matters of environmental and personal health and relentlessly marketed to them by offering the information they needed to remake their lifestyles. The company systematically studied its corner of the marketplace and used its insights to better market future titles. In an era of environmental and economic turmoil, Rodale's marketplace environmentalism focused on personal changes as a way for consumers to enact their environmental values in everyday life.

Judging from the stories of homesteaders and do-it-yourselfers that populated Rodale Press periodicals, remaking your lifestyle could be more enjoyable and rewarding than organizing political action or boycotting corporations. Readers no doubt found a measure of meaning in learning how to can their own jams, but for all its anti-consumerist trappings the Rodale Press gave agency and identity to a group of consumers whose very lifestyles often placed the greatest burden on ecosystems both near and far. The company taught modern Americans how to do more with less on idealized organic homesteads, and how to change their lifestyles as a response to environmental crises. Yet it focused on the households and domestic anxieties of middle-class families and offered its advice to those who could afford to subscribe to a periodical or join a book club. It offered individualized consumer solutions to environmental problems and sold a politics that told people they could make themselves and the earth better by interacting with consumer culture in certain ways.

In shifting toward a focus on lifestyle, the Press expanded beyond the compost heap but largely eschewed an environmental politics that pushed for regulation and citizen action. The Rodale Press had crafted its vision of the organic lifestyle as a frugal and pragmatic consumer response to the energy and pollution concerns of the 1970s. Yet the question of which style of life a consumer should live was itself the product of an economy of abundance. Only with the freedom provided by a wealth of choices—and the knowledge and capital required to make those choices—could a consumer value a niche set of consumer goods and habits. And in the decade to come the Spartan style of organic living in the 1970s would largely give way to the values of personal health, diet, and the elusive goal of a perfect body. Following the lead of its readers away from the health food stores and toward the supermarket checkout, the Rodale Press would change once again what it meant to be organic as its brand of environmentalism embraced the mass market.

FIVE

A WHOLE NEW YOU

Making the Marketplace Mainstream

EVEN WHEN HE WAS THE ONE THROWING THE PARTY, BOB RODALE could not help but stick out at a cocktail reception on Madison Avenue. Rodale admitted to a reporter that he would have preferred to be wearing his standard uniform of flannel shirt, bolo tie, and trusty Earth Shoes. But as both he and his company began courting mainstream advertisers ahead of the launch of a new magazine in 1982, he was not too concerned about his own fashion choices. Rodale wanted to show that both he and the company he inherited from his father were no longer country cousins in the backwaters of the publishing world, that the organic lifestyle was not all brown breads and tasteless carob desserts, and that the ideas and products at the center of Rodale's niche market could appeal to a broader swath of American consumers. The company was attempting to move beyond the ranks of mail-order publishing, and Bob Rodale wanted to show that people like him and his staff, devoted to healthy and environmentally conscious living, were not out of touch with contemporary life or incurably rigid. In the decade since J. I. passed away, Bob had sought to put some daylight between himself and his father, but he showed more than a little bit of his dad's humor when he stated on the record that his wife and daughters wore cosmetics, that on occasion he had eaten at McDonald's, and that he enjoyed a drink now and again. Rodale professed that his company was on a mission to make American consumers more conscious of their health—and more natural—but told the reporter for *New York* magazine, "We're not out to create some puritanical world. We live in the real world. I *don't* want to be considered the Jerry Falwell of the health movement."[1]

Yet it was not just the minds of mass-market advertisers that Bob Rodale wanted to change in the 1980s; he wanted the world of agricultural science and policy to respect his company as well. Amid the farm crisis of the late 1970s and early 1980s, the Rodale Press used its research and outreach divisions to draw popular attention to the questions the crisis raised about the future of the American food system. Seeking to demonstrate the effectiveness of organic methods at the scale of the farm, the company's nonprofit arm developed organic conversion trials at its Pennsylvania headquarters and sponsored new research and marketing efforts to support sustainable farming across the country. At the same time, Bob Rodale used his company's public relations skills to increase political support for organic farming initiatives, both in the United States and in other parts of the world.

These efforts in the early 1980s occurred during tense but auspicious years for US environmentalism. Americans elected Ronald Reagan as president in the fall of 1980, and the next year saw the appointment of new leaders to federal agencies that managed natural resources and enforced environmental laws. Reagan's appointees largely saw the progress made in protecting natural resources in the 1970s as an expansion of the regulatory state and began working to roll back many of the policies that had been instituted since the first Earth Day. Yet, in the face of these new challenges, the environmental community also experienced an upswing of support and expanded its political leverage. National environmental organizations broke membership and fundraising records in the early 1980s and developed into well-organized and well-funded political lobbies as a result. Groups like the Sierra Club and the Natural Resources Defense Council—much like their conservative counterparts—harnessed the power of direct mail to organize citizens and push back against Reagan's regulatory agenda. The Rodale Press, which had long been an ally of the environmental community, linked its support for reforming the food system with these efforts to safeguard the gains of the environmental movement.

However, the riddle here is that at the same moment the Rodale Press widened its scope and pushed for systematic reforms in the nation's food system in the 1980s, it also became increasingly devoted to personal health and fitness as ends onto themselves. Bob Rodale courted mainstream advertisers by remaking his company's image and launched a new set of magazine titles that emphasized the therapeutic themes of health and fitness more than environmental issues. These titles proved to be immensely popular in the mass marketplace; by the end of the 1980s the family-owned publishing house that had once been known for promoting compost heaps and bone meal tabs was better known for glossy magazines that championed six-pack abs and guided young men and women in their sex lives. Scrubbed of its hoary appearance and nearly any association with the environment, the company's gospel of personal health became a fixture in the mass marketplace—and one that would be not just tolerated but increasingly imitated in consumer culture.

Reforming America's food system, on the one hand, and the changing market for lifestyle magazines in the 1980s, on the other, might seem to have little in common, but taken together they speak to how Bob Rodale and his company combined a search for reform with a search for profit. Moreover, these threads of the Rodale story help explain how improving yourself as a path to improving the world became synonymous in marketplace environmentalism. In the face of opposition to new environmental laws and the regulatory state, environmentalists increasingly adopted individualized efforts over large-scale action. In the years to come, the virtues of organic food and a fit, healthy body— as both good for you and good for the planet—became assumptions beyond reproach in consumer culture. Yet both the Rodale company and marketplace environmentalism proved better equipped at responding to the ever-changing health anxieties of high-income consumers than addressing the deeper health and environmental imbalances created by modern food production. Bob Rodale and his company charted a course to Madison Avenue for organic food and personal fitness in the 1980s. But for all the new options it created for late twentieth-century consumers, the marketplace offered limited tools for reforming the food system and protecting the environment

CRISIS AND REGENERATION

"24,000 Tons of Broccoli." So read the headline of a column that appeared on the Op-Ed page of the *New York Times* on October 17, 1980.

According to the article, that number represented how much of the vegetable the New York region consumed in a year. However, the point of the column was how far that broccoli needed to travel to get to Gotham's plates. Despite the fact that it was a cool-weather crop that could be grown throughout the Northeast, most broccoli, like nearly all other fruits and vegetables consumed by the city, had been shipped across the country from California. The column claimed that New York's broccoli was symptomatic of a much larger imbalance in the nation's system of food production. For every two dollars Americans spent on food, they spent another dollar paying "to move it around." At least two decades before local food activists started counting food miles and calculating a salad's carbon footprint, the column claimed that such inefficiencies highlighted deeper issues of the food system: "It's a crazy-quilt pattern of unplanned food-growing and unrealistic distribution which cannot continue much longer. Our economy will be unable to survive the expense. Our energy system will be unable to supply the demand." Reforming this system meant not only moving less food across the country, but also supporting small farms close to the city so they could compete with cheap food from far away. To get a handle on the economic and environmental costs of the food system would require greater consumer understanding and new informational resources devoted to reforming agriculture. And in order to learn more, all an interested reader needed to do was send a letter—to Bob Rodale.[2]

The "broccoli column" was one of dozens the Rodale Press produced and printed between 1980 and 1982 in the editorial pages of the *New York Times* and other media outlets. These cleverly written "advertorials" were one of the most visible parts of a charm offensive the company undertook in the early 1980s. Some of these columns addressed other issues the company cared about, like the virtues of preventative medicine or promoting the use of seat belts. But it was the columns about the economic and environmental issues of the food system that gained the most public attention. These columns painted a picture of the Rodale Press and its ideas about food and farming as no longer outlandish or provincial. Quoting national statistics and the work of academics, the columns depicted the company as not simply a publishing house but the nation's epicenter for studying and reforming food systems. The company was certainly not alone in worrying over the fate of the nation's food producers in the early 1980s, as a debt crisis among small farmers brought increased public attention to the agricultural sector. That critical moment ultimately provided the Rodale Press with a new avenue for arguing the economic, social, and ecological benefits of organic farming.

The farm crisis of the 1980s was part of larger trends that had been reshaping food production for decades. Farmers in the United States had long been yoked with debt for the materials they needed to produce food and fiber. Taking on debt allowed farmers to add more land, adopt new technologies, and try new methods to improve yields and profits. However, each new bit of acreage and each new tractor or pesticide sprayer purchased on credit often helped accelerate a treadmill of increased production costs and debt. New equipment allowed farmers to save on labor and bring more land into cultivation, but rising payments on loans and mortgages could swamp gains in productivity. Any fluctuation in the price of agricultural commodities altered the entire equation, and farmers might find themselves increasing production just to meet debt payments. This cycle had long shaped land-use practices and farm economics in the United States, but it came to a head in 1980 when President Jimmy Carter announced an embargo on wheat to the Soviet Union in response to that country's invasion of Afghanistan. The action closed off an important avenue for American farm commodities at the very moment a depression in developing markets slowed demand for American agricultural products abroad. Despite rising energy costs and an inflated dollar making American farm exports unappealing in many parts of the world, commodity surpluses exploded and made already cheap prices even cheaper. With land prices collapsing in some parts of the country and rapidly rising in others, farm bankruptcies soared in the early 1980s. Nearly three hundred thousand farmers left the profession altogether.[3] Ultimately, the crisis of the 1980s accelerated the hollowing out of rural parts of the country that had been in the works for some time. As small producers failed, more and more of the agricultural system fell under the control of large-scale industrial operations.

Public attention to the debt crisis and the renewed attention to environmental issues on the heels of Reagan's election provided an opening for the Rodale Press and other enthusiasts to make the case for alternative farming practices. J. I. Rodale's ideas about producing foods without artificial chemicals had never achieved much standing beyond gardeners and their compost heaps. Certainly there were some farmers who applied organic methods on larger plots of land and a few scientists who championed nourishing soils with organic matter, but in agricultural commodity production and the science and policy that supported it, organic farming had barely made a dent in how most food was produced before 1980. Compared to the Rodale Press's success at popularizing gardening, natural health, and organic living among consumers in the 1960s and 1970s, its efforts to reach farmers had largely been a failure.

One place the company had succeeded was in providing a forum for the small circle of farmers who pursued organic practices as well as a crop of "agro-intellectuals" who emerged in the 1970s. Much like those who published soil jeremiads in the 1930s, these writers critiqued the economic, social, and environmental effects of modern farming methods and the impact of economic consolidation. Perhaps the best known of these critics was the Kentucky farmer and author Wendell Berry, who began publishing pieces in *Organic Gardening and Farming* in the early 1970s and became a regular contributor to the magazine in 1977. That same year Berry published *The Unsettling of America*, a book that highlighted the challenges faced by small farmers in rural America and made a moral case for farming methods that preserved the integrity of the land as well as agricultural communities.[4] Berry diverged from some of the organic orthodoxies of the Rodale Press, but his critique underscored the combined social and environmental costs of the modern food system. What the country needed, according to Berry and other writers who used Rodale publications as a forum, was to reform systems that worked against the environmental health of the land and the economic health of farmers and their families. As the farm crisis became acute, more farmers began paying attention to what Berry and others had been saying in the pages of Rodale Press publications.

Amid the farm crisis, the Rodale Press recast how it wrote about and promoted organic farming methods. After twenty-five years of publishing *Organic Gardening and Farming* as a single title with only a few articles devoted explicitly to farming, the Press dropped "farming" from the title in 1979 and launched a monthly magazine called the *New Farm* as a separate entity. The magazine reiterated critiques of modern agriculture that would have been familiar to existing organic enthusiasts and readers of the new agro-intellectuals. However, the *New Farm* also repurposed those critiques to appeal to farmers struggling with rising costs of energy and the power of large business interests in the farm economy. In particular, the magazine emphasized the low cost of organic management techniques and the premium prices farmers could charge for organic crops. As one early advertisement in January 1979 pitched the magazine:

> We'll be bringing you news and information that can really help independent-minded farmers like you. You'll be reading about *new markets* that pay premium prices for specialty crops that the "big boys" can't grow . . . *new techniques* that allow you to slash 30 percent off your production costs . . . *new energy sources* to reduce your "fuelish" dependence on large corporations . . . *new methods of insect control* . . . that free you from hazardous pesticides and environmental poisons . . . *new programs* . . . of low-interest financing and aid for farmers who know where and how to look.[5]

The magazine argued that "organic" methods meant not giving up on technology but choosing a different set of technological inputs for the farm. Another advertisement for the magazine promised, "THE NEW FARM is the only magazine today that brings you advice and information that will help you take advantage of proven, low-cost *organic* technology. *It will help you beat the out-of-sight costs of chemical fertilizers*, help you evaluate alternative crops and marketing possibilities, help you maximize your profit per acre and help you get more of the things you need from your land."[6] These were certainly hyperbolic marketing promises for a new magazine, but they suggest how in the 1980s the Rodale Press recast organic farming not as some pie-in-the-sky ideal, but as a pragmatic solution to the nation's farm crisis.

Organic farming practices also received a closer look by scientists in the late 1970s and early 1980s. Rising fuel and energy prices in the late 1970s led to some of the first peer-reviewed efforts to study organic methods as a viable alternative in agriculture. In September 1975 *Science* magazine reported on work by William Lockeretz at the Center for the

Biology of Natural Systems at Washington University that pointed to both the cost and energy efficiency of some organic production practices. The study compared sixteen organic farms with their conventional counterparts of a similar size and determined that organic practices required a third less energy. Lockeretz's study signaled the fact that despite opposition from federal agricultural officials and many scientists, a reappraisal of organic agriculture was underway in at least some corners of the scientific community. In yet another response to energy costs, a provision in the Food and Agriculture Act of 1977 called for a study of fossil fuel consumption in agriculture and explored the application of organic wastes as a method of doing so. Two years later the USDA began an unprecedented survey of organic farming. The study sought to determine the costs and benefits of organic production practices, reviewed the experiences of organic farmers, and surveyed the existing literature. In addition to case studies of twenty-three organic farms across the country, the study partnered with the Rodale Press to survey one thousand random subscribers of the *New Farm*. Through Rodale's publication the USDA received close to seven hundred responses from 95 organic farmers, 112 conventional farmers, and 204 farmers who identified as "combined conventional and organic."[7] While the study found some evidence that organic farms required less energy, the very fact that the USDA partnered with the Rodale Press to conduct the research was evidence itself that both organic methods and the company were no longer beyond the pale in the world of agricultural science and policy.

The farm crisis and the new efforts to study organic production practices helped spur an ambitious research project that Bob Rodale created in the early 1980s to assess the nation's food system. Known as the "Cornucopia Project," this endeavor used the company's research acumen to develop state-level assessments of the relationship between food producers and consumers. The project launched nationally in late 1980 with the advertorials that appeared in the *New York Times*, and the next year Bob Rodale reported that over ten thousand people had signed up for the project's newsletter. The response, he claimed, "gave us a great deal of encouragement, and convinced us we were on the right track. And one after another, the letter writers kept raising a basic question: What can *I* do about the problems of our food system?"[8] In June

1981 the Cornucopia Project hosted its first symposium, which brought together over four hundred attendees for two days at Lehigh University. The symposium outlined how the project would create state-by-state assessments of how much food was "imported" and "exported" and assemble profiles of the "vulnerability" of each state's food system. In his address to the group Bob Rodale described how the project grew out of questions about how organic farming could reform the larger food system and the energy imbalances of modern agricultural production. The project also emphasized that reforming food systems required consumers to push for more control. Cementing a link between individual consumer choices and systemic reforms, Rodale claimed in his remarks at the symposium, "The consumer's control has lessened, too, since it's no longer possible to make a meal from local foods as we could when I was a boy. We need to restore that capability. . . . We are all pilots with a little bit of power to change the trim paths of the American food system. Maybe we can arrange for it to have a soft landing into a better era than seems likely if it keeps going as it is."[9]

Like many of the company's endeavors over the years, the project centered on the marketplace as the avenue where individuals could exercise their power. Those who subscribed to the project's newsletter were encouraged to think about what *they* could do to help reform the food system: "Getting involved in this movement is easy. Begin by developing the ability to question your local food system—look at the facts. Just because you're not a scientist or Ph.D. (or even if you are) doesn't mean you can't research the problems within your own home or community. . . . Talk with other community people about where the local food system is vulnerable. Work together in experimenting with potential solutions—plan meals differently, start a garden, get involved in a food co-op or buying club."[10] Pushing readers to see themselves as "food voters" each time they went to the marketplace, the Cornucopia Project told consumers that they had a role in addressing the farm crisis and that they could make choices that benefited their regional food economy as well as their personal health.

Both the *New Farm* magazine and the Cornucopia Project's organizing efforts were central to Bob Rodale's attempt to put his own stamp on reforming the food system. Indeed, Rodale used the farm crisis and the popular attention to environmental issues in the 1980s as a backdrop for recasting organic farming as one piece of a broader vision he called "regeneration." Over the course of the decade, Rodale became something of an agro-intellectual himself, albeit one whose publishing company gave him the means to support research projects on his own. Rodale adopted the term "regeneration" as a catchall to describe how systems—food systems, local communities, the human body, even businesses—could recover from a crisis and return to health by relying on "internal resources" over outside inputs. With respect to the food system, regeneration developed into Bob Rodale's holistic concept for how farmers could rely on organic soil management techniques and how communities could restore their food-growing capacity. He suggested that regeneration was bigger than just organic farming. In a piece addressed to supporters of his firm's research efforts in the early 1980s, Rodale asked, "Can organic farming and gardening do the job? Only partly. Organic methods can help to make the soil more pure, more healthful, and more productive." However, a broader transformation of the agricultural system, he argued, would require something more: "But we need to do more than just improve the soil to get our method of growing food headed toward a state of permanent improvement and growth." Regeneration, he claimed, required restoring "all aspects of our capacity to produce on the land. We need a fully regenerative form of agriculture, we need a regenerative agriculture that draws productive strength from the land itself, from the sun and the rains and from an ever-growing community of healthy, productive people."[11]

When applied to food systems, regeneration sounded not unlike "sustainability," a term whose currency was on the rise in environmental circles in the 1980s. The *New Farm* magazine soon became devoted to "regenerative agriculture," and research on the company's farm aimed to adapt and refine regenerative concepts like cover crops and interplanting. Regeneration was also an attempt to put some distance between attempts to reform farming and the antediluvian associations of "organic" that had long dogged enthusiasts. Like sustainability, regeneration was also vague enough that Rodale and his company could apply the term to more than just farm-management practices. Over the course of the 1980s, Rodale and his company promoted regenerative technologies, regenerative communities, as well as the regeneration of the body and even the spirit. While researchers associated with the

Rodale Institute today still use the term to describe alternative farming methods, it never gained much currency beyond the Rodale orbit. Once the farm crisis receded from the headlines, regeneration largely faded as well.

Bob Rodale's attempt to popularize his philosophy of regeneration was another piece of redefining the Rodale Press. He worked not only to solidify himself as an agro-intellectual but also to recast his company as something more than just a business driven by profit alone. Whereas J. I. Rodale had spent much of his time clipping away at study after study that he could use to back up his existing ideas and rarely enjoyed an audience with experts, by the 1980s Bob increasingly spent time at conferences and rubbing elbows with scientists and policy makers. Bob Rodale told one interviewer in 1984, "I spend a lot of time traveling: going to medical meetings and visiting people I think of as *pioneers*— people involved in innovative thinking on health. Then I go home and try to get some of their ideas across to our readers." When asked to explain why he did not display his wealth with fancy houses and an extravagant office like the heads of other publishing firms, Rodale said he was driven by a desire to be "societally conscious." Money, he said, provided the means for making his company's mission achievable: "We can't ignore money altogether. Money and profit are constraints for us, to the extent that we have to at least balance our books to do what we feel we should be doing. But money is certainly not our main goal. It's deeply embedded in our corporate culture that we are here to do a job, we are here to fulfill a mission. And money is just a tool that allows us to do that."[12] In a 1982 profile piece in *Adweek*, Pamela Pietri Lawrence asserted that under Bob Rodale the firm was "far more" than just a media company. Lawrence called the company "a complex relay center for concepts aimed at doing nothing less than trying to save the world. Scientists, experts, visionaries and concerned citizens filter future-minded ideas through Rodale Press." In a sign of the company's growing influence, Lawrence said that the firm "reports these ideas not only to its readers, but to national science organizations, trade groups, the Department of Agriculture, Ralph Nader and the Reagan White House."[13] The Rodale Press recast itself as an organization with gravitas that served as a national conduit for big ideas about the future of food and health.

Bob Rodale also enlisted his firm's nonprofit arm to help grow his company's stature. What is known today as the Rodale Institute had been created in 1947 as the Soil and Health Foundation by J. I. Rodale. The organization initially sought to gather donations in support of scientific research in organic methods, but it became essentially a dead letter office until the late 1970s. In the fall of 1982 Bob Rodale announced that the society would split into two divisions, one known as the Regenerative Agriculture Association and the other called the People's Medical Society. The People's Medical Society would advocate on behalf of natural health consumers and readers of *Prevention*, while the Regenerative Agriculture Association would be devoted to sponsoring research in farming. In 1983 a full-page ad in *Organic Gardening* titled "S.O.S... an Urgent Message from Organic Gardening" asked readers to join the RAA with a fifteen-dollar contribution and to help fight to save both the soil and "America's agricultural heritage." Rodale suggested that government efforts to reform agriculture and address the farm crisis would always be limited by a close association with agribusiness, and that agribusiness would not change due to its concern for profits: "Agribusiness has shown it won't change from within. But it can be changed from without, through citizen action. Your action and mine. That's why I'm launching a people's action group that will fight for our soil, our health, and a self-renewing agriculture."[14] Although these efforts relied heavily on the coffers of the publishing company, the nonprofit divisions nonetheless provided a measure of legitimacy and authority for Bob Rodale that would have been unimaginable for his father just a decade or so earlier. Convening with state agricultural officials, speaking at scientific conferences, and supporting academic research, Bob developed the influence of the name Rodale and laid the foundation for a reconsideration of organic farming in 1980s agricultural circles.

Whether it was launching the *New Farm* or hosting national symposiums, the farm crisis and the surge of public interest and engagement with environmental issues in the 1980s provided the Rodale Press with an opportunity to make a renewed case for reforming the food system. As a privately held firm that did not need to meet the quarterly demands of shareholders, the company enjoyed the freedom to pursue projects that did not create immediate returns. To address the farm crisis, the company relied on the tools of the marketplace—events for media-savvy people, columns in national news outlets, and its own array of publications—to generate public support for reforming how food was grown, distributed, and consumed in the 1980s. Yet the impact of these efforts was limited at best. As the debt crisis waned and the environmental panic of the early Reagan years subsided, the company invariably moved on to new endeavors. These projects continued to rely on Bob Rodale's idea of regeneration but would more commonly use the term to reference rebuilding the health of the body, the mind, and the spirit. The Press showed that it could use the marketplace as an effective tool for publicizing issues of food and farming, but the company was better at reading the changing winds of consumer culture than it was at developing substantial changes to the nation's food system. And as the decade progressed and the recession of the early 1980s faded, those consumers who purchased the company's books and subscribed to its magazines showed they were less interested in revitalizing soils and American farm communities and more interested in the promise of a renewed self.

THE NEW HEALTHISM

In the same years the Rodale Press was working to develop new respect for its ideas about the food system, the company was also busy remaking its publications in order to attract mainstream advertisers. Not only did the company change the look and feel of its magazines by using higher-quality paper sources and adding more glossy photos, it emphasized the pursuit of health as a means of self-improvement and personal virtue. While personal health had long been central to the Rodale Press's focus on nutrition and food in *Prevention*, the company doubled down on the therapeutic promises of health in the 1980s as a way to capture mass-market advertising across all its titles. By the end of the decade millions of American consumers knew the company more for its guidance on how to craft a sculpted body than for its sage advice on growing tastier organic tomatoes. While this part of the Rodale company's transformation might appear far removed from environmental politics and organic farming, it demonstrates how idealized notions of the body and bodily health came to outstrip social and environmental concerns

Direct-mail envelope for *Organic Gardening*, n.d. Author's collection. Courtesy
of the Rodale Family Archives.

among consumers. Personal health became a defining—and limiting—
feature of Rodale's marketplace environmentalism in the 1980s.

Since the early 1940s the Rodale Press had been something of a curious outpost in the publishing world. Not only was the firm located in
rural Pennsylvania, literally outside the New York publishing sphere,
but it maintained a very small presence on newsstands as well. Moreover, for decades it had required that any products advertised in its
pages meet the strictures of its organic and natural health philosophies.
Despite these limitations, the Press had experienced remarkable growth
in sales of its books and its number of subscribers over the course of the
1970s as millions were drawn to its do-it-yourself titles and natural
health advice. Nonetheless, by the end of that decade it became clear
that such growth could not continue indefinitely and the company
would need to transform itself in order to keep pace.

A key factor that hampered the company was its reliance on advertising in *Prevention* for the bulk of its profits. According to the company's own history, *Our Roots Grow Deep*, the magazine accounted for

close to half its overall revenue in 1978 and a "disproportionate share" of its overall profits. More significantly, 80 percent of the advertising in *Prevention* still came from direct-response advertisements for natural vitamin and food supplements—the same products that had made the Press into a profitable business in the 1950s. This revenue model became increasingly precarious as natural food supplements found their way into supermarkets and vitamin shops in the late 1970s. Despite its robust circulation numbers, the engine that kept the company's publishing apparatus and its many extracurricular endeavors running was at risk of breaking down.[15]

This was the less-visible backdrop that had led to Bob Rodale's appearance on Madison Avenue and the series of advertorials the company ran in the *New York Times* in the early 1980s. The Press was not only trying to improve its public profile; it was also trying to diversify its revenue stream. Mass-market advertisers of name-brand products had once paid little attention to the relatively small number of environmentally and health-minded consumers who subscribed to titles like *Organic Gardening* or *Prevention*. That was beginning to change in the 1980s. In a 1980 story about the Rodale Press in *Business Week*, J. Kendrick Noble Jr. of the Madison Avenue advertising firm Paine Webber Mitchell Hutchins said, "I used to think they were just health food nuts. . . . But their numbers are becoming rather impressive."[16] After a decade that saw the firm's reported revenue rise from almost 8 million to 76 million dollars, Robert Teufel, president of the Rodale Press, told *Business Week* and many other publications in 1980 that it was now time for advertising revenue to catch up with the growth in circulation. Teufel declared that the company was taking a step away from what he called "our laid-back approach" as it aggressively courted mainstream advertisers, aiming to show that the company's consumers should not be ignored.[17]

Yet convincing advertisers of this market's potential was not easy. Foremost among advertisers' concerns was the lingering impression of *Prevention* as a backwater of offbeat health ideas. Despite the magazine's sustained popularity, *Business Week* declared that *Prevention* had a reputation "as reading material for everyone's eccentric grandparent."[18] Another concern for advertisers was the fact that the median age of *Prevention*'s readers in the early 1980s was close to fifty-five and that nearly

70 percent were women. But with circulation growing at a faster rate than any of the other top twenty consumer magazines of the time, the Rodale Press countered that these impressions belied the potential "sleeping giant" of its readership. The age of *Prevention*'s readers, the firm claimed, was counterbalanced by their income, their interest in health, and their devotion to the magazine. Based on the company's own readership studies, *Food and Beverage Marketing* reported in 1983 that *Prevention* readers spent more per person on health products than did readers of all other women's magazines. Moreover, readers spent more time with each issue and referred back to it at a higher rate, increasing what marketers called its "lifespan." Still, that same devotion to the magazine and the close relationship between its advertising and editorial content would make any drastic changes difficult to implement. In what one of the company's publishers called a "Catch-22," the Rodale Press could make some changes to accommodate advertisers, but large-scale change would have to happen very slowly.[19]

In order to accommodate mass-market products, the company reexamined the relationship between some of its closely held principles and its advertising policies. For decades the Press had prided itself on the many products that could *not* be advertised in its magazines. Indeed, by excluding many name-brand products, it had fostered a separate world of consumerism that aligned with its ideas about natural foods and health. In a 1982 piece on the firm's efforts to reach new advertisers, *New York* magazine noted, "Sometimes the company's behavior drives money away. [The] Rodale Press has what must be the longest list of advertising taboos in the business."[20] In an effort to make its publications more accessible to advertisers, in the late 1970s the company pared down its advertising guidelines from twelve pages to a half a page. It chose to maintain its restrictions on most over-the-counter remedies as well as the two largest sources of national advertising at the time—alcohol and tobacco products—but relaxed its restrictions on processed foods and other health products.

In addition to overhauling its advertising policies, the Press sought to capture a younger segment of the market with new titles that emphasized personal fitness as part of a healthy, natural lifestyle. It first attempted this in 1982 with a new women's magazine called *Spring*, which targeted "the 20-to-40-year-old high-energy woman who is trying to balance a family, a job and a relationship, plus any outside interests she might have." According to executive editor Emrika Padus, these types of "post-liberation" women of the 1980s had many options for how to live their lives, and a magazine like *Spring* was there to help make sense of it all. With glossy fashion layouts for clothes from L. L. Bean, Perry Ellis, and Abercrombie and Fitch, the products *Spring* featured were a clear departure from the Craftmatic adjustable beds and fish oil supplements that filled *Prevention*.[21] In an interview with *Adweek*, Robert Rodale noted, "*Spring* will have very practical lifestyle-improvement ideas for fitness, health, diet, clothing, travel, families, and work. It will present the techniques of the natural lifestyle."[22] In contrast to the 1970s when it was canning jars, wood stoves, homemade yogurt, and a do-it-yourself ethos that marked an organic lifestyle, *Spring* emphasized personal goals of health and fitness—and the name-brand products needed to achieve them—as essential to a "natural lifestyle" in the 1980s. This shift from "organic" to "natural" reflected something more than just changing fashions. In the same way that regeneration aimed to be a modern and forward-thinking farming method, the natural lifestyle the company created with *Spring* aimed to be an up-to-date alternative that could fit in at most supermarket checkouts.

The company also divorced the consumption habits of a natural lifestyle from broader social or political connotations. Indeed, the type of energy and environmental concerns that had animated the pages of *Organic Gardening and Farming* in the 1970s and even the Cornucopia newsletters in the 1980s were absent from the pages of *Spring*. An active, healthy lifestyle still involved consuming whole-wheat products, but that consumption was largely an end unto itself. *Spring* ultimately had a short life as a result of high production costs and the fact that it launched in the middle of the early 1980s recession. Yet that magazine became a harbinger of where the Rodale Press—and the mass market— were headed. Dieting, personal health, and fitness became national obsessions in the 1980s, which publishers and advertisers gladly facilitated. Indeed, at the same time the Rodale Press was trying to find a home on Madison Avenue with its new natural lifestyle, the mass market seemed to be moving in the direction of Emmaus.

The company's shift toward a depoliticized and market-friendly version of personal improvement reached a turning point a few years later with the launch of *Men's Health*. Although it had tested a range of fitness publications with different themes over the years, in 1984 the Rodale Press produced a newsletter devoted to what it called "health challenges that are uniquely male." Over the next several years the company grew the circulation of the newsletter and tested themes through various "one-shots," or single issues of a magazine designed to be sold in retail outlets. In 1986 *Prevention Magazine's Guide to Men's Health* appeared on newsstands; in a sign of the new types of products this lifestyle magazine could accommodate, the one-shot featured articles like "The Healthy Man's Guide to Beer" and "The Great Condom Test of 1986." As evidence of how responsive the marketplace was to this type of publication, the issue sold ninety thousand copies at retail outlets. The Press then followed these special issues with waves of direct-mail advertisements to build up circulation. By the time the magazine launched at ten issues per year in 1989 it had a base circulation of three hundred thousand readers.[23] By 1994 *Advertising Age* and others were reporting on the remarkable rise of *Men's Health*, which in just a few years passed one million monthly subscribers and outstripped the circulation of perennially popular men's magazines like GQ and *Esquire*.[24] The company also launched *Women's Health* in a similar fashion in the late 1980s and acquired other fitness titles like *Runner's World* and *Backpacker*, securing its place in the supermarket magazine rack as a leader among media outlets for health-minded and fitness-oriented consumers with an outdoor bent.

Even as these new titles targeted a segment of consumers like runners or bicyclists, the ads that filled the pages were for mass-market products. The Rodale Press used its direct-marketing tools to cultivate mass-market advertisers and to show them the potential of this fitness-and-health-minded marketplace. In the same way that it joined with the USDA to study organic farmers ten years earlier, in 1989 the company partnered with the Opinion Research Corporation to quantify the changing consumption patterns of American males. Using its still-nascent database of *Men's Health* subscribers, the group produced a study targeted at advertisers called *Men in the Marketplace*. The report claimed that many of the spaces of consumption that advertisers traditionally thought of as dominated by women were now frequently populated with men. As *Men's Health* executive editor Michael Lafavore claimed, "The stereotype of the American male as someone who rarely pokes his head into a supermarket, who is oblivious to differences between one brand of soup or cereal and another, who never buys anything but beer, razor blades and motor oil is outdated. It's just not true any longer." The reasons for this shift, the study found, was the rising number of two-career households, the increased willingness of American men to accept "flexible sex roles" in a household, and rising rates of divorce and bachelorhood.[25] This study—one of dozens the company conducted to attract mass-market advertisers—helped make the pages of Rodale magazines look barely distinguishable from any others at the supermarket checkout.

These new titles reveal the significant changes the company underwent as it shifted toward the mainstream in the 1980s. But they also reveal how an emphasis on improving the environment and the home through natural practices gave way to the pursuit of idealized images of the body and regimes of bodily self-management through practices like diet, exercise, and personal care. The Rodale Press had long promoted health-conscious behavior in *Prevention*, but its new fitness titles paid scant attention to any greater environmental concerns like toxins or a critique of the medical establishment. Instead, these magazines focused on the achievement of a fit body as an end unto itself. Both the stories and the products in these new publications visually emphasized lean, sculpted, and active bodies as the benchmark for what a consumer's body *should* be. This body-centered, individual ideal, which the sociologist Robert Crawford has called "healthism," mirrored broader changes in the American economy and culture in which a thin, fit, and well-managed body came to serve as a marker of both financial and personal success.[26] As Julie Guthman has argued, an obsessive focus on the fitness and thinness—not to mention whiteness—of the body divorced healthism from its more progressive roots in social movements of the 1960s and 1970s. Instead, the new healthism—and the media and marketing firms like Rodale that promoted it—normalized personal health and bodily fitness as an individual rather than collective responsibility.[27]

While the natural health philosophy of years' past was largely absent in *Men's Health* and its ilk, nature nonetheless provided a tool for normalizing what a body should look like and what a consumer should do in order to achieve that desired appearance. Of course, the Rodale company was hardly alone in its embrace of healthism. Consumers in the 1980s and in years to come encountered similar themes and images as they flipped to any channel or paged through any popular magazine. Yet the fact that the Rodale Press, a firm that had long been tied to environmental issues, would adopt healthism with such aplomb speaks to deeper changes in environmental attitudes and action in the 1980s. While letter-writing and fund-raising gave national environmental organizations clout in Washington, environmentalists increasingly focused on individual choices made at the checkout counter rather than more systematic reforms. Healthism helped seal the logic that in voting with their dollars, consumers could help the environment and the same time improve themselves.

J. I. Rodale had enlisted nature as a tool for building up the body's defenses against the threats of a synthetic world. By the 1980s natural foods served as yet another consumable gadget for achieving an idealized body. The firm had built its niche market around environmentally minded and natural consumption practices with therapeutic promises of health and happiness. It took those promises to the mainstream in the 1980s to accommodate brand-name advertising and to change advertisers' impressions. In making this move and adopting the new healthism—not only in *Men's Health* but across its publications in the late 1980s—the company found greater success than it ever had with composting and handyman books. Indeed, its mass-market success showed that the company was better equipped for responding to consumer desires than it was at creating lasting reforms of food production or public health. Marketplace environmentalism's greatest strength and its greatest weakness was its ability to respond and adapt to the mercurial trends of consumer culture. The therapeutic promises of fitness and healthism—and its profits—pointed toward improving consumers' bodies rather than the natural world. And at the very moment that millions of consumers began to question chemicals in their foods, the Rodale Press helped cement the marketplace as a site for environmental reforms that served some consumers more than others.

ALAR AND THE PYRRHIC VICTORY
OF MARKETPLACE ENVIRONMENTALISM

Organic enthusiasts as early as the 1940s had hoped a time would come when the nation would notice the dangers of pesticides and other synthetic chemicals in foods. J. I. Rodale had once publicly implored Upton Sinclair to write an exposé like *The Jungle* about chemical fertilizers in hopes that such a book would inspire the nation's regulatory authorities to respond. There were of course moments when the general public became alarmed about certain substances used in food production, such as when the chemical aminotriazole was detected in the nation's cranberry supply in 1959 and when *Silent Spring* was published in 1962. In these moments, J. I. Rodale and organic enthusiasts believed changes were finally in the offing. The hope that a wake-up call will one day change the status quo is central to any prophetic claim, and the prophecy of the organic movement was no exception. In truth, such moments of crisis often came and went. Indeed, the food system had become ever more reliant on the use of synthetic chemicals in farming and food processing since the 1940s. Even as the Rodale Press was gaining the ear of the USDA and organic foods were edging their way into some supermarkets in the 1980s, the amount of land farmed organically and the amount of organic food sold in the mainstream remained a very small fraction of overall food production.

By the end of the 1980s, both the Rodale Press and its allies in the environmental community were once again searching for a way to spark consumer interest and draw attention to the issue of pesticides in food production. That spark arrived at another moment of intense public scrutiny of chemicals used in food production, this time surrounding a compound used to ripen fruit known by its trade name as Alar. Yet in this moment the Rodale Press was no longer merely reacting to intense media attention to synthetic chemicals in foods—the company actively helped to create it. Publicity surrounding the risks of this compound created what would become known as the "Alar scare" in 1989. The scare ultimately transformed the work that Robert Rodale and other organic enthusiasts had been doing for years to create a market for organic foods. The public debate about Alar produced an explosion of media coverage and ultimately induced more consumers than ever before to seek out organic foods. The resulting spike in demand prodded more farmers and food producers to make the switch to organic methods and helped usher in the first national standards for organic foods. To a certain extent this moment represented a clear triumph for J. I. Rodale's prophecy and the type of market-oriented environmentalism his company promoted for decades. Indeed, it appeared to some enthusiasts that the moment J. I. Rodale had envisioned long ago had finally arrived. Yet whether those standards, and the growing marketplace for green products in general, could lead the way to more substantial—and more equitable— reforms remained harder to foresee.

Throughout the 1980s Bob Rodale applied his company's considerable financial resources to support alternative farming methods in both scientific research and national policy. He also routinely implored readers to write to their elected officials in support of federal initiatives on organic farming. Some of these initiatives led to few noticeable results. Others, such as the low-input and sustainable agriculture guidelines that were included in the 1985 Farm Bill, were important steps toward creating a national system of organic production standards. In addition, Bob routinely used his public platform to tell readers to consider their own power as consumers. In early 1988 Rodale described to readers how consumer demand was becoming an important part of changing the policy landscape: "Leverage is the reason. Consumers and voters are learning how to use it. Today they know how to press the spots in the system to get exactly what they want." He believed that a fragmenting marketplace would ultimately give consumers more power: "Consumers' desires keep changing, and organic food is clearly a new desire of many people." He went on to suggest that if readers shared his concerns they could contact lawmakers to support bills that limited pesticide contamination of groundwater, advocate for conservation reserves at the federal level, and buy whatever organic foods they could find at the supermarket.[28]

In a sign of how the Rodale Press had gained more allies over the years, it also partnered with national environmental groups to raise awareness about pesticides in food production. In June 1988 *Organic Gardening* published a multipage excerpt from the Natural Resources

Defense Council's *Pesticide Alert* guidebook for consumers. The article suggested that the guide could be used in the "short term" to "help make more informed choices," and told readers that "in the long term, use your power in the marketplace to encourage the reduction of the use of pesticides in agriculture."[29] This alliance with the NRDC became all the more visible in February 1989 when that group released a report titled *Intolerable Risk: Pesticides in Our Children's Food*. It was this report, and the highly coordinated media campaign that followed, that put Alar in the national spotlight and drew more consumers than ever to organic food.

As mentioned above, Alar was a chemical compound growers used as an aid in ripening fruit. While the NRDC's report focused on a range of different pesticides, it highlighted Alar as the substance with the greatest risk for causing cancer. Moreover, the NRDC's report highlighted the dangers for those who consumed large quantities of fruit products, particularly apples, and pointed to children as the consumers whose health was most at risk. The report made more systematic critiques of agricultural production methods, but the threat of Alar on apples to children's health became its prime takeaway. The study raised valuable questions about how the EPA developed and enforced pesticide tolerance levels, but the larger story became about how those findings made their way to the American public and how a popular fear of Alar and other agricultural chemicals transformed the organic food industry. The release of the NRDC report coincided with a 60 *Minutes* story and a coordinated national media blitz orchestrated by a public relations firm. In the days after the story aired and the report was published, other news outlets and talk shows picked up on the story and the reiterated its findings. From *Today* to the *MacNeil/Lehrer NewsHour*, from the *New York Times* to *USA Today*, stories about the dangers of Alar proliferated across the media landscape.[30]

The Rodale Press was fully in stride with these PR efforts. It used its own channels and its marketing tools to publicize the Alar story along with consumer demand for organic food. The editorial column of the March 1989 issue of *Organic Gardening* carried the same title as the NRDC's report, "Intolerable Risk," and restated its findings. Rodale publications also served as a platform for Mothers and Others for Pesticide Limits, an activist group founded by Meryl Streep, Wendy

Rockefeller, and the NRDC. Streep made appearances in a variety of news outlets and commercials in conjunction with the report and was featured on the cover of *Organic Gardening* in April 1989. The feature story, produced with the help of NRDC writers, described how Streep learned about the dangers of pesticides and how the first step she took was to bring those concerns to the manager of the produce section of her local supermarket. Streep said that after learning about pesticides, she felt it was "bizarre that the produce manager is more important to my child's health than the pediatrician."[31] The piece also claimed that Streep's group explicitly modeled itself on MADD (Mothers Against Drunk Driving) and that group's campaign for new state and federal laws in the late 1980s. Defining themselves as mothers and relying on images of children's vulnerable bodies, the group echoed traditional gender roles that made mothers responsible for making proper choices for the health and well-being of their children.[32] The combination of Streep's public profile and the coordinated media campaign led to a decline in apple sales and ultimately pushed the manufacturer to pull Alar from production.

The Alar scare certainly confirmed the anxieties of existing organic enthusiasts, but it also brought scores of new consumers into the organic marketplace for the first time. Indeed, the controversy proved a boon for getting organic produce into retail outlets. Yet that windfall also created lingering problems for the organic marketplace. Undoubtedly, more consumers than ever went to supermarkets in search of organic produce in the second half of 1989. But the surge in demand also caused the price of organic produce to spike and created new incentives for mislabeling and fraud, thereby providing detractors with a clear line of attack. Nearly a month after the *60 Minutes* story aired, the *Wall Street Journal* reported on the thousands of calls and letters grocery store chains were receiving about the safety of their produce, as well as the surging number of growers in California who were exploring how to convert their acreage to organic methods.[33] As Julie Guthman discusses in her work on organic farming in California, the Alar scare produced a wave of consumer demand and also growers who responded to that demand by becoming "instantly organic."[34] At the same time, the surge in demand highlighted the lack of enforcement and the unevenness of organic production standards across the country.

As the Rodale Press helped with the push for organic standards in the wake of the Alar scare, it combined its advocacy work on behalf of alternative agriculture with the marketing tools it had honed with the launch of fitness publications like *Men's Health*. In order to demonstrate the extent to which the consumer market for organic products was growing, in late 1988 the Rodale Press commissioned Louis Harris and Associates to conduct a national poll of American consumers and their interest in fruits and vegetables grown without chemicals. The study was first released to the public as the *Organic Index: Tracking America's Preference for Organic Food and a Clean Environment* in the spring of 1989 amid the Alar scare. The firm conducted the poll again in the fall of that year to capture how publicity surrounding pesticides and other chemicals had reshaped demand. Bullet points from the second study, released in March 1990, reported that as a result of the Alar scare 30 percent of consumers had changed their eating habits, 20 percent more had tried organic food, and 84 percent "still want organic."[35] At the same time, the study's press release endeavored to show that demand for organic had been consistent since before and after the scare and that those organic consumers were not responding out of fear. *Organic Gardening*'s editor Stevie Daniels pointed to the fact that the two polls showed such little change between the two years, claiming "that the organic mandate is not a passing fad fueled by fear, but a clear preference fueled by reason."[36]

Daniels also echoed the notion that in an era of regulatory gridlock and conflicting science, a consumers' choices about their own health were paramount. Daniels claimed that the demand for organic food was the result of individuals seeking to take matters of health and the environment into their own hands: "The message of this poll is clear. Americans are not willing to wait as government and environmental groups debate exactly what level of pesticide residue is safe for consumption. . . . They realize that [the] organic alternative is the answer, and they want government and conventional agriculture businesses to respond to their demands. What holds true for the home garden is also true on a larger scale—organic works."[37] Echoing the empirical experience of health and the body that had been foundational to J. I. Rodale's health ideas decades ago, the Rodale Press was now arguing that millions of consumers shared its concerns about chemicals in food production and urged the national marketplace to respond. These consumers did not need experts to validate their intuitions about health or the benefits of organic foods. They needed products to consume.

In many ways, these marketing studies were the culmination of the Rodale Press's efforts to make consumer choice the central method for changing the nation's food system. For years the Rodale Press had connected its coterie of organic gardeners and natural health enthusiasts with products, but at the start of the 1990s the company was able to influence the mainstream marketplace in ways it never had before. Using its tools of marketing research, the company sought to demonstrate that consumers across the nation had reached a consensus about the value and the merits of organic food. Interest in organic, the studies suggested, was no longer isolated to a small group of gardeners and back-to-the-landers; rather, it was now a firm part of the mainstream. However, just as the company's fitness magazines put personal health front and center, these efforts to support the national market for organic foods also elevated healthism as the most important value of organic food. Rather than highlighting the systematic risks of pesticide exposure for farm workers or the effects of conventional agricultural practices on the natural world, healthism put the bodies of consumers and *their* perceived risk of individual exposure at the forefront. Whether those risks were real or validated by science and policy was beside the point—the logic of healthism made the marketplace the site where Americans chose for themselves what was best for their own health and that of their families.

The notion that consumers, rather than policy makers or scientists, should drive change by asserting their preferences was hardly new by the 1990s. Yet as the Cold War came to end and the power of free markets became ascendant in American political culture, the will of consumers increasingly figured as the central agent for driving change in environmental politics and reform. Ultimately the Alar scare was proof positive that the marketplace was adept at responding to consumer demands. On the heels of the Alar imbroglio the Rodale Press and its allies worked to marshal public support for a national system of organic standards and the passage of the Organic Foods Production Act in 1990. In the years to come, organic foods became the fastest-growing segment of the food economy and an increased range of both food and nonfood items would carry a label that certified them as "organic." Yet in many ways that victory—and many of the organic and "green" products that followed in its wake—did more to benefit organic consumers and the businesses that catered to them than to alleviate the economic or ecological hazards of the modern food system for the natural world or farm communities. The marketplace could easily expand to offer more choices, but more sweeping changes in how the rest of the country's food was produced, let alone more fundamental social and environmental reforms, were another story.

The organic standards adopted in 1990 said nothing about labor conditions or the systems that processed and distributed food. Industry groups and activists battled fiercely over the new organic standards in the decade that followed, and ultimately the label that emerged for national certification focused on materials applied to soils and fed to animals rather than broader reforms of systems of labor or capital. The new label could signify the stuff used to grow a piece of produce, but it said nothing about whether the farm that produced it was large or small, whether that farm was owned by a family or a billion-dollar conglomerate with horrid labor practices, or whether that piece of food had traveled down the road or across the continent. The new organic standards allowed farmers to secure premium prices for organic goods but did little to address the underlying causes that led to the farm crisis of the 1980s or the imbalances that still influence agricultural production. The label winnowed down all the complexities of the American food system and its myriad effects on the natural world to a little green circle, convincing consumers to make the healthy choice for themselves. As for all those other food products on the shelf, both the organic standards and marketplace environmentalism had much less influence. For its part, the Rodale Press embraced the organic standards adopted in the 1990s and papered over divisions between factions of the organic movement and the rapidly growing business of organic food production.

In this way the Alar scare and the mainstream embrace of organic foods that followed in the late 1980s and 1990s represented a pyrrhic victory for the Rodale Press and all those gardeners and enthusiasts that had supported its efforts over the years. The expanding selection of organic produce that appeared in grocery stores in the 1990s and the growing number of consumers who adopted natural foods as the key to maintaining their personal health were certainly evidence that J. I. Rodale and Robert Rodale had been on to something for all those years. Indeed, those quirky aunts who read *Prevention* and those devoted gardeners who swore by the composting tips of *Organic Gardening* could feel validated by the growth and success of the organic marketplace after 1990.

The abundance of the organic marketplace today and the fact that organic foods are now common in even the largest supermarket chains serves to validate the long history of the Rodale Press. However, while the marketplace has proved adept at providing more and more products, it has struggled to produce evidence for many of the closely held beliefs of organic and natural health consumers. The empirical proof for the benefits of organic foods for both personal health and the environment remains highly contested. Likewise, the version of environmental reform that the Rodale Press championed has proven limited in its ability to drive more fundamental and equitable reforms. The marketplace has shown it can accommodate many different interests and produce an expanding array of products to align with consumers' changing health and environmental values. Yet the benefits of this type of environmentalism have largely flowed to those with the fiscal and social capital to purchase organic foods. For those left on the sidelines or those working in the field, the marketplace has had much less to offer.

• • •

The Rodale company not only produced new magazines in the 1980s but also found a home in the mass marketplace. To a certain extent this success came because the company tamped down on some of the excesses of its natural health philosophy and gave up on some of its most strident beliefs to accommodate mainstream advertisers and name-brand products. At the same time, the mass marketplace moved toward the Rodale Press. Matters of diet and fitness and the ideal of a toned, healthy body became ascendant features of consumer culture. The Rodale Press adapted its titles and launched new ones to fit this latest iteration of healthism. In periodicals like *Men's Health* and *Runner's World* the improvement of the self became an end unto itself, and the marketplace responded with a proliferating array of products to achieve that elusive goal.

In *Organic Gardening* the company merged improving the self with improving the environment. At the start of the 1980s the farm crisis and a surge in environmental activism had given new impetus to reforming the nation's food system. The Rodale Press's own Cornucopia Project initiated prescient studies of state-level food systems, and in their earliest incarnations Bob Rodale's regeneration programs linked the economic effects of modern farming with social and environmental reform. But by the end of the decade organic activism came to rely on what Finis Dunaway has characterized as "environmental spectacle" more than systematic reform.[38] With the Alar scare and its aftermath, the Rodale Press became entangled with the type of celebrity culture and carefully orchestrated PR campaigns that have increasingly defined environmental activism since the late 1980s. Moreover, the Alar scare cemented healthism as a dominant value for organic consumers and the growing ranks of green media outlets such as the Rodale Press.

The fact that the Organic Foods Production Act of 1990 created a national set of standards for producing and labeling organic foods was undoubtedly a victory for Bob Rodale and his company as well as the legions of growers, activists, and scientists that had pushed for the standards. Yet for consumers that label made their pursuit of environmental values and better health a matter of individual choice. The label lent a veneer of consumer agency to the decisions of daily life, yet it muted more systematic reforms. Both the Rodale Press and marketplace environmentalism succeeded in altering the aisles of supermarkets, but they could barely make a dent out in the fields.

CONCLUSION

A Consuming Vision

BOB RODALE AND HIS COMPANY ENJOYED GREATER STATURE THAN ever before in the 1980s. It was not just book sales and new magazine titles that helped make the name Rodale a force in the world of publishing and commerce; it was also in the company's growing influence in policy and scientific circles, where the company had once been unwelcome. That influence was evident in the number of places Bob Rodale visited and the audiences he enjoyed in the 1980s. Ever since he had taken a spontaneous journey to Mexico in 1949 when he was just nineteen Bob had been an inveterate traveler. A champion skeet shooter, he also traveled the globe for international shooting competitions. In his role as editor and president of the Press, he had made trips to India and China in the 1970s and reported to readers about the state of the food systems in those countries. In 1973 he learned about an ancient grain crop known as amaranth and began devoting his company's funds to breeding improved varieties. After paying the expenses of a group of students to travel to Mexico to collect seeds, Rodale spent over a million dollars over the next decade exploring the plant's properties and sponsoring scientific research into figuring out how it might help alleviate famine.[1]

These endeavors took both Bob Rodale and his ideas about agriculture even further afield in the 1980s. In 1983 he traveled to Tanzania with a delegation from the Rodale Research Center that was invited to the newly independent country by its president, Julius Nyerere. Describing both the difficult living conditions and the repeated failures of international aid, Rodale suggested that what he called regenerative farming methods offered the country an alternative.[2] In years to come, Bob made more trips to places like Zimbabwe, Costa Rica, and other developing corners of the globe. He created a new arm of his research organization called Rodale International that worked to educate farmers about applying organic methods as part of famine-prevention efforts. At the same time, he promoted farmland preservation in Pennsylvania and helped protect local landscapes from development. Even as the scope of his organic vision widened around the globe, he remained personally committed to protecting land, water, soil, and health at home.

Rodale was also eager to explore the Soviet Union in the waning years of the Cold War. He had been such an exceptional skeet shooter that he competed as part of the US Olympic team in 1968 and became friendly with some of his Soviet competitors. Rodale maintained those friendships for the next twenty years, and he made several journeys to Moscow in the late 1980s to meet with his old friends and to study the country's agricultural problems. As the Soviet Union was opening to the West, Rodale and many others were beginning to recognize the depth and extent of the agricultural and economic crises that country faced. The Soviets, Rodale felt, were going to need help developing different farming methods. He and his partners created a joint venture to publish a Russian magazine devoted to regenerative agricultural practices called the *New Farmer*. Hoping to lead the Russians away from chemicals and toward compost, Rodale saw his work in Russia as a continuation of the mission he had inherited from his father decades ago.[3]

Yet it was not only the company's nonprofit endeavors that Bob hoped to grow overseas in the 1980s. Just as the company was seeking to develop new audiences among younger American consumers with its new health and fitness titles, it was also seeking new audiences around the globe. Rodale wanted to bring regenerative agriculture to Russia, but he was also eager to cultivate a new market for publications such as *Prevention* and the company's expanding set of lifestyle magazines. With his Earth Shoes and his corduroy pants, Bob Rodale's appearance could betray the fact that he remained, like his father, a man of business. Bob had steered the Rodale Press toward profitability and oversaw its remarkable growth from a modest publishing venture into a company that reported over $250 million in revenue by the end of the 1980s. Likewise, in the same years that he was developing his ideas about regenerative agriculture in response to the farm crisis he also became a leader of the Magazine Publishers of America and the Direct Marketing Association. In Russia he was doing what the Rodale Press had always done: studying the market and testing for untapped opportunities. His vision, like that of his father, was as much about the marketplace as it was about soils.[4]

Sadly, Bob Rodale's journeys came to an abrupt end at this very moment when he and his company had their greatest influence. After an evening of celebrating the launch of a joint venture with his friends and business partners in September 1990, he began the long journey back to Emmaus. While en route to the airport, the van he was riding in was struck head-on when a bus swerved to avoid a vehicle that had pulled into traffic. Robert Rodale and two other passengers were killed instantly.

Rodale's tragic death in 1990 at the age of sixty came at a time when his company was no longer a quirky publishing house in the sticks of Pennsylvania but a rapidly expanding media brand in the world of Madison Avenue. Moreover, by 1990 the type of market-centered environmentalism the company had popularized had more subscribers than ever before. The Organic Foods Production Act passed in 1990, and that same year environmentally conscious shopping guides and the best seller *50 Simple Things You Can Do to Save the Earth* made personal consumption choices a hallmark of environmental action. The year also saw the rebirth of Earth Day, not as a day of coordinated grassroots action but as a national media event, complete with branded sponsors, TV specials, and merchandise. As other firms followed in its steps and merged environmental values and business in years to come, the Rodale Press could certainly feel that J. I. and Robert, and their organic vision, had not been so far out of the mainstream after all.

That Bob Rodale died working to change soil management practices while at the same time exploring new markets for health and lifestyle magazines provides a fitting coda to the story of his company and the making of marketplace environmentalism. Bob wanted people to grow food without relying on outside inputs like fertilizers and pesticides, to live their lives more simply, and to take care of their bodies. He wanted to show people how to make changes in their daily life and supported a vast array of endeavors to make those changes feasible. Yet he also wanted to bring more consumers into the marketplace—whether it was for books, magazine articles, or organic food. His vision of how to change the world ran straight through the marketplace.

In this way Bob shared a great deal with the socially and environmentally minded entrepreneurs who make headlines today with the latest gadgets to save the world or whose TED talks spread through social media. It is no longer strange for a business enterprise to have a social or environmental mission or for a CEO to sound like an activist. Bob Rodale's combination of business acumen and environmental concern paved the way for any number of today's "natural capitalists."[5] It also is not so strange for the consumer marketplace to be the site where Americans contend with their environmental values. Whether it is in the foods they buy, the media they consume, or the lifestyle they choose to live (with the help of many eco-friendly products and practices), millions of consumers now express their environmental values with the dollars they spend and the firms with which they develop a relationship. Indeed, Bob Rodale's life and his company's story help us understand where this now-ubiquitous type of environmentalism came from, how it evolved over time, its ability to empower consumers and spark the marketplace, as well as the ambiguities and limitations it has sustained.

RECKONING WITH PROPHECY AND PROFIT

J. I. Rodale returned to the newsstand once again in the spring of 2015. The cover of a special collector's issue of *Organic Gardening* featured an elegiac profile photo of the long-deceased Rodale and prominently displayed a quote of his from 1942: "One of these days, the public is going to wake up and will pay for eggs, meats, vegetables, etc., according to how they were produced." The issue highlighted the turning points of J. I. Rodale's life and the journey of the company he created as both were transformed from peculiar outposts in rural Pennsylvania to mainstream arbiters of the "green" marketplace. From the test plots based on Sir Albert Howard's methods that J. I. had built on the original farm in the 1940s through the advent of the Rodale Institute in the 1970s and the emergence of a national organic label in the 1990s, the Rodale Press and its gardening magazine had been there all along. With its perennial advice about battling garden insects and its endless lists of tips and tricks for making compost—not to mention its ads for food supplements and rototillers—*Organic Gardening* remained a standard bearer of marketplace environmentalism through the second decade of the twenty-first century.[6]

But the publishing business in 2015 was quite different from the one J. I. Rodale entered in the 1930s. Magazine stands were filled with titles devoted to health, diet, fitness, hobbies, and sports as well as a ceaseless scrum of celebrity news and entertainment. Yet those magazines, and printed paper in general, were also increasingly difficult to sell to consumers in a profitable manner. The steady decline of print advertising revenues since the early 2000s made it ever more challenging to sustain both newspapers and magazines, whether their aim was a national audience or a small community of readers.[7] Indeed, that February 2015 edition of *Organic Gardening* was a collector's edition because it was also the magazine's last. Taking its place after over seventy years was a website that hosted all the accumulated wisdom the Rodale Press had gathered over the years and served as a one-stop shop for the latest organic news and advice of interest to gardeners. Devoted readers and newcomers would no longer need to collect issues and build personal libraries to have advice readily available—they could tap their queries into a search bar and plunge themselves into an ocean of organic information.

The end of *Organic Gardening* as a print magazine was emblematic of broader changes in the ways that American consumers accessed news, information, and entertainment in the early twenty-first century. A special-interest magazine like *Organic Gardening* survived for decades because it connected readers with both information and products that were hard to find in the mass marketplace. The Internet, however, not only provided endless space for ever more refined and selective information, it privileged the same type of interactive marketplace in which the Rodale Press had thrived. Similarly, digital tools also transformed direct marketing into "interactive marketing." The type of information about consumers and their preferences that the Rodale Press once collected through waves of direct mail was now gleaned through sorting and analyzing billions of mouse clicks and data points. The company maintained a robust presence in the world of marketing with a division known as Rodale CCM (or custom-content marketing). This division relied on Rodale's brands like *Men's Health*, *Runner's World*, and *Prevention* as platforms for advertisers to reach their desired consumers. Even as profits from printed paper plunged, those conduits to an audience of health-seeking and fitness-minded consumers grew more valuable in a digital age. By 2017, Rodale no longer called itself a publisher, but rather "a global health and wellness content company."[8]

Yet it was not just the decline of printed ads that brought about the end of *Organic Gardening*. By the first decade of the twenty-first century, the market for organic ideas was no longer composters and health nuts but affluent and aspiring consumers who embraced "organic" as a fixture of their broader consumption habits. Emblematic of this shift was the magazine that replaced *Organic Gardening*, a new Rodale publication called *Organic Life*. Filled with sumptuous photographs of artisanal desserts and stories about the health and happiness to be found in farm-to-table foods, rustic kitchen tools, and the latest yoga poses, *Organic Life* embodied the evolution of marketplace environmentalism since the early 1990s. This magazine's target audience was not frugal seed savers, home canners, or little old ladies in tennis shoes. Instead, it aimed for consumers who could afford to pay more for heirloom tomatoes at farmers markets and organic cotton sheets of the highest thread count. The products that filled its pages likewise spoke to the ways that "organic" proved to be an ever-flexible theme that could define a range of products that by the early twenty-first century bore little to no relation to soils or agricultural methods whatsoever. *Organic Life* promoted products like copper garden trowels, Ayurvedic lip balms, tree swings made from reclaimed wood, classic French linen aprons, beechwood hairbrushes, and an array of colorful leggings, wraps, and shawls made with organic cotton. All these products—and many, many more—could also be found and purchased on Rodales.com, an e-commerce site the company launched in 2013 to sell goods directly to consumers that curated a refined aesthetic of luxurious and sustainable green consumption. A whole new ecosystem of green products has proliferated over the last decade, and the Rodale company still aims to steer the market that connects those products with consumers.[9]

It can be hard not to see J. I. Rodale's claim from the 1940s—about consumers paying more for products that reflected their values—as prescient or maybe even prophetic. He may not have been able to envision such a wide assortment of products that now carry an organic label, but he certainly understood the power of—and the profits in—defining a set of products and practices as natural. The word "organic," whether applied to compost methods or cheese puffs, served as a compelling means of invoking nature and the natural at a time when American consumers felt their lives and livelihoods were increasingly removed from the natural world. While it was first adopted by a group of gardeners and health enthusiasts, organic evolved to become a defining feature of marketplace environmentalism in the early twenty-first century. It became not just a set of regulatory standards but a way for environmentally minded consumers to consecrate some consumption habits as good for the natural world and human health and at the same time classify other consumption habits as bad. Of course, the catch here was that no consumers' lives or livelihoods were ever removed from the natural world. Moreover, it was often those same consumers that J. I. Rodale saw as being willing to pay extra for natural products whose very way of life put the greatest strain on natural resources. Marketplace environmentalism sanctified some products and practices and gave more choices to those consumers whose plates were already full.

Considering the distance between the compost pits on the old farm in Emmaus in the 1940s and a global media brand with hundreds of millions in yearly revenue at the turn of the century, or the distance from the first organic gardening clubs in the 1950s to the proliferation of organic personal care products in the 2000s, what are we to learn from the Rodale story?

Ultimately, the lesson lies in the tension between prophecy and profit. For some, J. I. Rodale remains a voice in the wilderness—a prophet who saw that organic methods were the path toward healthier soils and healthier human bodies. The fact that organic is a robust sector of the food economy and that diet, nutrition, and health are matters of popular debate serve as evidence that J. I. saw the truth in something that others did not; that his work of clipping, questioning, analyzing, and digesting the research of doctors and scientists for a popular audience made him a visionary, if unlikely, reformer. Likewise, Bob Rodale and the Rodale company deserve credit for making "organic" a household word and fusing together health and environmental concerns. The Rodale Press gave consumers the tools and knowledge they needed to take control of their health and improve their lives, and it helped to build the organic market in the United States and beyond. The legacy of Rodale, both the family and the company, lies in the many green product choices that surround us every time we walk into the supermarket and in the many outlets for information that help us make better decisions about the products and practices that define our daily lives. The moral of *that* story is that a company can grow its profits while also giving consumers the agency to improve the natural world. The Rodales demonstrate that the marketplace could be a powerful site for developing a popular critique of material ecology and for contesting scientific and medical understandings of health and the environment. Through their books and magazines as well as the consumption habits they promoted, they show how a firm brought environmentally minded consumers together and taught Americans how to grow, eat, and live in more environmentally friendly ways.

A different take on the Rodale story runs in the opposite direction, however, and puts profits ahead of prophecy. The freedom of the marketplace that gave the Rodales a platform also gave license to an untold number of dubious products and practices. J. I. Rodale critiqued the certainty of agricultural and medical scientists, but he did so by selling subscribers on the virtues of natural health and organic food and profiting from the ad revenue of questionable products. The publishing company flourished in the 1970s and 1980s by catering to the perennial demand for diet books and self-improvement advice and wrapping it in the garb of environmental action. If one legacy of the Rodales is the array of natural product choices that consumers now have, another is the array of impudent, unscientific, and dubious natural health "gurus" and media figures that peddle junk information about genetically modified foods and the merits of coconut water. The Rodales deserve some credit for curbside composting today, but they also bear some responsibility for Dr. Oz and the Food Babe. Marketplace environmentalism gave power to consumers, but that power has done more to strain the relationship between science and environmentalism than it has to initiate systematic reforms. Rodale's brand of environmentalism expanded rather than replaced the goods on the shelf in the wealthiest corners of consumer societies and sustained the commercial cacophony that often keeps the marketplace growing at the expense of more equitable reforms.

Each of those takes on the Rodale legacy could provide comfortable certainty and a reassuring takeaway about the Rodales and marketplace environmentalism more generally. Both stories—one could be called "Rodale as prophet" and the other "Rodale as shill"—offer a clear lesson about commercial culture and environmental history in the late twentieth century. In one, changing environmental values conquer the marketplace. In the other, environmental values are swamped by marketing and its populist excesses. And the same story lines could be applied to nearly any environmentally minded company or environmental group that has made its profits or its peace with the marketplace in recent decades. When a natural food company like Walnut Acres or Muir Glen is purchased by a food conglomerate like Kraft, or Burt's Bees is purchased by Clorox, the lesson could be about the triumph of environmental values or their failure. Likewise, when Wal-Mart starts selling organic soda or a group like the Nature Conservancy partners with Dow Chemical rather than suing it, the lesson—depending on your perspective—is often quite clear. Yet what should be evident from this deeper look at the Rodale enterprise and the roots of marketplace environmentalism over the decades is that such stark lessons do not reflect the more nuanced and unpredictable historical paths that have wedded consumption, commerce, and environmental values in the marketplace. Those clear-cut stories do not match the knotty realities.

Again, the deeper lesson lies in the tension between prophecy and profit. J. I. Rodale was both a reformer and a publisher, not to mention the owner of an electrical parts company. Raised with the bootstrapping ethos of the turn-of-the-century industrial capitalism and the folklore of personal improvement, Rodale worked within that culture rather than against it. His publishing company sold ad space and built a marketplace centered on the buying and selling of natural goods—one that connected far-flung organic gardeners and natural health consumers into civic action at the same time that it sold untested health advice and products. The company that Robert Rodale brought toward the mass market in the 1970s and 1980s made personal matters of lifestyle, diet, and health as important to helping the natural world as protecting wild spaces and species. Yet what allowed Bob Rodale to fund research into sustainable agriculture and push for national organic standards was the sales of diet books, health magazines, and an array of natural products and therapeutic advice. The marketplace proved more effective at addressing individual health concerns than creating public health interventions, but it also brought readers together and helped them navigate the changing material ecology of their lives in the late twentieth century. Ultimately, it is less important to determine whether the Rodales were prophets or shills and more important to understand the role of the marketplace as a contested yet vital site of environmental thought and action.

Rodale's magazines and books deserve a place on the shelf in our histories of environmentalism—not for any deep prophecy they contain, but because they were texts Americans consumed to feel better and to learn how to grow foods and keep themselves healthy in a world that seemed increasingly artificial and detrimental to health. Regardless of whether bone meal or rose hips or composting were definitively healthier for people and the planet is beside the point—the Rodales and their readers believed in those products and practices, and the market responded. The Rodales and their brand of marketplace environmentalism do not need to be debunked, nor do they need to be enshrined. Similarly, we do not need to stamp green consumers or green companies as dupes or all-powerful agents in order to see the marketplace as another site where Americans have grappled with environmental change. That marketplace undoubtedly had its limits. It was better at producing profits than it was at producing verifiable evidence, and it frequently promoted the improvement of the body as an end unto itself. It made room for voices on the margins yet too often remained quiet about persistent inequalities. Rodale's story does not resolve the tension between prophecy and profits, but it does illustrate the complexities of green consumerism and the many unresolved questions about the choices we face in an era of unprecedented environmental change.

GREEN CHOICES IN AN ERA OF GLOBAL CHANGE

Looking better, feeling better, living longer, doing more for yourself, gaining the respect of friends and family—these have long been the anthems of consumer culture and the ones that defined J. I. Rodale's work and his company's message. Over the decades those mantras convinced millions of consumers to try their hand at organic gardening and to make different choices in the marketplace. But can market-centered action effect change at a larger scale in a time of global environmental crisis? Indeed, it is worth asking whether the type of environmentalism the Rodales fostered has made it too easy to enjoy our nominally local and organic foods while ignoring the resource demands of consumer culture writ large. Does the existence of the organic aisle blind environmentally minded consumers to how the products in the rest of the store, not to mention their overstuffed homes, are produced? As we flip, stroll, and scroll our way through the endless "green" choices at our fingertips in the early twenty-first century, there remains an abiding riddle that the marketplace too frequently elides: are we making the natural world better with our choices, or just making ourselves feel better?

Most signs point to the latter. Given how few Americans make a living as farmers today compared with the 1940s, it is perhaps unsurprising that the organic movement took hold with consumers rather than producers. Large food producers have become more responsive to consumer demand in recent years, as evidenced by the fact that some have chosen to phase out artificial colors, hormones, preservatives, and antibiotics. Consumer demand for organic products has also generated a premium price for food products and convinced more commercial growers to adopt organic methods.[10] Even many large conventional farmers have adopted practices like cover cropping to reduce erosion and boost the biological life of their soils. Yet, for all the enthusiasm and media coverage that organic continues to draw, the amount of acreage devoted to organic methods remains a small slice of overall farm production. Moreover, it is unclear how well the constraints of organic standards will hold up as growing food becomes more unpredictable on a warming planet. Organic has succeeded at creating a great deal of sentiment and support among consumers, but its impact beyond a small segment has been limited at best.

Moreover, as organic food and green consumerism has gained a larger hold in the marketplace since the 1990s, that growth has coincided with the stalling out and rolling back of environmental policies.

As in so many other parts of contemporary life, in the absence of political momentum to remake the systems that produce, transport, and dispose of consumer goods, the marketplace has stepped in. There are now more labels and certifications around the globe than ever before that can help a consumer feel better about the fish they eat, the sneakers they wear, and the hybrid car they drive down the street—but fewer agreements about how to address global-scale environmental issues and even fewer mechanisms to enforce reforms. The green marketplace has produced an abundance of choices about which natural diet book and natural lifestyle magazine to buy—and a plethora of options for canned tuna—but little or no systematic reforms for the rest of the products on the shelf. The crowded marketplaces of consumer societies have succeeded in providing an array of choices at the exact same time that consumer societies have failed to tackle global climate change and many other issues of health, equity, and sustainability.

The green products and practices at the heart of marketplace environmentalism have not just failed as tools for responding to the globe's environmental crises, they have also made those issues more intractable. A well-heeled consumer can assert their agency by supporting companies that help the planet with organic cotton sheets and tasty dishes at farm-to-table restaurants—and the market will readily respond. But for those on the margins of the marketplace of American life, and those in the less-developed corners of the globe who are struggling to join the marketplace or bear the brunt of its effects on livelihoods and landscapes, the market has much less to offer. Consumers that can afford to subscribe to magazines and shop in specialty stores are often those with the benefits of education, health, and wealth, which have long privileged some with more choices than others. And it is often those consumers with the greatest array of choices whose very lifestyles place the most demand on the planet and its resources. As for those healthy children who have only ever consumed pesticide-free goldfish crackers and whose smiling, predominantly white faces figure prominently in green media outlets like Rodale publications and other websites, there is more evidence to verify that those children's good health is the result of a lack of exposure to violence, stress, and poverty than their lack of exposure to synthetic chemicals and GMOs. In the marketplace of consumer societies, knowledge itself has become a commodity, and for those with ready access to both knowledge and capital there are few barriers to the health and environmental amenities at their disposal. The marketplace has shown that it can provide more choices and the tools to improve ourselves. But the hope that it can sustain the health of *all* of us—including the natural systems on which we depend—is a demand for which the marketplace has no response.

NOTES

INTRODUCTION: BACK TO THE GARDEN, THROUGH THE MARKET

1   This sales number comes from Michael Kaplan, "Rodale's New Attitude," *Folio*, November 2000, 57. As a privately held firm, Rodale is not required to publicly disclose its earnings. *Organic Gardening* became *Organic Life* in 2015.

2   On environmentalism in the postwar era see Samuel P. Hays, *Beauty, Health, and Permanence: Environmental Politics in the United States, 1955–1985* (New York: Cambridge University Press, 1989); Robert Gottlieb, *Forcing the Spring: The Transformation of the American Environmental Movement*, rev. ed. (Washington, DC: Island Press, 2005); Adam Rome, *The Bulldozer in the Countryside: Suburban Sprawl and the Rise of American Environmentalism* (New York: Cambridge University Press, 2001); Rome, "'Give Earth a Chance': The Environmental Movement and the Sixties," *Journal of American History* 90, no. 2 (2003): 525–54; Adam Rome, *The Genius of Earth Day: How a 1970 Teach-In Made the First Green Generation* (New York: Hill and Wang, 2013); Jeff Crane and Michael Egan, eds., *Natural Protest: Essays on the History of American Environmentalism* (New York: Routledge, 2009); Christopher C. Sellers, *Crabgrass Crucible: Suburban Nature and the Rise of Environmentalism in Twentieth-Century America* (Chapel Hill: University of North Carolina Press, 2012); Andrew Kirk, *Counterculture Green: The Whole Earth Catalog and American Environmentalism* (Lawrence: University Press of Kansas, 2007); Frank Zelko, *Make It a Green Peace! The Rise of Countercultural Environmentalism* (New York: Oxford University Press, 2013); James Longhurst, *Citizen Environmentalists* (Lebanon, NH: University Press of New England, 2012).

3   The concept of marketplace environmentalism draws from scholars who have sought out sites of popular and mass consumer culture as places to analyze social and political change. In particular, Davarian Baldwin's notion of "marketplace intellectual life" in his work on commerce and ideas in Chicago's African American community in the interwar years has been critical, and my use of the term marketplace environmentalism is meant to reflect that debt. See Davarian Baldwin, *Chicago's New Negroes: Modernity, the Great Migration, and Black Urban Life* (Durham: University of North Carolina Press, 2007).

4   Andrew Szasz, *Shopping Our Way to Safety: How We Changed from Protecting the Environment to Protecting Ourselves* (Minneapolis: University of Minnesota Press, 2007), 1–8, 134–52; Julia Guthman, *Weighing In: Obesity, Food Justice, and the Limits of Capitalism* (Berkeley: University of California Press, 2011), 147–62.

5   Lawrence B. Glickman, *Buying Power: A History of Consumer Activism in America* (Chicago: University of Chicago Press, 2009), 3–6.

6   The best example of this perspective can be seen in James C. Whorton, *Crusaders for Fitness: The History of American Health Reformers* (Princeton, NJ: Princeton University Press, 1982), 332–39.

7   Michael Pollan, *Second Nature: A Gardener's Education* (New York: Dell, 1991), 79–83; Pollan, *The Omnivore's Dilemma: A Natural History of Four Meals* (New York: Penguin, 2005), 41–151.

8   For earlier assessments on the history of natural foods see Warren J. Belasco, *Appetite for Change: How the Counterculture Took on the Food Industry, 1966–1988* (New York: Pantheon, 1989). The most in-depth history of the organic movement in the United States remains Suzanne Peters, "The Land in Trust: A Social History of the Organic Farming Movement" (PhD diss., McGill University, 1979). An important critique of the history and practice of organic farming can be found in Julie Guthman, *Agrarian Dreams: The Paradox of Organic Farming in California* (Berkeley: University of California Press, 2004). On organic gardening see David M. Tucker, *Kitchen Gardening in America: A History* (Ames: Iowa State University Press, 1993). On composting see Barton Blum, "Composting and the Roots of Sustainable Agriculture," *Agricultural History* 66, no. 2 (1992): 171–88. More recent works that use parts of the Rodale story include Joshua J. Frye, "The Transnational Origin, Diffusion, and Transformation of 'Organic' Agriculture: A Study in Social Movement Framing and Outcomes" (PhD diss., Purdue University, 2007). More popular works that tell parts of the Rodale story include Samuel Fromartz, *Organic, Inc.: Natural Foods and How They Grew* (Orlando, FL: Harcourt, 2006).

9   Paul Sutter, *Driven Wild: How the Fight against Automobiles Launched the Modern Wilderness Movement* (Seattle: University of Washington Press, 2002), 10. Important exceptions to this trend come from histories focused on the organic movement both in the United Kingdom and throughout the world. See Philip Conford, *The Origins of the Organic Movement* (Edinburgh: Floris Books, 2001); Matthew Reed, *Rebels for the Soil: The Rise of the Global Organic Food and Farming Movement* (Washington, DC: Earthscan, 2010).

10   See Thomas Jundt, *Greening the Red, White, and Blue: The Bomb, Big Business, and Consumer Resistance in Postwar America* (New York: Oxford University Press, 2014); Robin O'Sullivan, *American Organic: A Cultural History of Farming, Gardening, Shopping, and Eating* (Lawrence: University Press of Kansas, 2015); Michelle Mart, *Pesticides, a Love Story: America's Enduring Embrace of Dangerous Chemicals* (Lawrence: University Press of Kansas, 2015).

11   Jundt, *Greening the Red, White, and Blue*, 62.

12   O'Sullivan, *American Organic*, 50.

13   Geoffrey Jones, *Profits and Sustainability: A History of Green Entrepreneurship* (New York: Oxford University Press, 2017), 3.

14   Adam Rome, "The Ecology of Commerce: Environmental History and the Challenge of Building a Sustainable Economy," in *Green Capitalism? Business and the Environment in the Twentieth Century*, ed. Adam Rome and Hartmut Berghoff (Philadelphia: University of Pennsylvania Press, 2017), 10.

15   Christine Meisner Rosen and Christopher C. Sellers, "The Nature of the Firm: Towards an Ecocultural History of Business," *Business History Review* 73, no. 4 (1999): 577–600.

16   Ulrich Beck, *Ecological Enlightenment: Essays on the Politics of the Risk Society* (Atlantic Highlands, NJ: Humanities Press, 1995), 3.

17   My thinking about Rodale's texts draws from Lawrence Levine's treatment of popular culture in his seminal essay "The Folklore of Industrial Society," in that it aims to understand American attitudes through materials in the past that were "widely accessible and widely accessed." Like Levine, I argue that popular culture cannot be understood as one imposed solely by cultural producers, but instead as one that emerged in the interaction between an audience and the texts. See Lawrence W. Levine, *The Unpredictable Past: Explorations in American Cultural History* (New York: Oxford University Press, 1993), 293.

CHAPTER ONE: PAY DIRT

1   On the Delaney Commission, see Philip J. Hilts, *Protecting America's Health: The FDA, Business, and One Hundred Years of Regulation* (New York: Knopf, 2003), 11–18, 38–52. On Harvey Wiley and early food and drug regulation, see James Harvey Young, *The Medical Messiahs: The History of Health Quackery in Twentieth-Century America* (Princeton, NJ: Princeton University Press, 1967), 32–52.

2   House Select Committee to Investigate the Use of Chemicals in Food Products, *Chemicals in Food Products: Hearings Before the House Select Committee to Investigate the Use of Chemicals in Food Products* (Washington, DC: Government Printing Office, 1951), 836.

3   Ibid., 845. On the extent of additives in foods after 1945, see Nancy Langston, *Toxic Bodies: Hormone Disruptors and the Legacy of DES* (New Haven, CT: Yale University Press, 2011), 80.

4   House Select Committee, *Chemicals in Food Products*, 852.

5   Ibid., 853.

6   Ibid., 857–58.

7   Ibid., 866.

8   Rodale Inc., *Our Roots Grow Deep* (Emmaus, PA: Rodale, 2009), 11–16.

9   Oliver Field to Kenneth Anglemire, November 4, 1965, Historical Health Fraud Collection, American Medical Association, Chicago. The AMA, among other critics, routinely pointed out Rodale's lack of training. The organization went so far as to challenge the *Who's Who in American Business* entry on Rodale in the mid-1960s because it stated he had attended NYU. Because of his name change there was no record of Rodale having taken courses.

10   J. I. Rodale, *Autobiography* (Emmaus, PA: Rodale Press, 1965), 19.

11   J. I. Rodale, "All Right, So I'm a Sucker," Box 265 "J. I. Autobiography," Rodale Press Archives, Emmaus, PA (hereafter RPA).

12   J. I. Rodale, "The History of My Colds," *Prevention*, April 1954, 8.

13   Rodale Inc., *Our Roots Grow Deep*, 15; J. I. Rodale, "Chapter 2," Box 265 "J. I. Autobiography," RPA.

14   Rodale, "Chapter 2."

15   Jerome Irving Cohen to Louis Ludwig, March 13, 1919, Box 265 "J. I. Autobiography," Folder "People: Letters to Ludwig, 1919," RPA.

16   Rodale Inc., *Our Roots Grow Deep*, 21.

17   Rodale, *Autobiography*, 25.

18   J. I. Rodale, "Autobiography Notes," n.d., Box 265 "J. I. Autobiography," Folder "Biographical Notes, Father," RPA.

19   Rodale Inc., *Our Roots Grow Deep*, 28–29; Rodale, *Autobiography*, 57.

20   Rodale, *Autobiography*, 33–35. Rodale produced dozens of variations on his "word finder" system, including the verb finder, an adverb finder, a word-at-a-time system, and countless others. A popular line of thesauruses known as *The Synonym Finder* still bears J. I. Rodale's name but has been heavily revised by professional editors.

21   Rodale Inc., *Our Roots Grow Deep*, 22–35.

22   Rodale, *Autobiography*, 37.

23   Ibid., 36–38.

24   Carlton Jackson, *J. I. Rodale: Apostle of Nonconformity* (New York: Pyramid, 1974), 62.

25   On the popularity of the digest format, see John Heidenry, *Theirs Was the Kingdom: Lila and Dewitt Wallace and the Story of Reader's Digest* (New York: Norton, 1993), 59–73; John William Tebbel and Mary Ellen Zuckerman, *The Magazine in America, 1741–1990* (New York: Oxford University Press, 1991), 182–85.

26   Rodale Inc., *Our Roots Grow Deep*, 41.

27   Paul K. Conkin, *A Revolution Down on the Farm: The Transformation of American Agriculture since 1929* (Louisville: University Press of Kentucky, 2008), 97–122.

28   Daniel J. Hillel, *Out of the Earth: Civilization and the Life of the Soil* (New York: Free Press, 1991).

29   Steven Stoll, *Larding the Lean Earth: Soil and Society in Nineteenth-Century America* (New York: Hill and Wang, 2002), 13–40.

30   F. H. King, *Farmers of Forty Centuries: Permanent Agriculture in China, Korea, and Japan* (1911; repr., Emmaus, PA: Rodale Press, 1990), iv.

31   Ibid., 13.

32   Vaclav Smil, *Enriching the Earth: Fritz Haber, Carl Bosch, and the Transformation of World Food Production* (Cambridge, MA: MIT Press, 2001).

33   On Howard's life and research, see Louise E. Howard, *Sir Albert Howard in India* (London: Faber and Faber, 1953); Gregory Barton, "Sir Albert Howard and the Forestry Roots of the Organic Farming Movement," *Agricultural History* 75, no. 2 (2001): 168–87; Philip Conford, *The Origins of the Organic Movement* (Edinburgh: Floris Books, 2001), 53–59.

34   Albert Howard, *The Soil and Health: A Study of Organic Agriculture* (New York: Devin-Adair, 1947), 7.

35   J. I. Rodale, "Introduction to Organic Farming," *Organic Farming and Gardening*, May 1942, 1.

36   Randal S. Beeman and James A. Pritchard, *A Green and Permanent Land: Ecology and Agriculture in the Twentieth Century* (Lawrence: University Press of Kansas, 2001), 10–17. Beeman and Pritchard draw their definition of the "soil jeremiad" from Sacvan Bercovitch, *The American Jeremiad* (Madison: University of Wisconsin Press, 1978).

37   Paul S. Sutter, *Let Us Now Praise Famous Gullies: Providence Canyon and the Soils of the South* (Athens: University of Georgia Press, 2015), 83–90.

38   Beeman and Pritchard, *Green and Permanent Land*, 49–50.

39   Louis Bromfield, *Out of the Earth* (1950; repr., Wooster, OH: Wooster Book Co., 2003), 298–99.

40   Randal Beeman, "The Trash Farmer: Edward Faulkner and the Origins of Sustainable Agriculture in the United States, 1943–1953," *Journal of Sustainable Agriculture* 4, no. 1 (1993): 98–99.

41   Beeman and Pritchard, *Green and Permanent Land*, 49–53.

42   Carlton Jackson, "Robert Rodale Interview," n.d., 7, Carlton Jackson MSS Box 17, Carlton Jackson Papers, Kentucky Building Manuscripts, Western Kentucky University, Bowling Green (hereafter KBM). Jackson interviewed Rodale family members in 1973. The transcripts of the interview are typed onto index cards, which are part of Jackson's papers.

43   Dona Brown, *Back to the Land: The Enduring Dream of Self-Sufficiency in Modern America* (Madison: University of Wisconsin Press, 2011), 143.

44   Rebecca Kneale Gould, *At Home in Nature: Modern Homesteading and Spiritual Practice in America* (Berkeley: University of California Press, 2005), 184.

45   On Macfadden's *Liberty* magazine, see Mark Adams, *Mr. America: How Muscular Millionaire Bernarr Macfadden Transformed the Nation through Sex, Salad, and the Ultimate Starvation Diet* (New York: HarperCollins, 2009), 165–76. For Macfadden's role in popularizing the 1930s back-to-the-land movement, see Brown, *Back to the Land*, 142; Robert Ernst, *Weakness Is a Crime: The Life of Bernarr Macfadden* (Syracuse, NY: Syracuse University Press, 1991), 137–40.

46 "Robert Rodale Interview: Part II," YouTube video, 8:31, an interview of Robert Rodale by Jane Potter Gates, November 21, 1989, posted by "Alternative Farming Systems Information Center," December 31, 2008, https://youtu.be/zGhVImfmHKU?list=PL6E4E8B90527762C8.

47 Gould, *At Home in Nature*, 24–27.

48 Rodale, *Autobiography*, 42. This conversion narrative appears repeatedly in Rodale's articles and books in the 1960s, particularly after the publication of Carson's *Silent Spring*.

49 House Select Committee, *Chemicals in Food Products*, 866.

50 For a useful introduction to the concept of "vernacular science," see Ron Eglash, "Appropriating Technology: An Introduction," in *Appropriating Technology: Vernacular Science and Social Power*, ed. Ron Eglash et al. (Minneapolis: University of Minnesota Press, 2004), 5–32.

51 On the concept of an "open text," see Umberto Eco, *The Role of the Reader: Explorations in the Semiotics of Texts* (Bloomington: Indiana University Press, 1979), 3–5.

52 J. I. Rodale, "Introduction to Organic Farming," *Organic Farming and Gardening*, May 1942, 3–5; "Letters from Readers," *Organic Farming and Gardening*, May 1942, 15. After several issues as *Organic Farming and Gardening*, Rodale dropped "farming" as the focus and published the magazine as *Organic Gardening*. In 1949, Rodale launched the *Organic Farmer* as a separate publication, but then folded it back into *Organic Gardening* as *Organic Gardening and Farming* in 1954. This arrangement stayed in place until the late 1970s when the farming portion became a separate publication called the *New Farm*.

53 "The Chemical Fertilizer Shortage," *Organic Gardening*, June 1943, 11. Many articles in Rodale's magazines were unattributed. Rodale routinely reprinted work from many sources but did not always say from where the piece was reprinted.

54 Howard, *Soil and Health*, 212.

55 See the back page of *Organic Gardening*, August 1945; and *Organic Gardening*, October 1944, 2.

56 Albert Howard, "Introduction," in *Pay Dirt: Farming and Gardening with Composts*, by J. I. Rodale (New York: Devin-Adair, 1945), vii.

57 Louis Bromfield, "Letter to J. I. Rodale," April 2, 1944, Celebrity Correspondence Folder, RPA; Louis Bromfield, "Letter to J. I. Rodale," March 24, 1945, Celebrity Correspondence Folder, RPA. The two men apparently met for lunch in New York in June 1943 and Bromfield followed the development of *Organic Gardening* with some interest. Their correspondence ends in 1946 with Bromfield telling Rodale he is too busy to read more materials. Bromfield seems to have agreed with Rodale's claims about building up organic matter in topsoil but departed from the health claims of the "organic school."

58 Russell Lord, "A Cure for Devil's Dust," *New York Times*, December 16, 1945, sec. Book Review, 3.

59   Rodale, *Pay Dirt*, 93–104.
60   A. F. Schell, "Organic Farming Leads to Prosperity and Health," *Organic Gardening*, April 1948, 72–73.
61   J. I. Rodale, "'Answer to Our Critics (Part III): Agriculture of Olden Times,'" *Organic Gardening*, November 1950, 15.
62   J. I. Rodale, "Looking Back," *Organic Gardening*, May 1952, 14.
63   "Application of Organic Methods to Farms," *Organic Gardening*, August 1947, 25.
64   A. J. Gilardi, "Mistakes I Have Made," *Organic Gardening*, March 1952, 28.
65   "Sunflower Plants on Our Farm," *Organic Gardening*, September 1944; "New Zealand Boxes," *Organic Gardening*, September 1944, 13–14; "Compost Making at the Experimental Farm," *Organic Gardening*, March 1946, 21; "Rodale's Composting Center," *Organic Gardening*, October 1946, 9–10.
66   Heinrich Meyer, "Some Recollections of J. I. Rodale," 1973, Carlton Jackson Correspondence 73–74, Carlton Jackson MSS Box 13, KBM. Meyer recalls one worker keeping a hidden stash of pesticides to control insects without Rodale's knowledge.
67   Rodale, *Autobiography*, 44.
68   "Soil and Health Foundation," *Organic Gardening*, November 1947, 14.
69   "Proof!" *Organic Gardening*, January 1948, 32.
70   Bingham Small, "Interesting Letters Department," *Organic Gardening*, February 1946, 37; Louis Sherman, "Champion Composter," *Organic Gardening*, May 1946, 21.
71   "Join Our Garden Seminar," *Organic Gardening*, December 1947, 49.
72   "Results," *Organic Gardening*, April 1945, 24.
73   "Take the Initiative," *Organic Gardening*, February 1946, 4.
74   "Memorandum," *Organic Gardening*, June 1947, 18.
75   "Friends of Organic Gardening Can Help Build Its Circulation by Handing Out Our Free Subscription Booklets," *Organic Gardening*, September 1947, 44.
76   "Do You Want to Help the Organic Cause?" *Organic Gardening*, June 1946, 4; "You Can Help the Organic Cause," *Organic Gardening*, July 1947, 15.
77   "Friends of Organic Gardening Can Help Build Its Circulation by Handing Out Our Free Subscription Booklets," 44.
78   Tebbel and Zuckerman, *Magazine in America*, 191.
79   Rodale Inc., *Our Roots Grow Deep*, 60.
80   Heinrich Meyer, "Some Recollections of J. I. Rodale," 1973, Correspondence 73–74, KBM. Meyer's reference to "trips around the world" refers to J. I.'s extensive travels in the 1950s. Rodale chronicled his travels frequently in his editorials for both magazines, as would Robert Rodale in years to come.
81   Thomas Jundt, *Greening the Red, White, and Blue: The Bomb, Big Business, and Consumer Resistance in Postwar America* (New York: Oxford University Press, 2014), 54–59.
82   Meyer, "Some Recollections of J. I. Rodale."

1   J. I. Rodale, *Walk, Do Not Run, to the Doctor* (Emmaus, PA: Rodale Books, 1967), 9.

2   Ibid., 21.

3   J. I. Rodale, *Cancer: Can It Be Prevented?* (Emmaus, PA: Rodale Press, 1950). This quote appears on the back cover of the booklet in an advertisement for *Prevention*.

4   J. I. Rodale, "Is Cancer Related to Artificial Fertilizers?" *Organic Gardening*, May 1949, 12. For an overview of cancer, see James T. Patterson, *The Dread Disease: Cancer and Modern American Culture* (Cambridge, MA: Harvard University Press, 1987); on the politics of knowledge surrounding cancer, see Robert Proctor, *Cancer Wars: How Politics Shapes What We Know and Don't Know about Cancer* (New York: Basic Books, 1995); Devra Davis, *The Secret History of the War on Cancer* (New York: Basic Books, 2009).

5   J. I. Rodale, "Cancer: Part 2," *Organic Gardening*, June 1949, 16.

6   "Robert Rodale Interview: Part X," YouTube video, 4:21, an interview of Robert Rodale by Jane Potter Gates, November 21, 1989, posted by "Alternative Farming Systems Information Center," December 31, 2008, https://youtu.be/jwfu6B9j_ZE.

7   J. I. Rodale, "With the Editor," *Prevention*, July 1950, 63–64.

8   Ibid.

9   J. I. Rodale, "Editor's Note," *Prevention*, July 1950, 11.

10 J. I. Rodale, "Adventures in Self-Analysis towards Health," *Prevention*, March 1951, 26–29. Sleeping positions and their influence on health was a routine Rodale subject and one of the first health systems he created. See J. I. Rodale, *Sleep and Rheumatism* (Emmaus, PA: Rodale Press, 1940).

11 J. I. Rodale, "That Subject of Soap Again," *Prevention*, 1951, 1–7.

12 J. I. Rodale, *This Pace Is Not Killing Us* (Emmaus, PA: Rodale Press, 1954), 85–96.

13 J. I. Rodale, "The History of My Colds," *Prevention*, April 1954, 8.

14 James C. Whorton, *Nature Cures: The History of Alternative Medicine in America* (New York: Oxford University Press, 2002), 10–13.

15 Conevery Bolton Valencius, *The Health of the Country: How American Settlers Understood Themselves and Their Land* (New York: Basic Books, 2002), 53–84.

16 Nancy Tomes, *The Gospel of Germs: Men, Women, and the Microbe in American Life* (Cambridge, MA: Harvard University Press, 1998), 9–13.

17 J. I. Rodale, *Autobiography* (Emmaus, PA: Rodale Press, 1965), 68.

18 David M. Oshinsky, *Polio: An American Story* (Oxford, UK: Oxford University Press, 2005), 93. See also Naomi Rodgers, *Dirt and Disease: Polio before FDR* (New Brunswick, NJ: Rutgers University Press, 1992).

19 "Does the Polio Virus Come from Without?" *Prevention*, July 1951, 25. Many

of the early articles in *Prevention* carry no author unless they were reprints from other publications.

20   "Poison Sprays on Fruits and Vegetables as Possible Cause of Polio," *Prevention*, June 1951, 3.

21   Brian Allen Drake, *Loving Nature, Fearing the State: Environmentalism and Antigovernment Politics before Reagan* (Seattle: University of Washington Press, 2013), 52–79.

22   J. I. Rodale, "Natural or Synthetic?" *Prevention*, July 1952, 6.

23   Ivan T. Anderson, "The Good Dirt: A Few Facts about Soap," *Prevention*, October 1950, 21–22.

24   "The Antihistamines Are on Trial," *Prevention*, November 1950, 32.

25   Allan Brandt and Martha Gardener, "The Golden Age of Medicine?" in *Medicine in the Twentieth Century*, ed. Roger Cooter and John Pickstone (Amsterdam: Harwood Academic Publishers, 2000), 22–26.

26   John C. Burnham, "American Medicine's Golden Age: What Happened to It?" in *Sickness and Health in America: Readings in the History of Medicine and Public Health*, 3rd ed., ed. Ronald L. Numbers and Judith W. Leavitt (Madison: University of Wisconsin Press, 1997), 284–88.

27   Susan Lederer and Naomi Rodgers, "Media," in *Medicine in the Twentieth Century*, ed. Roger Cooter and John Pickstone (Amsterdam: Harwood Academic Publishers, 2000), 492.

28   See J. I. Rodale and Staff, eds., *Prevention Method for Better Health* (Emmaus, PA: Rodale Books, 1960), 893–906.

29   "Prevention Readers Prevent Respiratory Disorders," *Prevention*, April 1954, 85.

30   "Tell Us Your Health Story . . . ," *Prevention*, May 1953, 51.

31   "Out of the Mailbag," *Prevention*, May 1954; "Out of the Mailbag," *Prevention*, January 1955; "Out of the Mailbag," *Prevention*, April 1955; "Out of the Mailbag," *Prevention*, May 1955.

32   "Out of the Mailbag," *Prevention*, May 1955.

33   Morton Simon, "Statement of Morton J. Simon," n.d., Carlton Jackson MSS Box 13, Folder 4 "Rodale Anecdotes," Carlton Jackson Papers, Kentucky Building Manuscripts, Western Kentucky University, Bowling Green.

34   Janice A. Radway, *A Feeling for Books: The Book-of-the-Month Club, Literary Taste, and Middle-Class Desire* (Chapel Hill: University of North Carolina Press, 1997), 135.

35   See Gary Taubes, *The Case against Sugar* (New York: Knopf, 2016).

36   Gregg Mitman, Michelle Murphy, and Christopher Sellers, "Introduction: A Cloud over History," *Osiris*, 2nd ser. 19 (2004): 13.

37   "Dos and Don'ts for Health," *Prevention*, October 1953, 45–53.

38   Rodale and Staff, "Foreword," in *Prevention Method for Better Health*, ed. Rodale and Staff.

39 See the back page of early copies of *Prevention*—most featured a one-page directory of organic suppliers.

40 Rodale and Staff, eds., *Prevention Method for Better Health*, 13.

41 Ibid., 547.

42 Ibid., 567.

43 Rima D. Apple, *Vitamania: Vitamins in American Culture* (New Brunswick, NJ: Rutgers University Press, 1996), 54–75.

44 Philip J. Hilts, *Protecting America's Health: The FDA, Business, and One Hundred Years of Regulation* (New York: Knopf, 2003), 282–83.

45 "Memo Re: Points of Agreement and under Consideration between J. I. Rodale of Allentown, Pennsylvania, and Rudolf Weissgerber . . . ," n.d., Box 265 "J. I. Autobiography," Folder "Madaus Co. and Rudolf Weissgerber," Rodale Press Archives, Emmaus, Pennsylvania (hereafter RPA).

46 Dr. Madaus Co. to Jerry Rodale, June 8, 1951; J. I. Rodale to Rudolph Weissgerber, August 7, 1951; J. I. Rodale to Dr. Madaus and Co., August 14, 1951, Box 265 "J. I. Autobiography," Folder "Madaus Co. and Rudolf Weissgerber," RPA.

47 See *Prevention*, July 1950, through *Prevention*, November 1950.

48 J. I. Rodale, "What Don't You Like about Prevention?" *Prevention*, January 1953, 5.

49 Ibid., 9.

50 Ibid., 7.

51 In England, where food and drug laws were less restrictive with respect to vitamins, there was a brand of Rodale vitamins. Documentation on this side of the business is scarce, although it is mentioned in the company's own history (*Our Roots Grow Deep*) and a handful of other places.

52 For an analysis of the history of direct-selling organizations, see Nicole Woolsey Biggart, *Charismatic Capitalism: Direct Selling Organizations in America* (Chicago: University of Chicago Press, 1989). For direct marketing more generally, the best introductions are commercial rather than scholarly. See Walter Weintz, *The Solid Gold Mailbox: How to Create Winning Mail-Order Campaigns* (New York: Wiley, 1987); Joan Throckmorton, *Winning Direct Response Advertising: How to Recognize It, Evaluate It, Inspire It, Create It* (Englewood Cliffs, NJ: Prentice-Hall, 1986).

53 In the case of the Rodale Press, many of these materials have only been preserved as a result of the AMA's investigation files and the files of the 1964 FTC action against the Press. See the Historical Health Fraud Collection, American Medical Association, Chicago (hereafter HHF); and the FTC trial documents in the Rodale Press Archives.

54 See James R. Hare, "Memo of James Hare," August 6, 1963, Box 12 "FTC Papers 1951–1964," Folder "Federal Trade Commission, 1962–1979," RPA. In this memo Hare states that many of the earlier records of the Press's mailings were destroyed. Between 1955 and 1963, the press sold 137,228 copies of *The Health Finder* of 160,000 printed. The majority of the remaining 23,000 copies

were sold to bookstores and "other retailers" (likely health food stores). In that same time, the Press mailed 7.619 million mailings in support of the book, peaking in 1956 with 2.9 million mailings.

55   "At Last! The Truth about How to Stop Disease," n.d., Circulars 1953–57, HHF; for examples of early Rodale circulars see the "Direct Mail Archives" folder in RPA.

56   *Guide to the American Medical Association Historical Health Fraud and Alternative Medicine Collection* (Chicago: American Medical Association, 1992), 1–13.

57   Morris Fishbein, *Fads and Quackery in Healing: An Analysis of the Foibles of the Healing Cults, with Essays on Various Other Peculiar Notions in the Health Field* (New York: Blue Ribbon Books, 1932), 29.

58   Oliver Field to Dr. Harry N. Moore, October 12, 1955, Box 673 "Prevention Magazine Correspondence, 1955," HHF.

59   The nature of the AMA's archive collection makes it difficult to know the full extent of the association's involvement with actions against Rodale. Nonmembers of the AMA have limited access to the association's records, and only the HHF is open to the public.

60   "Prevention Correspondence, n.d.," Folder 0672-07 "Prevention Magazine Correspondence, 1955," HHF. The classic tomes on health quackery remain James Harvey Young, *The Medical Messiahs: The History of Health Quackery in Twentieth-Century America* (Princeton, NJ: Princeton University Press, 1967); and James Harvey Young, *The Toadstool Millionaires: A Social History of Patent Medicines in America before Federal Regulation* (Princeton, NJ: Princeton University Press, 1961).

61   See the AMA Bureau of Investigation correspondence files, especially those covering 1955–65, HHF.

62   Oliver Field to John F. Kiser, August 24, 1959, Folder 0673-01 "Prevention Magazine Correspondence, 1959," HHF.

63   Harry Davis to Oliver Field, August 15, 1958, Folder 0672-10 "Prevention Magazine Correspondence, 1958," HHF.

64   Letter of Miss Anne E. Jackson, November 2, 1962, Box 673 "Prevention Magazine Correspondence, 1962," HHF.

65   Oliver Field to George Mott, November 13, 1959, Box 673 "Prevention Magazine Correspondence, 1959," HHF.

66   Nancy Tomes, "Merchants of Health: Medicine and Consumer Culture in the United States, 1900–1940," *Journal of American History* 88, no. 2 (2001): 519–47.

67   National Congress on Medical Quackery, American Medical Association, and United States Food and Drug Administration, *Proceedings: National Congress on Medical Quackery* (Chicago: American Medical Association, 1962), 1.

68   Ibid., 68.

69   US Congress, Senate, Special Committee on Aging, *Frauds and Quackery Affecting the Older Citizen: Hearings before the Special Committee on Aging,*

United States Senate, Eighty-Eighth Congress, First Session (Washington, DC: Government Printing Office, 1963), 43.

70   National Congress on Medical Quackery, American Medical Association, and United States Food and Drug Administration, *Proceedings: Second National Congress on Medical Quackery* (Washington, DC: Government Printing Office, 1963), 19.

71   Morton Simon, "Correspondence with Robert Rodale and Staff," Box 12 "FTC Papers 1951–1964," Folder "Federal Trade Commission, 1962–1979," RPA.

72   Federal Trade Commission, "Order Denying Request for Permission to File Interlocutionary Appeal," n.d., Box 9 "FTC Papers, 1964," RPA.

73   Robert Rodale to Thurmond Arnold, November 16, 1963, Box 12 "FTC Papers 1951–1964," Folder "Federal Trade Commission, 1962–1979," RPA.

74   J. I. Rodale, "How I Came to Compile the Health Finder," n.d., Box 12 "FTC Papers 1951–1964," Folder "Federal Trade Commission, 1962–1979," RPA.

75   "The Following Learned Papers . . . ," n.d., Box 12 "FTC Papers 1951–1964," Folder "Federal Trade Commission, 1962–1979," RPA.

76   "Letters from Readers, 1965," various dates, Box 12 "FTC Papers 1951–1964," Folder "Federal Trade Commission, 1962–1979," RPA.

77   James J. Kilpatrick, "Bureaucrats in Stew over Food Fad Book," *Miami Herald*, August 21, 1965.

78   Robert Rodale to Raymond Treadwell, February 8, 1965, Box 12 "FTC Papers 1951–1964," Folder "Federal Trade Commission, 1962–1979," RPA.

79   "1st Amendment Limits FTC's Ad Rule: Arnold," *Advertising Age*, October 4, 1965.

80   In addition to *The Health Finder*, J. I. Rodale's books *How to Eat for a Healthy Heart* and *This Pace Is Not Killing Us* were cited in the FTC action. For all intents and purposes these books can be treated as one and the same; although the "heart books" contained advice on preventing heart disease, much of their contents are the same as *The Health Finder* and other *Prevention* books. The FTC seized on the heart books in the trial, likely because they were much shorter than *The Health Finder*.

81   *Official Transcript of the Proceedings before the Federal Trade Commission, Docket No. 8619, in the Matter of Rodale Press, Inc.* (Washington, DC: Ward and Paul, 1964), 160, 177.

82   Ibid., 235.

83   Ibid., 392–94.

84   In an undated note in Robert Rodale's handwriting, Rachel Carson's name is listed as a potential witness. Carson died in April 1964, over six months before the hearing began. See Box 12 "FTC Papers 1951–1964," Folder "Federal Trade Commission, 1962–1979," RPA.

85   *Official Transcript of the Proceedings before the Federal Trade Commission*, 515.

86   Gregg Mitman, *Breathing Space: How Allergies Shape Our Lives and Landscapes* (New Haven, CT: Yale University Press, 2007), 192–94.

87   *Official Transcript of the Proceedings before the Federal Trade Commission*, 644.

88   Ibid., 649.

89   Theron G. Randolph, *Human Ecology and Susceptibility to the Chemical Environment* (Springfield, IL: C. C. Thomas, 1962).

90   Michelle Murphy, *Sick Building Syndrome and the Problem of Uncertainty: Environmental Politics, Technoscience, and Women Workers* (Durham, NC: Duke University Press, 2006), 160.

91   Brandt and Gardener, "Golden Age of Medicine?" 23.

92   Linda Nash, *Inescapable Ecologies: A History of Environment, Disease, and Knowledge* (Berkeley: University of California Press, 2007), 127–69.

93   The trial is covered in great depth in Carlton Jackson, *J. I. Rodale: Apostle of Nonconformity* (New York: Pyramid, 1974), 148–90.

94   Tomes, "Merchants of Health," 53.

95   Dana Frank, *Purchasing Power: Consumer Organizing, Gender, and the Seattle Labor Movement, 1919–1929* (New York: Cambridge University Press, 1994), 1–15.

CHAPTER THREE: OUR POISONED EARTH AND SKY

1   *The World's Happiest Gardeners* (Emmaus, PA: Rodale Press Inc., 1959), 7–8. The pamphlet was offered free as part of a prepublication offer for Rodale's *Encyclopedia of Organic Gardening*.

2   See the table of contents in J. I. Rodale and Staff, *Our Poisoned Earth and Sky* (Emmaus, PA: Rodale Press, 1964).

3   Ibid., 272.

4   Samuel P. Hays, *Beauty, Health, and Permanence: Environmental Politics in the United States, 1955–1985* (New York: Cambridge University Press, 1989), 205–6.

5   Raymond Williams, *Keywords: A Vocabulary of Culture and Society*, rev. ed. (New York: Oxford University Press, 1985), 78.

6   Ulrich Beck, *Ecological Enlightenment: Essays on the Politics of the Risk Society* (Atlantic Highlands, NJ: Humanities Press, 1995), 16.

7   J. I. Rodale, "Farm Economics," *Organic Gardening and Farming*, July 1955, 12–13.

8   J. I. Rodale, "The Organic Creed," *Organic Gardening and Farming*, March 1956, 72, 75.

9   J. I. Rodale, "Food: A Plan," *Organic Gardening and Farming*, May 1956, 19.

10   J. I. Rodale and Staff, *How to Grow Fruits and Vegetables with the Organic Method* (Emmaus, PA: Rodale Press, 1961).

11   "How to Spend Your Garden Dollar," *Organic Gardening and Farming*, November 1954, 50–53.

12   "Readers Report on the Organic Method, Part 2," *Organic Gardening and Farming*, October 1955, 50–53.

13   Gordon L'Allemend, "Compost for the West Coast," *Organic Gardening and Farming*, October 1956, 34–35; Jeanne Wellenkamp, "Where Fall Is Spring," *Organic Gardening and Farming*, October 1956, 31–32; Eleanor Gilman, "Good Practices, Good Results," *Organic Gardening and Farming*, October 1956, 30–31.

14   "Gardening from a Haystack," *Organic Gardening and Farming*, February 1957, 52–53; Ruth Stout, "Will You Walk into My Garden?" *Organic Gardening and Farming*, April 1956, 28–32. Stout's articles from 1953 to 1971 are reprinted in Ruth Stout, *The Ruth Stout No-Work Garden Book* (Emmaus, PA: Rodale Press, 1971). Stout is frequently cited today as one of the first to popularize what is now called "permaculture."

15   "Organic World: Homesteading the Modern Way," *Organic Gardening and Farming*, April 1957, 2; on lawn machines in postwar America, see Ted Steinberg, *American Green: The Obsessive Quest for the Perfect Lawn* (New York: Norton, 2007), 17–37.

16   Ernest Colwell, "Choosing Your Garden Tools," *Organic Gardening and Farming*, August 1954, 26–27. Advertisements for rototillers in particular were ubiquitous in the magazine. The February 1956 issue alone featured eleven ads for tillers, including color ads on the inside and back side of the cover stock.

17   Jerome Olds, "The Changing Scene at Deer Valley Farm," *Organic Gardening and Farming*, December 1959, 65–66.

18   Thomas Powell, "The New Exodus," *Organic Gardening and Farming*, December 1954, 43–45. See also Jerome Olds, "Sunset Farming Versus Suburbia," *Organic Gardening and Farming*, December 1958, 62–64.

19   J. I. Rodale, "Health and the Organic Homestead," *Organic Gardening and Farming*, April 1957, 18.

20   Robert Rodale, "Every Man a Homesteader," *Organic Gardening and Farming*, May 1961, 16.

21   Ibid., 17.

22   J. I. Rodale, "What Does Organic Mean?" *Organic Gardening and Farming*, December 1958, 14–15.

23   Organic Directory, *Organic Gardening and Farming*, January 1954.

24   Audrey Stephan, "Your Garden Club Goals for '56," *Organic Gardening and Farming*, January 1956, 34–37.

25   Robert M. Stoll, "Michigan Round-Up Draws National Interest," *Organic Gardening and Farming*, January 1956, 64–67.

26   Jerry A. Minnich, "Problems of Marketing Organic Foods," *Organic Gardening and Farming*, May 1956, 58–60.

27   Cash Asher, "This Garden Grew a Store," *Organic Gardening and Farming*, November 1955, 41–43.

28 Warren J. Belasco, *Appetite for Change: How the Counterculture Took on the Food Industry, 1966–1988* (New York: Pantheon, 1989), 16–19.

29 Michael Ackerman, "Science and the Shadow of Ideology in the American Health Foods Movement, 1930s–1960s," in *The Politics of Healing: Histories of Alternative Medicine in Twentieth-Century North America*, ed. Robert D. Johnston (New York: Routledge, 2004), 55–70.

30 "Organic World," *Organic Gardening and Farming*, June 1958.

31 "Organic World," *Organic Gardening and Farming*, August 1955. The first few years of "Organic World" carry no author, while after 1957 it is initialed by Robert Rodale as "R. R." Executive editors that followed, such as Jerome Goldstein and M. C. Goldman, did the same.

32 "Organic World: Wisconsin Legislature Needs Checking," *Organic Gardening and Farming*, September 1957, 3.

33 "Organic World: 250,000 Ton Compost Pile," *Organic Gardening and Farming*, December 1957, 2; "Organic World: Pumpkins Really Grow!" *Organic Gardening and Farming*, March 1956, 7.

34 "Organic World: This Is Your Magazine," *Organic Gardening and Farming*, July 1955, 3.

35 Robert Rodale, "Organic World: Organic Gardening in the U.S.," *Organic Gardening and Farming*, February 1958, 3.

36 Lawrence B. Glickman, *Buying Power: A History of Consumer Activism in America* (Chicago: University of Chicago Press, 2009), 3–6.

37 For a discussion of pre-1945 pesticide use, see James C. Whorton, *Before Silent Spring: Pesticides and Public Health in Pre-DDT America* (Princeton, NJ: Princeton University Press, 1975), 3–35.

38 Edmund Russell, *War and Nature: Fighting Humans and Insects with Chemicals from World War I to Silent Spring* (New York: Cambridge University Press, 2001).

39 "Needless Death versus Organics," *Organic Gardening and Farming*, May 1954, 23.

40 "Connecticut Organization Fights DDT Spraying—and Wins," *Organic Gardening and Farming*, October 1954, 67.

41 "Organic World: More Than Insects Are Killed," *Organic Gardening and Farming*, February 1956, 3.

42 "Organic World: DDT Kills Canadian Salmon," *Organic Gardening and Farming*, May 1956, 2.

43 On battles against gypsy moths, see Mark L. Winston, *Nature Wars: People vs. Pests* (Cambridge, MA: Harvard University Press, 1997), 19–39. On agricultural spraying, see Pete Daniel, *Toxic Drift: Pesticides and Health in the Post–World War II South* (Baton Rouge: Louisiana State University Press, 2007).

44 "Organic World: Aerial Spraying Is Big Business," *Organic Gardening and Farming*, August 1957, 2.

45 Robert Rodale, "The Gypsy Moth Tragedy!" *Organic Gardening and Farming*, August 1957, 25.

46   J. I. Rodale, "The Spray Gun against Man," *Organic Gardening and Farming*, November 1957, 13–15.

47   Thomas Powell, "The Battle to Halt Mass Poisoning Is On," *Organic Gardening and Farming*, December 1957, 52.

48   "Funds Needed for Gypsy Moth Trial," *Organic Gardening and Farming*, November 1957, 68; "DDT Fund Progress," *Organic Gardening and Farming*, January 1958, 87; "Organic World: DDT Trial Date Is Set," *Organic Gardening and Farming*, February 1958, 2.

49   Marjorie Spock, "Letters: DDT Trial News," *Organic Gardening and Farming*, March 1958, 9.

50   Christopher Sellers, "Body, Place, and State: The Making of an 'Environmentalist' Imaginary in the Post–World War II U.S.," *Radical History Review* 74 (Spring 1999): 35.

51   On fire ants see Joshua Blu Buhs, *The Fire Ant Wars: Nature, Science, and Public Policy in Twentieth-Century America* (Chicago: University of Chicago Press, 2010).

52   Marilyn Sibley, "The Imported Fire Ant: Will It Bring Back Poisoned Air Sprays?" *Organic Gardening and Farming*, May 1958, 60.

53   "Organic World," *Organic Gardening and Farming*, September 1958.

54   Thomas Powell, "Conservation Is Your Business," *Organic Gardening and Farming*, August 1958, 22.

55   Jerome Olds, "Power of Positive Conservation," *Organic Gardening and Farming*, August 1958, 37; Audrey Stephan, "Every Garden a Bird Sanctuary," *Organic Gardening and Farming*, August 1958, 61.

56   "Organic Club Notes," *Organic Gardening and Farming*, August 1958, 78.

57   Kendra Smith-Howard, *Pure and Modern Milk: An Environmental History since 1900* (New York: Oxford University Press, 2014), 121–46.

58   "Organic World: You Can Prevent Strontium Poisoning," *Organic Gardening and Farming*, August 1958, 2.

59   M. C. Goldman, "What You Can Do about Strontium-90," *Organic Gardening and Farming*, May 1958, 24.

60   J. I. Rodale, "Is the Strontium 90 (Fall Out) in Bone Meal Dangerous?" *Prevention*, December 1961; Robert Rodale, "The Safety Factor in Bone Meal," *Prevention*, December 1961, 43–45.

61   Ruth Adams to Carlton Jackson, June 4, 1973, Carlton Jackson MSS Box 13, Folder 4 "Rodale Anecdotes," Carlton Jackson Papers, Kentucky Building Manuscripts, Western Kentucky University, Bowling Green (hereafter KBM). The extent of Barrett's claims can be found in correspondence with the AMA and the FTC. Barrett charged that the Rodale Press fought fluoridation in Allentown and elsewhere because of the amount of revenue it earned from bone meal advertising.

62   "This Month's Cover," *Organic Gardening and Farming*, July 1959, 8; "The Case against Poison Spray," *Organic Gardening and Farming*, July 1959, 22–24;

Thomas Powell, "The People Who Sued the Government," *Organic Gardening and Farming*, July 1959; "Spraying and the Law," *Organic Gardening and Farming*, July 1959, 33.

63 Each of these letters can be found in "Response to Poison Spray Survey," *Organic Gardening and Farming*, September 1959, 6.

64 Jerome Olds, "What to Do in a Spray Emergency," *Organic Gardening and Farming*, November 1959, 44. Jerome Olds was the pseudonym used by long-time Rodale editor Jerome Goldstein. Goldstein later left the Rodale company and founded *BioCycle* magazine.

65 The public relations efforts included vice president Richard Nixon eating cranberry sauce on camera. For an introduction to this story, see Christopher J. Bosso, *Pesticides and Politics: The Life Cycle of a Public Issue* (Pittsburgh, PA: University of Pittsburgh Press, 1987), 96–100.

66 J. I. Rodale, "Cranberries," *Organic Gardening and Farming*, March 1960, 21–24; Winston, *Nature Wars*, 159–160.

67 On the publication and reception of Carson's book, see Priscilla Coit Murphy, *What a Book Can Do: The Publication and Reception of Silent Spring* (Amherst: University of Massachusetts Press, 2005). For an overview of the book's relationship to the environmental movement, see Mark H. Lytle, *The Gentle Subversive: Rachel Carson, Silent Spring, and the Rise of the Environmental Movement* (New York: Oxford University Press, 2007).

68 "Organic World: Short Notes from All Over," *Organic Gardening and Farming*, February 1960, 2.

69 "Organic World: Chemicals from Birth to Death," *Organic Gardening*, September 1962, 2; Robert Rodale, "Rachel Carson's Masterpiece," *Organic Gardening and Farming*, September 1962, 17–19.

70 Jerome Olds, "The New Year and 'Silent Spring,'" *Organic Gardening and Farming*, December 1962, 14. See also "Organic World: The Reaction Has Begun," *Organic Gardening and Farming*, October 1962, 2.

71 J. I. Rodale, "Adventures in Self-Analysis towards Health," *Prevention*, May 1951, 38–43.

72 J. I. Rodale, "Nature in Action," *Organic Gardening and Farming*, August 1959, 15; "Out of the Mailbag," *Prevention*, June 1955, 94–98.

73 J. I. Rodale, "Notes on Biography," n.d., Box 265, "J. I. Autobiography," Rodale Press Archives, Emmaus, Pennsylvania (hereafter RPA).

74 J. I. Rodale, "Founder's Day Speech, 1966," n.d., ibid.

75 J. I. Rodale, "Twenty Years Ago," *Organic Gardening and Farming*, February 1963, 98–102.

76 Frank Graham Jr. to Carlton Jackson, August 28, 1972; and Shirley Biggs to Carlton Jackson, September 14, 1972, both in Carlton Jackson MSS Box 13, Folder 4 "Rodale Anecdotes," KBM; "Organic Gardening Reader Survey Response of Rachel Carson," n.d., Folder 5 "Miscellaneous," KBM. Jackson claims that some of Carson's supporters felt Rodale tried to "cash in" on

Carson's fame and success. See Carlton Jackson, *J. I. Rodale: Apostle of Non-conformity* (New York: Pyramid, 1974), 242.

77 Carlton Jackson, "Robert Rodale Interview," Box 17, "Miscellaneous Notes," KBM.

78 "Organic World: Organizing the Opposition," *Organic Gardening and Farming*, April 1963, 2.

79 Robert Rodale, "1963: A Year for Action," *Organic Gardening and Farming*, September 1963, 16.

80 Robert Rodale, "Our Shabby Treatment of Migrant Farm Workers," *Organic Gardening and Farming*, November 1963, 17–19.

81 "Our Poisoned Earth and Sky (Advertisement)," *Organic Gardening and Farming*, April 1964, 96.

82 Robert Rodale, "The Next 25 Years," *Organic Gardening and Farming*, May 1967, 25.

83 Ibid., 26.

84 "Table of Contents," *Organic Gardening and Farming*, June 1968, 4.

85 "Organic World: Short Notes from All Over," *Organic Gardening and Farming*, June 1968, 3; Jerome Olds, "Do We Really Want Pollution Control?" *Organic Gardening and Farming*, June 1968, 78.

86 Hays, *Beauty, Health, and Permanence*, 427–90.

87 Robert Rodale, "Is Conservation in the Constitution?" *Organic Gardening and Farming*, March 1968, 34–35.

88 Robert Rodale, "Vote Organically This Fall," *Organic Gardening and Farming*, November 1968, 19.

89 Ibid., 21.

90 Robert Rodale, "Chemical Fertilizers Cause New Concern," *Organic Gardening and Farming*, March 1969, 31. See also Maurice Franz, "Inorganic Nitrates Threaten Health and Cause Widespread Pollution," *Organic Gardening and Farming*, March 1968.

91 Barry Commoner to Carlton Jackson, October 17, 1972, Carlton Jackson MSS Box 13, Folder 2 "J. I. Rodale Apostle of Nonconformity—Correspondence Jan. 26, 1971–Dec. 29, 1972," KBM; on Commoner's ideas about science and expertise, see Michael Egan, *Barry Commoner and the Science of Survival: The Remaking of American Environmentalism* (Cambridge, MA: MIT Press, 2007), 109–38.

92 Robert Rodale, "Are We Prisoners of Technology?" *Organic Gardening and Farming*, December 1965, 17.

93 Rodale Robert, "Your Garden in the Year 2000," *Organic Gardening and Farming*, June 1966, 21.

94 Robert Rodale, "How Big Is the Organic Idea?" *Organic Gardening and Farming*, October 1968, 19–20.

95 Robert Rodale, "Your Garden Is on the Front Line," *Organic Gardening and Farming*, October 1969, 21, 24.

96   Jerome Olds, "Organic Living for Half a Million People," *Organic Gardening and Farming*, March 1970, 41.

97   See *Rodale's Environmental Action Bulletin*, June 2, 1970.

98   "Santa Barbara Group Builds Eco-Center, Grows Victory Garden," *Rodale's Environmental Action Bulletin*, September 5, 1970, 5; "Guide for Eco-Action Groups," *Rodale's Environmental Action Bulletin*, October 31, 1970.

99   "National Network of Ecology Centers Is Developed at St. Louis Meeting," *Rodale's Environmental Action Bulletin*, December 19, 1970, 2–3.

100 "Organic Foods Symposium Reveals Rapidly-Expanding Market Demand," *Rodale's Environmental Action Bulletin*, June 6, 1970, 2; "How're You Going to Keep Them Down on the Farm?" *Rodale's Environmental Action Bulletin*, June 6, 1970, 3.

101 "The Social Significance of Organic Foods," *Rodale's Environmental Action Bulletin*, June 6, 1970, 2.

102 Robert Rodale, "Prevention Is One Man: J. I. Rodale," *Prevention*, June 1970, 140–51.

103 Rodale, "Founder's Day Speech, 1966."

104 J. I. Rodale, "Organic Food and Health," *Organic Gardening and Farming*, December 1970, 106.

105 Eleanor Perényi, "Apostle of the Compost Heap," *Saturday Evening Post*, July 30, 1966, 31–33.

106 Eleanor Perényi, *Green Thoughts: A Writer in the Garden* (New York: Vintage, 1981), 41–46.

107 James J. Kilpatrick, "Bureaucrats in Stew over Food Fad Book," *Miami Herald*, August 21, 1965.

108 Peter Tonge, "'Cabbages as Big as Basketballs,'" *Christian Science Monitor*, April 3, 1971.

109 Rodale, "Prevention Is One Man," 140.

110 Gay Bryant, "J. I. Rodale: Pollution Prophet," *Penthouse*, June 1971, 42.

111 Wade Greene, "Guru of the Organic Food Cult," *New York Times Magazine*, June 6, 1971, 31.

112 Ibid., 54–57; Perényi, *Green Thoughts*.

113 *A World of Sense: The Life Journey of Bob Rodale*, directed by Scott Schmidt (Emmaus, PA: Rodale Productions, 1994), VHS.

114 Dick Cavett, "When That Guy Died on My Show," *New York Times Opinionator*, May 3, 2007.

CHAPTER FOUR: ORGANIC LIVING

1   *Our Roots Grow Deep* (Emmaus, PA: Rodale, 2009), 155.

2   John O'Rourke, "'Hip' to Health Foods," *Organic Gardening and Farming*, October 1969, 60–62. Euell Gibbons had a monthly column in *OG&F* for many years called the "Organic Nature Lover." For a classic profile of Gibbons, see

John McPhee, *A Roomful of Hovings and Other Profiles*, 5th ed. (New York: Farrar, Straus and Giroux, 1979), 65–118.

3   Sam Binkley, *Getting Loose: Lifestyle Consumption in the 1970s* (Durham, NC: Duke University Press, 2007), 116–26.

4   Wade Greene, "Guru of the Organic Food Cult," *New York Times Magazine*, June 6, 1971, 68.

5   Robert Rodale, "Relieve Tension," *Washington Post*, September 16, 1971, sec. D; Robert Rodale, "Organic Living: Get Close to Nature," *Salt Lake Tribune*, September 12, 1971, Sunday ed. These two columns are the same, but only the *Tribune* version features the phrase "fight tension organically."

6   Robert Rodale, "An Ecology Test," *Washington Post*, May 16, 1972, sec. C.

7   Robert Rodale, "What Air Pollution Is Doing to Your Head, Heart, Eyes . . . ," *Washington Post*, March 9, 1972, sec. C.

8   Robert Rodale, "Letters Can Lead the Way to Organic Living," *Washington Post*, May 18, 1972, sec. D.

9   Robert Rodale, *Sane Living in a Mad World: A Guide to the Organic Way of Life* (Emmaus, PA: Rodale Press, 1972), 258–60.

10   Greene, "Guru of the Organic Food Cult," 68.

11   Rodale, *Sane Living in a Mad World*, 44–45.

12   Ibid., ix–xiv.

13   "'Organic Living': Special Section in Every Issue," *Organic Gardening and Farming*, October 1973, 4.

14   M. C. Goldman, "New Guide to the Back-to-the-Kitchen Movement," *Organic Gardening and Farming*, October 1973, 82.

15   Nancy Albright, *The Rodale Cookbook* (Emmaus, PA: Rodale Press, 1973), 7.

16   Goldman, "New Guide to the Back-to-the-Kitchen Movement," 84.

17   Carol Hupping Stoner, ed., *Stocking Up: How to Preserve the Foods You Grow, Naturally* (Emmaus, PA: Rodale Press, 1973), xi.

18   Robert Rodale, "Seeking a Better Way," *Organic Gardening and Farming*, April 1975, 47.

19   Ibid., 49.

20   Ibid., 46.

21   Ibid., 47.

22   Staff of *Environmental Action Bulletin*, Staff of *Organic Gardening and Farming*, and Staff of *Fitness for Living*, *The Organic Guide to Colleges and Universities* (Emmaus, PA: Rodale Press, 1973), 81.

23   Thomas Fegeley and Bud Souders, *The Organic Classroom: Introduction to Environmental Education the Organic Way, an Interdisciplinary Approach*, ed. Rita Reemer (Emmaus, PA: Rodale Press, n.d.), 1–2.

24   Jerome Goldstein, "Organic Force," in *The New Food Chain: An Organic Link between Farm and City*, ed. Jerome Goldstein (Emmaus, PA: Rodale Books, 1973), 2.

25   On the emergence of self-liberation from the social movements of the 1960s,

see Bruce J. Schulman, *The Seventies: The Great Shift in American Culture, Society, and Politics* (Cambridge, MA: Da Capo Press, 2002), 78–101; Debra Michals, "From 'Consciousness Expansion' to 'Consciousness Raising': Feminism and the Countercultural Politics of the Self," in *Imagine Nation: The American Counterculture of the 1960s and '70s*, ed. Peter Braunstein and Michael William Doyle (New York: Routledge, 2002), 41–68.

26 Michael Sobel, *Lifestyle and Social Structure: Concepts, Definitions, Analyses* (New York: Academic Press, 1981), 28; Annamarie Jagose, "The Invention of Lifestyle," in *Interpreting Everyday Culture*, ed. Fran Martin (London: Arnold, 2003), 110.

27 On the transformation of the magazine industry see John William Tebbel and Mary Ellen Zuckerman, *The Magazine in America, 1741–1990* (New York: Oxford University Press, 1991), 243–65. For the end of mass-market periodicals, see Stephen Holder, "The Death of the *Saturday Evening Post*, 1960–1969: A Popular Culture Phenomenon," in *New Dimensions in Popular Culture*, ed. Russel B. Nye (Bowling Green, OH: Bowling Green University Popular Press, 1972), 78–89; David Abrahamson and Carol Polsgrove, "The Right Niche: Consumer Magazines and Advertisers," in *A History of the Book in America: The Enduring Book: Print Culture in Postwar America*, vol. 5, ed. David Paul Nord, Joan Shelley Rubin, and Michael Schudson (Chapel Hill: University of North Carolina Press, 2009), 107–18.

28 Theodore Peterson, *Magazines in the Twentieth Century*, 2nd ed. (Urbana: University of Illinois Press, 1964); David Abrahamson, *Magazine-Made America: The Cultural Transformation of the Postwar Periodical* (Cresskill, NJ: Hampton Press, 1996), 19–31.

29 Lizabeth Cohen, *A Consumers' Republic: The Politics of Mass Consumption in Postwar America* (New York: Vintage, 2003), 292–309.

30 The most comprehensive overview of the development of lifestyle research in marketing is Patrick T. Wehner, "Living in Style: Marketing, Media, and the Discovery of Lifestyles" (PhD diss., Emory University, 2000), 88–120. For an introduction to lifestyle marketing application to business, see Bernard Cathelat, *Socio-Lifestyles Marketing: The New Science of Identifying, Classifying, and Targeting Consumers Worldwide* (Chicago: Probus, 1994).

31 Laurence P. Feldman, "Societal Adaptation: A New Challenge for Marketing," *Journal of Marketing* 35, no. 3 (1971): 59.

32 Leslie M. Dawson, "The Human Concept: New Philosophy for Business," *Business Horizons*, December 1969, 29.

33 Ibid., 36.

34 Wehner, "Living in Style," 133–35.

35 William Lazer, "Life Style Concepts and Marketing," in *Proceedings of the Winter Conference of the American Marketing Association* (Chicago: American Marketing Association, 1963), 130.

36 William Lazer, "Marketing's Changing Social Relationships," *Journal of Marketing* 33, no. 1 (1969): 4.

37 Jerome Goldstein, *How to Manage Your Company Ecologically* (Emmaus, PA: Rodale Press, 1971), 11.

38 Ibid., 15.

39 Jerome Goldstein, "Are We Burying the Organic Food Industry?" *Organic Gardening and Farming*, September 1972, 45.

40 Goldstein, "Organic Force," 26.

41 Jennifer Price, *Flight Maps: Adventures with Nature in Modern America* (New York: Basic Books, 2000), 198.

42 Chris Roberts, "Publisher Taps Goldmine in 'How-to-Do-It' Books," *Gazette Telegraph*, April 28, 1977, sec. B.

43 *Our Roots Grow Deep*, 162–64.

44 Roberts, "Publisher Taps Goldmine in 'How-to-Do-It' Books."

45 "Most Book Clubs Promise You Big Savings . . . ," *Organic Gardening and Farming*, January 1971, 80.

46 Reprinted in Joan Throckmorton, *Winning Direct Response Advertising: How to Recognize It, Evaluate It, Inspire It, Create It* (Englewood Cliffs, NJ: Prentice Hall, 1986), 235–38.

47 Walter Weintz, *The Solid Gold Mailbox: How to Create Winning Mail-Order Campaigns* (New York: Wiley, 1987), 1–3.

48 Ibid., 11.

49 Janice A. Radway, *Reading the Romance: Women, Patriarchy, and Popular Literature* (Chapel Hill: University of North Carolina Press, 1991), 55; Frank Leopold Schick, *The Paperbound Book in America: The History of Paperbacks and Their European Background* (New York: R. R. Bowker, 1958), 48–50.

50 William Goldstein, "A Healthy Staff Makes for Healthy Profits: That's the Organic Approach at Rodale," *Publishers Weekly*, November 5, 1982, 54.

51 Ibid.

52 Ibid., 54–55.

53 Ibid., 55.

54 Editors of *Prevention*, *Healing with Nature* (Emmaus, PA: Rodale Press, 1979); *Prevention's Quick and Natural Kitchen Medicine* (Emmaus, PA: Rodale Press, 1979), Pamphlet Collection, Rodale Press Archives, Emmaus, Pennsylvania. Many of these types of small booklets do not contain an ISBN number, and aside from cover art and an introduction they largely recycle previously published content from other Rodale books.

55 Goldstein, "Healthy Staff Makes for Healthy Profits," 55. Bricklin's natural health encyclopedias are a clear demonstration of how the press cultivated its relationship with readers to develop products. The books are largely based on tips and folk-wisdom that readers sent to the press over the years interspersed with evidence from medical sources and organized around themes.

56 Research Department of *Prevention*, *Health Food Store Shoppers: A Lifestyle and Product Usage Profile* (Emmaus, PA: Rodale Press, n.d.), introduction. See also

Research Department of *Prevention, Diet as a Lifestyle: A Profile of American Women* (Emmaus, PA: Rodale Press, 1983).

57 David Bell and Joanne Hollows, "Making Sense of Ordinary Lifestyles," in *Ordinary Lifestyles: Popular Media, Consumption and Taste*, ed. David Bell and Joanne Hollows (New York: Open University Press, 2005), 5; Anthony Giddens, *Modernity and Self Identity: Self and Society in the Late Modern Age* (Cambridge, UK: Polity Press, 1991); Mike Featherstone, "Lifestyle and Consumer Culture," *Theory, Culture & Society* 4, no. 1 (1987): 55–70; Douglas B. Holt, "Poststructuralist Lifestyle Analysis: Conceptualizing the Social Patterning of Consumption in Postmodernity," *Journal of Consumer Research* 23, no. 4 (1997): 326–50; Cathelat, *Socio-Lifestyles Marketing*; David Bell and Joanne Hollows, eds., *Historicizing Lifestyle: Mediating Taste, Consumption, and Identity from the 1900s to 1970s* (Burlington, VT: Ashgate, 2006).

58 Nancy Bubel, *Have a Natural Christmas* (Emmaus, PA: Rodale Press, 1979). These pamphlets were produced and distributed yearly in the late 1970s and early 1980s. The company also produced a woodworking and quilting magazine at this time.

59 Juliet B. Schor, "In Defense of Consumer Critique: Revisiting the Consumption Debates of the Twentieth Century," *Annals of the American Academy of Political and Social Science* 611, no. 1 (2007): 25.

CHAPTER FIVE: A WHOLE NEW YOU

1 Bernice Kanner, "Rich and Wholesome," *New York*, May 10, 1982, 19.

2 Cornucopia Project of the Rodale Press, *Empty Breadbasket? The Coming Challenge to America's Food Supply and What We Can Do about It* (Emmaus, PA: Rodale Press, 1981), 158.

3 Paul K. Conkin, *A Revolution Down on the Farm: The Transformation of American Agriculture since 1929* (Louisville: University Press of Kentucky, 2008), 132–34.

4 On Wendell Berry's relationship to the Rodale Press, see Jeffrey M. Filipiak, "Learning from the Land: Wendell Berry and Wes Jackson on Knowledge and Nature" (PhD diss., University of Michigan, 2004), 305–22.

5 "Advertisement: Grow Healthier with Us!" *New Farm*, January 1979, 81.

6 "Advertisement: The Only Place You'll Find the Non-chemical Point of View!" *New Farm*, January 1981, 69.

7 USDA Study Team on Organic Farming, *Report and Recommendations on Organic Farming Prepared by USDA Study Team on Organic Farming, United States Department of Agriculture* (Washington, DC: United States Department of Agriculture, 1980).

8 "The Cornucopia Project Newsletter Is Our Response to Your Letters," *Cornucopia Project Newsletter*, n.d., 8, author's collection. This first newsletter of

the Cornucopia Project carried no date but was sent to those who responded to the company's advertorials in the fall of 1980.

9   Robert Rodale, "Shaping Our Food Future," in *The Cornucopia Project Symposium*, ed. Brenda Bortz (Emmaus, PA: Cornucopia Project of Rodale Press, 1981), 11.

10 "Cornucopia Action," *Cornucopia Project Newsletter*, Winter 1981, 1, author's collection.

11 Robert Rodale, "A Look at Our Past—and Our Plans for the Future," *Soil and Health News*, November 1982, 3–4.

12 Tom Ferguson, "A Conversation with Robert Rodale," *Medical Self-Care*, Fall 1984, 43.

13 Pamela Pietri Lawrence, "Robert Rodale Shapes Up a Flabby Society," *Adweek: Magazine Report*, February 1982, M.R. 64.

14 "Advertisement: SOS . . . an Urgent Message from Organic Gardening," *Organic Gardening*, June 1983, 73.

15 *Our Roots Grow Deep* (Emmaus, PA: Rodale, 2009), 168.

16 "Rodale Reaches Out for the Mainstream," *Business Week*, October 27, 1980, 85. For a humorous look at Rodale at the end of the 1970s, see Calvin Trillin, "U.S. Journal: Emmaus, Pa.: Mowing the Lawn," *New Yorker*, December 10, 1979, 164–74.

17 "Rodale Reaches Out for the Mainstream," 85.

18 Ibid.

19 "Prevention Comes Out on Top in 'Cost Per Mind,'" *Food and Beverage Marketing* 2, no. 10 (1983): 25.

20 Kanner, "Rich and Wholesome," 18.

21 Gretchen Ewing, "Marketing Gets Rodale's 'Spring' off to Good Start," *Morning Call*, April 5, 1982, 3.

22 Lawrence, "Robert Rodale Shapes Up a Flabby Society," 66.

23 Francis Davis, "Men's Health: Direct Mail Marketing Campaign," in *Encyclopedia of Major Marketing Campaigns*, ed. Thomas Riggs (Farmington, MI: Gale Group, 2000), 1534–37. On "new" men's magazines see Peter Jackson, Nick Stevenson, and Kate Brooks, *Making Sense of Men's Magazines* (Malden, MA: Blackwell, 2001), 1–18, 74–102.

24 Scott Donaton, "Boys Will Be Boys but, Says 'Men's Health,' It's No Fad," *Advertising Age*, March 7, 1994, 3S; Shaifali Puri, "Men's Health Advises and Conquers," *Fortune*, January 12, 1992, 40; Halie Mummert, "Rodale Press: Naturally Successful," *Target Marketing*, March 1994, 10.

25 *Men in the Marketplace: A Reflection of Changing Social Roles in America* (Emmaus, PA: Men's Health, 1989), 2, 17, 19.

26 Robert Crawford, "Healthism and the Medicalization of Everyday Life," *International Journal of Health Services: Planning, Administration, Evaluation* 10, no. 3 (1980): 365–88.

27 Julie Guthman, *Weighing In: Obesity, Food Justice, and the Limits of Capitalism* (Berkeley: University of California Press, 2011), 52–56.

28 Robert Rodale, "Pesticides and You," *Rodale's Organic Gardening*, January 1988, 18–19.

29 Lawrie Mott and Karen Snyder, "Pesticide Alert," *Organic Gardening*, June 1988, 78.

30 Bradford H. Sewell, Robin M. Whyatt, and Natural Resources Defense Council, *Intolerable Risk: Pesticides in Our Children's Food: Summary* (New York: Natural Resources Defense Council, 1989); "How a PR Firm Executed the Alar Scare," *Wall Street Journal*, October 3, 1989.

31 James C. McCullagh, "A Mother's Crusade," *Organic Gardening*, April 1989, 35.

32 Finis Dunaway, *Seeing Green: The Use and Abuse of American Environmental Images* (Chicago: University of Chicago Press, 2015), 210–22.

33 Sonia L. Nazario, "Big Firms Get High on Organic Farming: Pesticide Scare Reinforces Shift in Techniques," *Wall Street Journal*, March 21, 1989.

34 Julie Guthman, *Agrarian Dreams: The Paradox of Organic Farming in California* (Berkeley: University of California Press, 2004), 113.

35 Louis Harris and Associates, *2nd Annual Organic Index: Tracking America's Preference for Organic Food and a Clean Environment* (Emmaus, PA: Rodale Press, 1990), 1.

36 Ibid., 3.

37 Ibid.

38 Dunaway, *Seeing Green*, 187–89.

CONCLUSION: A CONSUMING VISION

1 Bob Whitman, "The Person of the Century: Robert Rodale," *Morning Call*, January 1, 2000; Amaranth Conference and Rodale Press, *Proceedings of the Second Amaranth Conference* (Emmaus, PA: Rodale Press, 1980); John N. Cole, *Amaranth, from the Past for the Future* (Emmaus, PA: Rodale Press, 1979).

2 Robert Rodale, "The Compost Revolution," *Organic Gardening*, August 1983, 27.

3 Deirdre Carmody, "Rodale's Soviet Venture: Sausages and a Magazine," *New York Times*, February 11, 1991.

4 Ibid.

5 For the origins of this term, see Paul Hawkin, Amory Lovins, and L. Hunter Lovins, *Natural Capitalism: Creating the Next Industrial Revolution* (New York: Little, Brown and Company, 1999).

6 See *Organic Gardening*, February–March 2015.

7 Derek Thompson, "The Print Apocalypse and How to Survive It," *The Atlantic*, November 3, 2016.

8   Rodale Inc., "About Us," accessed June 23, 2017, www.rodale.com/about-us.

9   See Rodale Inc., "Home," accessed June 23, 2017, www.rodales.com.

10   US Department of Agriculture, Economic Research Service, "Organic Market Overview," accessed June 23, 2017, https://www.ers.usda.gov/topics /natural-resources-environment/organic-agriculture/organic-market -overview.

SELECTED BIBLIOGRAPHY

MANUSCRIPT COLLECTIONS

Carlton Jackson Papers. Kentucky Building Manuscripts Collection. Western Kentucky University, Bowling Green.
Historical Health Fraud Collection. American Medical Association, Chicago.
Rodale Family and Press Archives, Emmaus, Pennsylvania.

RODALE PERIODICALS

Organic Gardening
Organic Gardening and Farming
Prevention
Rodale's Environmental Action Bulletin

BOOKS, ARTICLES, AND DISSERTATIONS

Abrahamson, David. *Magazine-Made America: The Cultural Transformation of the Postwar Periodical*. Cresskill, NJ: Hampton Press, 1996.
Abrahamson, David, and Carol Polsgrove. "The Right Niche: Consumer Magazines and Advertisers." In *A History of the Book in America: The Enduring Book: Print Culture in Postwar America*, vol. 5, edited by David Paul Nord, Joan Shelley Rubin, and Michael Schudson, 107–18. Chapel Hill: University of North Carolina Press, 2009.
Ackerman, Michael. "Science and the Shadow of Ideology in the American Health Foods Movement, 1930s–1960s." In *The Politics of Healing: Histories of Alternative Medicine in Twentieth-Century North America*, edited by Robert D. Johnston, 55–70. New York: Routledge, 2004.
Adams, Mark. *Mr. America: How Muscular Millionaire Bernarr Macfadden Transformed the Nation through Sex, Salad, and the Ultimate Starvation Diet*. New York: HarperCollins, 2009.
Albright, Nancy. *The Rodale Cookbook*. Emmaus, PA: Rodale Press, 1973.
Amaranth Conference and Rodale Press. *Proceedings of the Second Amaranth Conference*. Emmaus, PA: Rodale Press, 1980.

Apple, Rima D. *Vitamania: Vitamins in American Culture*. New Brunswick, NJ: Rutgers University Press, 1996.

Baldwin, Davarian. *Chicago's New Negroes: Modernity, the Great Migration, and Black Urban Life*. Chapel Hill: University of North Carolina Press, 2007.

Barton, Gregory. "Sir Albert Howard and the Forestry Roots of the Organic Farming Movement." *Agricultural History* 75, no. 2 (2001): 168–87.

Beck, Ulrich. *Ecological Enlightenment: Essays on the Politics of the Risk Society*. Atlantic Highlands, NJ: Humanities Press, 1995.

Beeman, Randal. "The Trash Farmer: Edward Faulkner and the Origins of Sustainable Agriculture in the United States, 1943–1953." *Journal of Sustainable Agriculture* 4, no. 1 (1993): 91–102.

Beeman, Randal, and James A. Pritchard. *A Green and Permanent Land: Ecology and Agriculture in the Twentieth Century*. Lawrence: University Press of Kansas, 2001.

Belasco, Warren J. *Appetite for Change: How the Counterculture Took on the Food Industry, 1966–1988*. New York: Pantheon, 1989.

Bell, David, and Joanne Hollows, eds. *Historicizing Lifestyle: Mediating Taste, Consumption, and Identity from the 1900s to 1970s*. Burlington, VT: Ashgate, 2006.

———. "Making Sense of Ordinary Lifestyles." In *Ordinary Lifestyles: Popular Media, Consumption and Taste*, edited by David Bell and Joanne Hollows, 1–20. New York: Open University Press, 2005.

Biggart, Nicole Woolsey. *Charismatic Capitalism: Direct Selling Organizations in America*. Chicago: University of Chicago Press, 1989.

Binkley, Sam. *Getting Loose: Lifestyle Consumption in the 1970s*. Durham, NC: Duke University Press, 2007.

Blum, Barton. "Composting and the Roots of Sustainable Agriculture." *Agricultural History* 66, no. 2 (1992): 171–88.

Bosso, Christopher J. *Pesticides and Politics: The Life Cycle of a Public Issue*. Pittsburgh: University of Pittsburgh Press, 1987.

Brandt, Allan, and Martha Gardener. "The Golden Age of Medicine?" In *Medicine in the Twentieth Century*, edited by Roger Cooter and John Pickstone, 22–26. Amsterdam: Harwood Academic Publishers, 2000.

Bromfield, Louis. *Out of the Earth*. 1950. Reprint, Wooster, OH: Wooster Book Co., 2003.

Brown, Dona. *Back to the Land: The Enduring Dream of Self-Sufficiency in Modern America*. Madison: University of Wisconsin Press, 2011.

Bryant, Gay. "J. I. Rodale: Pollution Prophet." *Penthouse*, June 1971.

Bubel, Nancy. *Have a Natural Christmas*. Emmaus, PA: Rodale Press, 1979.

Buhs, Joshua Blu. *The Fire Ant Wars: Nature, Science, and Public Policy in Twentieth-Century America*. Chicago: University of Chicago Press, 2010.

Burnham, John C. "American Medicine's Golden Age: What Happened to It?" In *Sickness and Health in America: Readings in the History of Medicine and Public*

Health, 3rd ed., edited by Ronald L. Numbers and Judith W. Leavitt, 284–88. Madison: University of Wisconsin Press, 1997.

Carmody, Deirdre. "Rodale's Soviet Venture: Sausages and a Magazine." *New York Times*, February 11, 1991.

Cathelat, Bernard. *Socio-Lifestyles Marketing: The New Science of Identifying, Classifying, and Targeting Consumers Worldwide*. Chicago: Probus, 1994.

Cavett, Dick. "When That Guy Died on My Show." *New York Times Opinionator*, May 3, 2007.

Cohen, Lizabeth. *A Consumers' Republic: The Politics of Mass Consumption in Postwar America*. New York: Vintage, 2003.

Cole, John N. *Amaranth, from the Past for the Future*. Emmaus, PA: Rodale Press, 1979.

Conford, Philip. *The Origins of the Organic Movement*. Edinburgh: Floris Books, 2001.

Conkin, Paul K. *A Revolution Down on the Farm: The Transformation of American Agriculture since 1929*. Louisville: University Press of Kentucky, 2008.

Cornucopia Project of the Rodale Press. *Empty Breadbasket? The Coming Challenge to America's Food Supply and What We Can Do about It*. Emmaus, PA: Rodale Press, 1981.

Crane, Jeff, and Michael Egan, eds. *Natural Protest: Essays on the History of American Environmentalism*. New York: Routledge, 2009.

Crawford, Robert. "Healthism and the Medicalization of Everyday Life," *International Journal of Health Services: Planning, Administration, Evaluation* 10, no. 3 (1980): 365–88.

Daniel, Pete. *Toxic Drift: Pesticides and Health in the Post–World War II South*. Baton Rouge: Louisiana State University Press, 2007.

Davis, Devra. *The Secret History of the War on Cancer*. New York: Basic Books, 2009.

Davis, Francis. "Men's Health: Direct Mail Marketing Campaign." In *Encyclopedia of Major Marketing Campaigns*, edited by Thomas Riggs, 1534–37. Farmington, MI: Gale Group, 2000.

Dawson, Leslie M. "The Human Concept: New Philosophy for Business." *Business Horizons*, December 1969.

Drake, Brian Allen. *Loving Nature, Fearing the State: Environmentalism and Antigovernment Politics before Reagan*. Seattle: University of Washington Press, 2013.

Dunaway, Finis. *Seeing Green: The Use and Abuse of American Environmental Images*. Chicago: University of Chicago Press, 2015.

Eco, Umberto. *The Role of the Reader: Explorations in the Semiotics of Texts*. Bloomington: Indiana University Press, 1979.

Egan, Michael. *Barry Commoner and the Science of Survival: The Remaking of American Environmentalism*. Cambridge, MA: MIT Press, 2007.

Eglash, Ron. "Appropriating Technology: An Introduction." In *Appropriating Technology: Vernacular Science and Social Power*, edited by Ron Eglash, Jennifer L. Croissant, Giovanna Di Chiro, and Rayvon Fouché, 5–32. Minneapolis: University of Minnesota Press, 2004.

Ernst, Robert. *Weakness Is a Crime: The Life of Bernarr Macfadden*. Syracuse, NY: Syracuse University Press, 1991.

Featherstone, Mike. "Lifestyle and Consumer Culture." *Theory, Culture & Society* 4, no. 1 (1987): 55–70.

Fegeley, Thomas, and Bud Souders. *The Organic Classroom: Introduction to Environmental Education the Organic Way, an Interdisciplinary Approach*. Edited by Rita Reemer. Emmaus, PA: Rodale Press, n.d.

Feldman, Laurence P. "Societal Adaptation: A New Challenge for Marketing." *Journal of Marketing* 35, no. 3 (1971): 54–60.

Filipiak, Jeffrey M. "Learning from the Land: Wendell Berry and Wes Jackson on Knowledge and Nature." PhD diss., University of Michigan, 2004.

Fishbein, Morris. *Fads and Quackery in Healing: An Analysis of the Foibles of the Healing Cults, with Essays on Various Other Peculiar Notions in the Health Field*. New York: Blue Ribbon Books, 1932.

Frank, Dana. *Purchasing Power: Consumer Organizing, Gender, and the Seattle Labor Movement, 1919–1929*. New York: Cambridge University Press, 1994.

Fromartz, Samuel. *Organic, Inc.: Natural Foods and How They Grew*. Orlando, FL: Harcourt, 2006.

Frye, Joshua J. "The Transnational Origin, Diffusion, and Transformation of 'Organic' Agriculture: A Study in Social Movement Framing and Outcomes." PhD diss., Purdue University, 2007.

Giddens, Anthony. *Modernity and Self Identity: Self and Society in the Late Modern Age*. Cambridge, UK: Polity Press, 1991.

Glickman, Lawrence B. *Buying Power: A History of Consumer Activism in America*. Chicago: University of Chicago Press, 2009.

Goldstein, Jerome. *How to Manage Your Company Ecologically*. Emmaus, PA: Rodale Press, 1971.

———. "Organic Force." In *The New Food Chain: An Organic Link Between Farm and City*, edited by Jerome Goldstein, 1–19. Emmaus, PA: Rodale Books, 1973.

Goldstein, William. "A Healthy Staff Makes for Healthy Profits: That's the Organic Approach at Rodale." *Publisher's Weekly*, November 5, 1982.

Gottlieb, Robert. *Forcing the Spring: The Transformation of the American Environmental Movement*. Rev ed. Washington, DC: Island Press, 2005.

Gould, Rebecca Kneale. *At Home in Nature: Modern Homesteading and Spiritual Practice in America*. Berkeley: University of California Press, 2005.

Greene, Wade. "Guru of the Organic Food Cult." *New York Times Magazine*, June 6, 1971.

Guide to the American Medical Association Historical Health Fraud and Alternative Medicine Collection. Chicago: American Medical Association, 1992.

Guthman, Julie. *Agrarian Dreams: The Paradox of Organic Farming in California.* Berkeley: University of California Press, 2004.

———. *Weighing In: Obesity, Food Justice, and the Limits of Capitalism.* Berkeley: University of California Press, 2011.

Hays, Samuel P. *Beauty, Health, and Permanence: Environmental Politics in the United States, 1955–1985.* New York: Cambridge University Press, 1989.

Heidenry, John. *Theirs Was the Kingdom: Lila and Dewitt Wallace and the Story of Reader's Digest.* New York: Norton, 1993.

Hillel, Daniel J. *Out of the Earth: Civilization and the Life of the Soil.* New York: Free Press, 1991.

Hilts, Philip J. *Protecting America's Health: The FDA, Business, and One Hundred Years of Regulation.* New York: Knopf, 2003.

Holder, Stephen. "The Death of the *Saturday Evening Post*, 1960–1969: A Popular Culture Phenomenon." In *New Dimensions in Popular Culture*, edited by Russel B. Nye, 78–89. Bowling Green, OH: Bowling Green University Popular Press, 1972.

Holt, Douglas B. "Poststructuralist Lifestyle Analysis: Conceptualizing the Social Patterning of Consumption in Postmodernity." *Journal of Consumer Research* 23, no. 4 (1997): 326–50.

House Select Committee to Investigate the Use of Chemicals in Food Products. *Chemicals in Food Products: Hearings Before the House Select Committee to Investigate the Use of Chemicals in Food Products.* Washington, DC: Government Printing Office, 1951.

Howard, Albert. *The Soil and Health: A Study of Organic Agriculture.* New York: Devin-Adair, 1947.

Howard, Louise E. *Sir Albert Howard in India.* London: Faber and Faber, 1953.

Jackson, Carlton. *J. I. Rodale: Apostle of Nonconformity.* New York: Pyramid, 1974.

Jackson, Peter, Nick Stevenson, and Kate Brooks. *Making Sense of Men's Magazines.* Malden, MA: Blackwell, 2001.

Jagose, Annamarie. "The Invention of Lifestyle." In *Interpreting Everyday Culture*, edited by Fran Martin, 109–23. London: Arnold, 2003.

Jones, Geoffrey. *Profits and Sustainability: A History of Green Entrepreneurship.* New York: Oxford University Press, 2017.

Jundt, Thomas. *Greening the Red, White, and Blue: The Bomb, Big Business, and Consumer Resistance in Postwar America.* New York: Oxford University Press, 2014.

Kanner, Bernice. "Rich and Wholesome." *New York*, May 10, 1982.

Kaplan, Michael. "Rodale's New Attitude." *Folio*, November 2000.

King, F. H. *Farmers of Forty Centuries: Permanent Agriculture in China, Korea, and Japan.* 1911. Reprint, Emmaus, PA: Rodale Press, 1990.

Kirk, Andrew G. *Counterculture Green: The Whole Earth Catalog and American Environmentalism.* Lawrence: University Press of Kansas, 2007.

Langston, Nancy. *Toxic Bodies: Hormone Disruptors and the Legacy of DES.* New Haven, CT: Yale University Press, 2011.

Lazer, William. "Life Style Concepts and Marketing." In *Proceedings of the Winter Conference of the American Marketing Association*, 130–39. Chicago: American Marketing Association, 1963.

Lederer, Susan, and Naomi Rodgers. "Media." In *Medicine in the Twentieth Century*, edited by Roger Cooter, and John Pickstone, 487–502. Amsterdam: Harwood Academic Publishers, 2000.

Levine, Lawrence W. *The Unpredictable Past: Explorations in American Cultural History*. New York: Oxford University Press, 1993.

Lord, Russell. "A Cure for Devil's Dust." *New York Times*, December 16, 1945.

Louis Harris and Associates. *2nd Annual Organic Index: Tracking America's Preference for Organic Food and a Clean Environment*. Emmaus, PA: Rodale Press, 1990.

Lytle, Mark H. *The Gentle Subversive: Rachel Carson, Silent Spring, and the Rise of the Environmental Movement*. New York: Oxford University Press, 2007.

Mart, Michelle. *Pesticides, a Love Story: America's Enduring Embrace of Dangerous Chemicals*. Lawrence: University Press of Kansas, 2015.

Men in the Marketplace: A Reflection of Changing Social Roles in America. Emmaus, PA: Men's Health, 1989.

Michals, Debra. "From 'Consciousness Expansion' to 'Consciousness Raising': Feminism and the Countercultural Politics of the Self." In *Imagine Nation: The American Counterculture of the 1960s and '70s*, edited by Peter Braunstein and Michael William Doyle, 41–68. New York: Routledge, 2002.

Mitman, Gregg. *Breathing Space: How Allergies Shape Our Lives and Landscapes*. New Haven, CT: Yale University Press, 2007.

Mitman, Gregg, Michelle Murphy, and Christopher Sellers. "Introduction: A Cloud over History." *Osiris*, 2nd ser., 19 (2004): 1–17.

Mummert, Halie. "Rodale Press: Naturally Successful." *Target Marketing*, March 1994.

Murphy, Michelle. *Sick Building Syndrome and the Problem of Uncertainty: Environmental Politics, Technoscience, and Women Workers*. Durham, NC: Duke University Press, 2006.

Murphy, Priscilla Coit. *What a Book Can Do: The Publication and Reception of Silent Spring*. Amherst: University of Massachusetts Press, 2005.

Nash, Linda. *Inescapable Ecologies: A History of Environment, Disease, and Knowledge*. Berkeley: University of California Press, 2007.

National Congress on Medical Quackery, American Medical Association, and United States Food and Drug Administration. *Proceedings: National Congress on Medical Quackery*. Chicago: American Medical Association, 1962.

——. *Proceedings, Second National Congress on Medical Quackery*. Washington, DC: Government Printing Office, 1963.

Official Transcript of the Proceedings before the Federal Trade Commission, Docket No. 8619, in the Matter of Rodale Press, Inc. (Washington, DC: Ward and Paul, 1964), 160, 177.

Oshinsky, David M. *Polio: An American Story*. Oxford, UK: Oxford University Press, 2005.

O'Sullivan, Robin. *American Organic: A Cultural History of Farming, Gardening, Shopping, and Eating*. Lawrence: University Press of Kansas, 2015.

Perényi, Eleanor. "Apostle of the Compost Heap." *Saturday Evening Post*, July 30, 1966.

———. *Green Thoughts: A Writer in the Garden*. New York: Vintage, 1981.

Peters, Suzanne. "The Land in Trust: A Social History of the Organic Farming Movement." PhD diss., McGill University, 1979.

Peterson, Theodore. *Magazines in the Twentieth Century*. 2nd ed. Urbana: University of Illinois Press, 1964.

Pollan, Michael. *The Omnivore's Dilemma: A Natural History of Four Meals*. New York: Penguin, 2005.

"Prevention Comes Out on Top in 'Cost Per Mind.'" *Food and Beverage Marketing* 2, no. 10 (1983): 25.

Price, Jennifer. *Flight Maps: Adventures with Nature in Modern America*. New ed. New York: Basic Books, 2000.

Proctor, Robert. *Cancer Wars: How Politics Shapes What We Know and Don't Know about Cancer*. New York: Basic Books, 1995.

Puri, Shaifali. "Men's Health Advises and Conquers." *Fortune*, January 12, 1992.

Radway, Janice A. *A Feeling for Books: The Book-of-the-Month Club, Literary Taste, and Middle-Class Desire*. Chapel Hill: University of North Carolina Press, 1997.

———. *Reading the Romance: Women, Patriarchy, and Popular Literature*. Chapel Hill: University of North Carolina Press, 1991.

Randolph, Theron G. *Human Ecology and Susceptibility to the Chemical Environment*. Springfield, IL: C. C. Thomas, 1962.

Reed, Matthew. *Rebels for the Soil: The Rise of the Global Organic Food and Farming Movement*. Washington, DC: Earthscan, 2010.

Research Department of *Prevention*. *Diet as a Lifestyle: A Profile of American Women*. Emmaus, PA: Rodale Press, 1983.

———. *Health Food Store Shoppers: A Lifestyle and Product Usage Profile*. Emmaus, PA: Rodale Press, n.d.

Roberts, Chris. "Publisher Taps Goldmine in 'How-to-Do-It' Books." *Gazette Telegraph*, April 28, 1977.

Rodale, J. I. *Autobiography*. Emmaus, PA: Rodale Press, 1965.

———. *Cancer: Can It Be Prevented?* Emmaus, PA: Rodale Press, 1950.

———. *Facts on Fluoridation*. Emmaus, PA: Rodale Press, 1954.

———. "Introduction to Organic Farming." *Organic Farming and Gardening*, May 1942.

———. *Pay Dirt: Farming and Gardening with Composts*. New York: Devin-Adair, 1945.

———. *Sleep and Rheumatism*. Emmaus, PA: Rodale Press, 1940.

————. *This Pace Is Not Killing Us*. Emmaus, PA: Rodale Press, 1954.

————. *Walk, Do Not Run, to the Doctor*. Emmaus, PA: Rodale Books, 1967.

Rodale, J. I., and Staff. *Our Poisoned Earth and Sky*. Emmaus, PA: Rodale Press, 1964.

————. *Prevention Method for Better Health*. Emmaus, PA: Rodale Books, 1960.

Rodale, Robert. "An Ecology Test." *Washington Post*, May 16, 1972.

————. "Letters Can Lead the Way to Organic Living." *Washington Post*, May 18, 1972.

————. "A Look at Our Past—and Our Plans for the Future." *Soil and Health News*, November 1982.

————. "Organic Living: Get Close to Nature." *Salt Lake Tribune*, September 12, 1971, Sunday ed.

————. "Relieve Tension." *Washington Post*, September 16, 1971.

————. *Sane Living in a Mad World: A Guide to the Organic Way of Life*. Emmaus, PA: Rodale Press, 1972.

————. "Shaping Our Food Future." In *The Cornucopia Project Symposium*, edited by Brenda Bortz, 8–11. Emmaus, PA: Cornucopia Project of Rodale Press, 1981.

————. "What Air Pollution Is Doing to Your Head, Heart, Eyes . . ." *Washington Post*, March 9, 1972.

Rodale Inc. *Our Roots Grow Deep*. Emmaus, PA: Rodale, 2009.

"Rodale Reaches Out for the Mainstream." *Business Week*, October 27, 1980.

Rodgers, Naomi. *Dirt and Disease: Polio before FDR*. New Brunswick, NJ: Rutgers University Press, 1992.

Rome, Adam. *The Bulldozer in the Countryside: Suburban Sprawl and the Rise of American Environmentalism*. New York: Cambridge University Press, 2001.

————. "The Ecology of Commerce: Environmental History and the Challenge of Building a Sustainable Economy." In *Green Capitalism? Business and the Environment in the Twentieth Century*, edited by Adam Rome and Hartmut Berghoff, 3–12. Philadelphia: University of Pennsylvania Press, 2017.

————. *The Genius of Earth Day: How a 1970 Teach-In Made the First Green Generation*. New York: Hill and Wang, 2013.

Rosen, Christine Meisner, and Christopher C. Sellers. "The Nature of the Firm: Towards an Ecocultural History of Business." *Business History Review* 73, no. 4 (1999): 577–600.

Russell, Edmund. *War and Nature: Fighting Humans and Insects with Chemicals from World War I to Silent Spring*. New York: Cambridge University Press, 2001.

Schick, Frank Leopold. *The Paperbound Book in America: The History of Paperbacks and Their European Background*. New York: R. R. Bowker, 1958.

Schor, Juliet B. "In Defense of Consumer Critique: Revisiting the Consumption Debates of the Twentieth Century." *Annals of the American Academy of Political and Social Science* 611, no. 1 (2007): 16–30.

Schulman, Bruce. *The Seventies: The Great Shift in American Culture, Society, and Politics*. Cambridge, MA: Da Capo Press, 2002.

Sellers, Christopher C. "Body, Place, and State: The Making of an 'Environmentalist' Imaginary in the Post–World War II U.S." *Radical History Review* 74 (Spring 1999): 31–64.

———. *Crabgrass Crucible: Suburban Nature and the Rise of Environmentalism in Twentieth-Century America*. Chapel Hill: University of North Carolina Press, 2012.

Sewell, Bradford H., Robin M. Whyatt, and Natural Resources Defense Council. *Intolerable Risk: Pesticides in Our Children's Food*. New York: Natural Resources Defense Council, 1989.

Smith-Howard, Kendra. *Pure and Modern Milk: An Environmental History since 1900*. New York: Oxford University Press, 2014.

Sobel, Michael. *Lifestyle and Social Structure: Concepts, Definitions, Analyses*. New York: Academic Press, 1981.

Staff of *Environmental Action Bulletin*, Staff of *Organic Gardening and Farming*, and Staff of *Fitness for Living*. *The Organic Guide to Colleges and Universities*. Emmaus, PA: Rodale Press, 1973.

Steinberg, Ted. *American Green: The Obsessive Quest for the Perfect Lawn*. New York: Norton, 2007.

Stoll, Steven. *Larding the Lean Earth: Soil and Society in Nineteenth-Century America*. New York: Hill and Wang, 2002.

Stoner, Carol Hupping, ed. *Stocking Up: How to Preserve the Foods You Grow, Naturally*. Emmaus, PA: Rodale Press, 1973.

Stout, Ruth. *The Ruth Stout No-Work Garden Book*. Emmaus, PA: Rodale Press, 1971.

Sutter, Paul. *Driven Wild: How the Fight against Automobiles Launched the Modern Wilderness Movement*. Seattle: University of Washington Press, 2002.

———. *Let Us Now Praise Famous Gullies: Providence Canyon and the Soils of the South*. Athens: University of Georgia Press, 2015.

Szasz, Andrew. *Shopping Our Way to Safety: How We Changed from Protecting the Environment to Protecting Ourselves*. Minneapolis: University of Minnesota Press, 2007.

Tebbel, John William, and Mary Ellen Zuckerman. *The Magazine in America, 1741–1990*. New York: Oxford University Press, 1991.

Throckmorton, Joan. *Winning Direct Response Advertising: How to Recognize It, Evaluate It, Inspire It, Create It*. Englewood Cliffs, NJ: Prentice Hall, 1986.

Tomes, Nancy. *The Gospel of Germs: Men, Women, and the Microbe in American Life*. Cambridge, MA: Harvard University Press, 1998.

———. "Merchants of Health: Medicine and Consumer Culture, 1900–1940." *Journal of American History* 88, no. 2 (2001): 519–47.

Tucker, David M. *Kitchen Gardening in America: A History*. Ames: Iowa State University Press, 1993.

US Congress, Senate, Special Committee on Aging. *Frauds and Quackery Affecting the Older Citizen: Hearings before the Special Committee on Aging,*

United States Senate, Eighty-Eighth Congress, First Session. Washington, DC: Government Printing Office, 1963.

USDA Study Team on Organic Farming. *Report and Recommendations on Organic Farming Prepared by USDA Study Team on Organic Farming, United States Department of Agriculture.* Washington, DC: United States Department of Agriculture, 1980.

Valencius, Conevery Bolton. *The Health of the Country: How American Settlers Understood Themselves and Their Land.* New York: Basic Books, 2002.

Wehner, Patrick T. "Living in Style: Marketing, Media, and the Discovery of Lifestyles." PhD diss., Emory University, 2000.

Weintz, Walter. *The Solid Gold Mailbox: How to Create Winning Mail-Order Campaigns.* New York: Wiley, 1987.

Whitman, Bob. "The Person of the Century: Robert Rodale." *Morning Call,* January 1, 2000.

Whorton, James C. *Before Silent Spring: Pesticides and Public Health in Pre-DDT America.* Princeton, NJ: Princeton University Press, 1975.

———. *Crusaders for Fitness: The History of American Health Reformers.* Princeton, NJ: Princeton University Press, 1984.

———. *Nature Cures: The History of Alternative Medicine in America.* New York: Oxford University Press, 2002.

Williams, Raymond. *Keywords: A Vocabulary of Culture and Society.* Rev. ed. New York: Oxford University Press, 1985.

Winston, Mark L. *Nature Wars: People vs. Pests.* Cambridge, MA: Harvard University Press, 1997.

The World's Happiest Gardeners. Emmaus, PA: Rodale Press, 1959.

Young, James Harvey. *The Medical Messiahs: The History of Health Quackery in Twentieth-Century America.* Princeton, NJ: Princeton University Press, 1967.

INDEX

Abernathy, Thomas, 19

Ackerman, Michael, 115

activism: the Alar scare and its aftermath, 200–201, 202–6, 208; consumers' pocketbook power, 120, 199, 201, 205; the Cornucopia Project and other Rodale organizing efforts of the 1980s, 187–88, 191, 201–2, 208; the Long Island aerial spraying lawsuit, 121–22, 125; personal choices viewed as, 154, 155, 159, 160–61, 179, 211; Rodale calls to action in the 1950s, 99, 118–19, 120, 127; *Rodale's Environmental Action Bulletin*, 139–41, 159; Rodale's organizing role, ix–x, 101–2, 131, 134–35, 139–41. *See also* environmentalism; food systems reform; organic farming advocacy

Adams, Ruth, 124

advertising: in conventional farming magazines, 103; First Amendment rights and, 84–85, 88–89, 94–95; and magazine industry changes in the 1960s and 1970s, 150, 162–63; in *Organic Gardening*, 43, 108, 129, 163, 167, 236n16; in *Prevention*, 57, 72, 76–78, 124, 162, 167, 193–94; recent decline of print advertising, 213; Rodale's 1980s pursuit of mass-market advertisers, 194–95, 197–98; supplement health claims regulation, 74, 75–76, 78. *See also* Federal Trade Commission actions; marketing; Rodale marketing techniques

Advertising Age, 197

Adweek, 190, 196

aerial spraying of pesticides, 119–22, 124–27, 131

agricultural chemicals: advertising of, 103; the Alar scare of 1989 and its aftermath, 200–201, 202–6, 208; Delaney Commis-

sion hearings on, 17–19, 37; emergence and impact on American agriculture, vii–viii, 20, 28–29, 37; J. I. Rodale's and *Prevention's* critiques of, 58–62, 103; linked with poor health/nutrition, viii–ix, 35, 37, 45–46; the move from farm to home use, 118; organic enthusiasts' rejection of, 43–44, 100–101, 112–13; *Organic Gardening* readers' experiences with, 43–44; *Organic Gardening* reporting on effects of, 119, 131–32; war-related shortages, 40. *See also* fertilizers, chemical; organic methods; pesticides; synthetic chemicals; *specific chemicals*

agricultural economics, 32–33, 103–4, 184, 206; the 1980s farm crisis, 184–85, 188–89, 191–92. *See also* food systems reform

agricultural establishment: support for new tools and chemical use, 29; views of organic agriculture, 19, 20, 43, 44, 185, 186–87

agricultural reform: agro-intellectual critiques of the 1970s, 185; King's work, 30–31; post–Dust Bowl concerns and reformist sentiment, vii, 29, 30–34, 37, 41. *See also* food systems reform; Howard, Albert; organic farming advocacy

agricultural research: mainstream research into organic methods, 43, 44, 186–87; Rodale research projects, 45–46, 181, 187, 191, 209

agriculture, American: mid-twentieth century changes, 20, 28–29, 37. *See also* conventional agriculture; organic farming; organic methods; *related entries immediately above*

air pollution, 133, 153. *See also* aerial spraying

Alar scare (1989) and its aftermath, 200–201, 202–6, 208

Albright, Nancy, 156, 157

alcohol advertising, 195

Aldrin, 119, 122

Allen, Floyd, 148

AMA (American Medical Association), 17, 76, 82–85, 226n9, 232n53, 233n59

amaranth, 209

American Marketing Association, 164

American Medical Association (AMA), 17, 76, 82–85, 226n9, 232n53, 233n59

aminotriazole, 128, 200

An Agricultural Testament (Howard), 32, 36

Andrews, Anna. *See* Rodale, Anna Andrews

Arnold, Thurman, 89, 95

Asian agriculture: Howard's work in India, 32; King's study of, 30–31

Audubon Society, 123, 125, 130

Backpacker, 197

back-to-the-land movements and sentiment, 35, 36, 109–11, 138. *See also* homesteading

Bailey, Liberty Hyde, 31

Barrett, Stephen, 124, 238n61

Beck, Ulrich, 102

Beeman, Randal, 33

Behold Our Land (Lord), 41

Belasco, Warren, 115

Berry, Wendell, 185

Bicycling!, 167

Binkley, Sam, 150

biodynamic methods, 39, 40

biological pest control, 131

Blood, Ruth, 69

bone meal, 123–24

Borsodi, Ralph, 35

Bosch, Carl, 31

Brandt, Allen, 93

Bricklin, Mark, 174, 175

Brockenbrough, Eugene, 17–18

Bromfield, Louis, 33–34, 41, 52, 228n57

Browand, Earl, 126–27

Bryant, Gay, 143

Business Horizons, 164

Business Week, 194

calcium, 123

cancer, 58–59, 90

Cancer: Can It Be Prevented? (J. I. Rodale), 58–59

canning. *See* food preservation

Carson, Rachel, 130–31, 234n84; *Silent Spring*, x, 101, 121, 125, 126, 128–31, 146, 239–40n76

Carter, Jimmy, 184

Cavett, Dick, 3, 145

chemicals. *See* agricultural chemicals; fertilizers, chemical; pesticides; synthetic chemicals

Cheraskin, Emmanuel, 91

children's health: the Alar scare and its aftermath, 200–201, 202–6, 208

chlordane, 122

chronic illnesses, 64

citizen action. *See* activism; food systems reform; organic farming advocacy

climate change challenges, marketplace environmentalism and, 219–21

clinical ecology, 91–92

Cohen, Jerome. *See* Rodale, J. I. (born Jerome Cohen)

Cohen, Joseph, 24, 51

Cohen, Lizabeth, 163

cold prevention, 63, 69

common cold, 63, 69

Commoner, Barry, 135–37

compost and composting: farm-scale composting, 109; Howard's work, 32, 39, 40, 43; J. I. Rodale's experiments and writings, 38, 39, 40–42; King's research, 30–31; organic gardeners' focus on, 100, 102; *Organic Gardening* readers' experiences, 42–45, 107–8. *See also* soil health

congressional hearings, 17–19, 37, 85–86; the Delaney commission (1950), 17–19, 37; on medical fraud and quackery (1963), 85–86

conservation: *Organic Gardening's* conservation advocacy, 122–23, 133–39. *See also* environmentalism

consumer culture and consumption choices: consumer agency, ix–x, 8, 177–78; consumer choices viewed as environmental activism, 154, 155, 159, 160–61, 179, 211; consumerist aspects of the organic lifestyle, 167, 176, 177, 179, 215; the fickleness of consumer culture, 161, 176–77, 199; identifying consumer needs and desires, 171–72; marketplace changes of

the 1970s, 161–65; natural health consumers in the 1960s, 95–97. *See also* activism; lifestyle marketing; marketplace
environmentalism; organic lifestyle
consumer networks, 118; Rodale as builder
of, ix–x, 8, 14–15, 19–20, 38. *See also
Organic Gardening* readers; *Prevention*
readers; Rodale consumer community
Consumer Reports, 124
conventional agriculture, vii; agro-
intellectual critiques of the 1980s, 185;
J. I. Rodale's critiques of, 103–4; and
the 1980s farm crisis, 184; synthetic
chemicals and, 20, 28–29, 37, 200. *See
also* agriculture *entries;* pesticides; synthetic chemicals
cookbooks and recipes, 156, 157, 175
cooperatives, 104, 115, 131
Cornucopia Project, 187–88, 208, 245–46n8
cover cropping, 34
cranberry scare (1959), 127–28, 200, 239n65
Criscitiello, Modestino, 90
crop rotation, 34

Daniels, Stevie, 204
Darby, William J., 17
Darwin, Charles, 39
Davis, Harry, 84
Dawson, Leslie, 164
DDT, 62, 119, 120, 121–22, 134, 144
Delaney, James, 17, 19
Delaney Commission, 17–19, 37
Dick Cavett Show, 3, 144–45
dieldrin, 122
diet and nutrition: J. I. Rodale's ideas on
diet and cancer, 58–59; organic foods
seen as nutritionally superior, 35, 37,
45–46, 72; viewed as key to personal
health, 60, 73. *See also* personal health;
Prevention entries
dietary supplements: health claims and
health claims regulation, 74–75, 76–79,
80; new advertising opportunities of the
1970s, 150; potential Rodale production
partnership, 74–76; *Prevention* as marketplace for, 57–58, 72–79, 93–94, 124,
162, 194; Rodale vitamin products in
England, 232n51; synthetic vs. natural,
73–74. *See also* vitamins
*Diet as a Lifestyle: A Profile of American
Women,* 175
digest magazines, 26, 39

Diggers, 115
digital media platforms, 213–14
direct marketing, 79–80, 85–86, 171–72,
176; Rodale direct-mail operations, 1950s
and 1960s, 79–85, 86, 94–95, 232nn53–54;
Rodale direct-mail operations, 1970s and
1980s, 167, 172–75, 176, 194, 197; through
digital media platforms, 213–14. *See also*
Federal Trade Commission actions
Direct Marketing Association, 211
disease: cancer, 58–59, 90; polio, 65–66;
in *Prevention's* pages, 63, 65–66, 69;
twentieth-century medical advances
and, 64, 68–69. *See also* personal health
drinking water fluoridation, 66–67, 124,
238n61
Dubos, Rene, 154
Dunaway, Finis, 208

Earth Day, 139, 146, 211
ecology: clinical ecology, 91–92; Rodale's
embrace of, 135–37, 138
Ehrlich, Paul, 154
Ellul, Jacques, 137–38, 154–55
Emmaus, Pennsylvania: Rodale Manufacturing Company's move to, 25; Rodale's
Emmaus campus in the 1970s, 156–57, 158,
168. *See also* Rodale farms
empiricism, 63–65. *See also* vernacular
science
endangered species preservation, 134
energy use and costs, 154, 158, 171, 186–87,
188
environmental activism. *See* activism; environmentalism; food systems reform;
organic farming advocacy
environmental community: 1980s growth
of, 181; *Rodale's Environmental Bulletin*
as organizing tool, 139–40; Rodale's role
in creating, x, 112–13, 117–19, 122, 133–35,
146–47
Environmental Defense Fund, 134
environmental health: linked with organic
methods, 133–34, 140–41; linked with
personal health, viii–ix, 95–96, 153, 182
environmentalism: chemical scares as
wake-up calls, 127–28, 200–201, 202–3;
environmental anxieties of the early
1970s, 153–54; impact of the Long Island
DDT lawsuit, 121–22, 125; as a marketing opportunity, 150, 165–66; market
mainstreaming of, 211; the regeneration

environmentalism (*continued*)
notion, 188–90, 192; the Rodale community's environmental awakening, 101–2, 112–13, 118; science and, 94, 96–97; systemic reforms vs. individual action, 182, 199, 205, 206, 208, 218, 220–21. *See also* activism; marketplace environmentalism; organic lifestyle; pesticides; pollution; synthetic chemicals

environmental medicine, 91

environmental organizations, 181; Rodale partnerships with, 201–2. *See also specific organizations*

environmental protection: government policy and regulation, 134, 181, 219–20; marketplace environmentalism's failure to effect real change, 219–21. *See also* environmentalism

Environmental Protection Agency (EPA) pesticide risk assessments, 202

exercise, 63

Eyster, William, 46

Fact Digest, 39

Fads and Quackery in Healing: An Analysis of the Foibles of the Healing Cults, with Essays on Various Other Peculiar Notions in the Health Field (Fishbein), 82–83

Farmers of Forty Centuries: Permanent Agriculture in China, Korea, and Japan (King), 30–31

farm workers, 13, 131–32, 205, 207

Faulkner, Edward, 34

FDA (Food and Drug Administration), 17, 74, 85, 117, 128

federal organic standards, ix, 205, 206, 208, 211

Federal Trade Commission (FTC) actions against Rodale Press, 14, 86–95, 232n53, 234n80; background, 80–81, 85–86; hearings and final outcome, 88–95, 234n84; Robert Rodale's role, 12, 86–88; Rodale reader responses to, 87–88

Federated Organic Clubs of Michigan, 114

Feldman, Laurence, 163–64

fertilizers, chemical: critiques and opposition to, 31–32, 40, 43–44, 135–37; growth in use of, 28, 31–32, 102; J. I. Rodale's investigations of a cancer link, 58–59; *Silent Spring's* failure to discuss, 130. *See*

also agricultural chemicals; synthetic chemicals

fertilizers, natural/organic: as key to soil health, 60. *See also* compost; soil health

Field, Oliver, 83

50 Simple Things You Can Do to Save the Earth, 211

fire ant eradication programs, 122, 126, 129

First Amendment rights, advertising and, 84–85, 88–89, 94–95

First National Congress on Medical Quackery, 85

Fishbein, Morris, 82–83

fitness and sports publications, 167, 197–99. *See also* personal health

Fitness House and test kitchen, 156–57, 168

Flemming, Arthur, 128

fluoride, 66–67, 124, 238n61

food additives and preservatives, 59, 116–17

food advertising, in Rodale publications, 195

food and cooking: as part of the organic lifestyle, 156; Rodale publications and research, 156–58, 175. *See also* organic foods/products marketplace; *health food entries*

Food and Drug Administration (FDA), 17, 74, 85, 117, 128

food cooperatives, 115, 131

food preservation, 105–6, 157–58

food safety: Delaney Commission hearings on (1950), 17–19, 37; nutrition supplements and, 74

food systems reform, 15, 181, 182–92; the Alar scare and Rodale's organic farming advocacy, 200–207, 208; current scholarly views on the organic movement, 10–12; and the 1980s farm crisis, 184–85, 188–89, 191–92; the regeneration notion, 188–90, 192; Robert Rodale's personal efforts, 12, 187–91, 209–11; Rodale alliances with environmental organizations, 201–2; Rodale consumer organizing initiatives, 187–88, 191, 201–2, 208, 245–46n8; Rodale research and assessment efforts, 181, 187–88; Rodale's related advertorials and other marketing techniques, 182–84, 187, 191–92, 194; systemic reforms vs. individual action, 182, 199, 205, 206, 208, 218. *See also* agricultural reform; *organic farming entries*

Franz, Maurice, 135

free speech rights, 84–85, 88–89, 94–95

frugality, 98–99, 105–6

FTC. *See* Federal Trade Commission

gardening: vs. agriculture, 37–38. *See also* *Organic Gardening* entries

gardening clubs, 101, 113–15, 123, 131

garden tools and machinery, 108, 236n16

Gardner, Martha, 93

Giddens, Anthony, 176–77

Gilardi, A. J., 44–45

Glickman, Lawrence, 118

Goldman, M. C., 157

Goldstein, Jerome (Jerome Olds), 109, 123, 127, 128, 134, 159, 165–66, 239n64

Goldstein, William, 173

Gould, Rebecca Kneale, 36

Graham, Frank, Jr., 130

Graham, Sylvester, 79

green consumerism. *See* marketplace environmentalism; organic lifestyle

Greene, Wade, 143–44, 151, 154

Green Thoughts (Perényi), 142

grocery stores, 120, 165–66; health food stores, 115, 143, 150, 156, 232–33n54. *See also* organic foods/products marketplace

Guthman, Julie, 198, 203

gypsy moth eradication program, 119–20

Haber, Fritz, 31

Harper, Marion, 165

Hays, Samuel, 101

health. *See* environmental health; personal health; *health entries immediately below*; *natural health entries*; *Prevention* entries

health advice: as protected commercial speech, 84–85, 88–89, 94–95. *See also* *Prevention* entries

The Health Bulletin, 117, 130, 139

health care costs and delivery, 65, 85

health claims: federal regulation of, 74, 75–76, 78; First Amendment rights and, 84–85, 88–89, 94–95; in Rodale advertising and publications, 76–79, 80. *See also* Federal Trade Commission actions

The Health Finder, 80, 87, 232–33n54; mar-

keting of, 80, 81, 83, 86, 88. *See also* Federal Trade Commission actions

health food advocacy: before the 1960s, 35, 115; recipes and cooking advice in Rodale publications, 156, 157, 175. *See also* food systems reform; organic farming advocacy

health food stores, 115, 143, 150, 156, 232–33n54. *See also* organic foods/products marketplace

Health Food Store Shoppers: A Lifestyle and Product Usage Profile, 175

health fraud and faddism: the AMA's anti-quackery crusade, 82–85; government investigations into, 85–86; J. I. Rodale's and *Prevention's* reputations for, 10, 12, 58, 70, 82–85, 130, 144; J. I. Rodale's early experiments with, 22–23; the Rodale legacy and, 216–17. *See also* Federal Trade Commission actions; vernacular science

healthism, 9, 198–99, 205, 207–8. *See also* personal health; self-improvement

heart health, J. I. Rodale's books on, 63, 234n80

Hebble, Lois, 98–99, 105

herbicides: the aminotriazole cranberry scare of 1959, 127–28, 200, 239n65. *See also* agricultural chemicals; pesticides; synthetic chemicals

The Hidden Persuaders (Packard), 163

hobbyists, as a target market, 171, 173. *See also* lifestyle marketing

homeopathy, 82–83

homesteading and homesteading litera-ture, 35–36, 110–11, 138; Rodale demon-stration projects of the 1970s, 158

Howard, Albert, Sir, viii, 18, 32, 40–41, 43; influence on Bromfield, 33; as influ-ence on J. I. Rodale, viii, 18, 36, 37, 39, 129, 142

How to Eat for a Healthy Heart (J. I. Rodale), 234n80

How to Grow Fruits and Vegetables by the Organic Method, 105

How to Manage Your Company Ecologically (Goldstein), 165

Human Ecology and Susceptibility to the Chemical Environment (Randolph), 92

Huttner, Richard, 173

India, Howard's work in, 32

Indore process, 32

14, 130–31, 176; in the twenty-first century, 6, 15, 214–15, 218–21; vs. environmental activism, 177. *See also* consumer culture; consumer networks; environmentalism; organic foods/products marketplace

Martin, William Coda, 116

mass market, Rodale's 1980s shift toward, 15, 180–81, 194–99, 207–8, 217–18

media and publishing industry: book clubs, 169–71; digest magazines, 26; environmental impacts of, 13, 167, 176; homesteading literature of the 1930s and 1940s, 35; industry and media assessments of Rodale Press, 173, 194, 195, 197; industry changes of the 1960s and 1970s, 150, 161–65; J. I. Rodale's earliest publishing endeavors, 26–28; Rodale Press's uniqueness, 173, 193; in the twenty-first century, 213. *See also* advertising; marketing; mass market; Rodale (company); *specific authors and book and magazine titles; specific titles*

medical advances, 63–64, 68–69, 89

medical establishment: policing of threats to its authority, 81, 82; *Prevention* and J. I. Rodale as challengers of, 57, 58, 63–66, 89, 92–94. *See also* American Medical Association; science

medical quackery. *See* health fraud and faddism

Men in the Marketplace, 197–98

men's magazines, 197; *Men's Health,* 197–98, 199, 207–8

Meyer, Heinrich, 51, 52, 229n80

Michigan organic gardening clubs, 114

milk, strontium-90 in, 123

Mothers and Others for Pesticide Limits, 202–3

Murphy, Michelle, 92

Murphy, Robert Cushman, 121, 125

National Audubon Society, 123, 125, 130

"natural," as term, 60, 195–97

The Natural Healing Cookbook (Bricklin), 175

natural health advocacy: People's Medical Society, 191. *See also* Rodale, J. I.; *Prevention* entries

natural health marketplace: consumer behavior and choice in, 95–97; new competition in, in the 1970s, 150–51; *Prevention* as, 57–58, 72–79, 93–94, 97; Rodale

natural health books of the 1970s and 1980s, 174–75; role of direct marketing in, 79–80. *See also* dietary supplements; *Prevention* entries

Natural Resources Defense Council (NRDC), 181, 201–3

New Farm, 158

The New Farm (magazine), 185–86, 187, 188–89, 228n52

The New Farmer, 210

The New Food Chain: An Organic Link between Farm and City, 159

New York, 180–81, 195

New Yorker, 128

New York Times, 3, 41, 143–44, 151, 154, 182–83

nitrogen fertilizers, 31–32. *See also* fertilizers, chemical

Nixon, Richard, 239n65

Noble, J. Kendrick, Jr., 194

no-till farming methods, 34; Ruth Stout's methods, 107–8

NRDC (Natural Resources Defense Council), 181, 201–3

nuclear testing fallout, 123–24

nutrition. *See* diet and nutrition

nutritional supplements. *See* dietary supplements; vitamins

Nyerere, Julius, 209

Ogden, Michael, 119

Olds, Jerome (Jerome Goldstein), 109, 123, 127, 128, 134, 159, 165–66, 239n64

Opinion Research Corporation, 197–98

"organic," as term, 40, 102, 215

organic certification, 148, 205–6, 220

The Organic Farmer (magazine), 104, 228n52

organic farming: before World War II, vii; current status of, 219; and demand increases after the Alar scare, 203; economic cases for, 186–87; establishment views of, 19, 20, 43, 44, 185, 186–87; framed as regenerative, 188–90. *See also* food systems reform; organic certification; organic farming advocacy; organic methods; organic standards

organic farming advocacy: J. I. Rodale as a visionary/prophet, 5, 9, 10–11, 52, 129, 140–46, 215; J. I. Rodale's emergence and prominence as a reformer, 19–20, 29–30, 34–37; and the 1980s farm crisis, 184–85,

polio, 65–66, 90

political engagement. *See* activism; food systems reform; organic farming advocacy; *environment entries*

politics: J. I. Rodale's lack of political ambition, 143; and *Organic Gardening's* environmental advocacy in the 1970s, 134–35; and U.S. environmental policy, 134, 181, 219–20

pollution, 133, 135, 153; *Rodale's Environmental Bulletin* coverage of, 139–40. *See also* environmental health; environmental protection

The Population Bomb (Ehrlich), 154

Powell, Thomas, 109–10, 122–23

Practical Encyclopedia of Natural Healing (Bricklin), 174

Prevention, x, 14, 55–97, 61; advertiser concerns about, in the 1980s, 194–95; advertising in, 57, 72, 76–78, 124, 162, 167, 193–94; and the American Medical Association, 82–85, 232n53, 233n59; articles and single-issue spin-offs as test marketing technique, 174, 197; bone meal tablet recommendations, 123–24; as challenger of establishment opinion, 56–57, 58, 63–66, 89, 92–94; chemical opposition in, 56–57, 59–62, 66–67, 78–79, 124, 238n61; commercial and financial success of, x, 14, 58, 162; focus on diet and nutrition, 61–62, 64, 72–75; focus on prevention rather than treatment, 60–62, 74–75, 85, 90–91; founding and growth of, 56, 59, 150, 173; grounding in personal experiences and anecdotal evidence, 46–47, 56, 58, 62–65, 78, 93, 95–96; polio-focused issues, 65–66; as a product marketplace, 57–58, 72–79, 93–94, 97, 124, 162, 194; related direct-mail operations, 80–85, 81, 86, 94–95, 194, 232nn53,54; Robert Rodale's characterization of, 86–87; Robert Rodale's writing in, 124, 142; rules for personal health, 61–62, 71–73; vs. Rodale's later health and fitness magazines, 198. *See also Prevention* books; *Prevention* readers; Rodale marketing techniques; *natural health entries*

Prevention books, 57–58, 79; *Practical Encyclopedia of Natural Healing* and its followup publications, 174–75.

See also Federal Trade Commission actions; *The Health Finder; other specific titles*

Prevention readers: as a community, 56–57, 68–71; and the magazine's advertising, 76–77; and the 1960s FTC action, 87–88; in the 1980s, 194–95

Price, Jennifer, 167

Pritchard, James, 33

public health: aerial pesticide spraying concerns and opposition, 119–22, 124–27, 131; radioactive fallout hazards, 123–24

Publishers Weekly, 173, 174

publishing. *See* media and publishing industry; Rodale (company)

quackery. *See* health fraud and faddism

radioactive fallout, 123–24

Radway, Janice, 70–71, 173

Randolph, Theron, 91–92, 93

Reader's Digest, 26

Reagan, Ronald, 181, 184

regeneration and regenerative agriculture, 188–90, 192, 208, 210

Regenerative Agriculture Association, 191

Richards, Mary, 121, 125

risk society, 13

Robinson, Ella, 125–26

Rockefeller, Wendy, 202–3

Rodale (company): educational services division, 159; environmental impacts of its operations, 13, 167, 176; film division, 148; financial status and revenue figures, 6, 51, 58, 124, 173–74, 193–94; J. I. Rodale's retirement from, 129; the nonprofit divisions, 6, 19, 46, 58, 191, 209–10; origins in J. I. Rodale's early publishing endeavors, 26–28; Robert Rodale as president and CEO, 12, 86, 151, 190, 210–12. *See also* marketplace environmentalism; Rodale Manufacturing Company; Rodale marketing techniques; Rodale publications; *specific publications*

—IN THE 1950S AND 1960S: AMA inquiries into Rodale activities, 82–85, 232n53, 233n59; FTC actions, 81, 86–95, 232n53, 234nn80,84; Rodale and the publication of *Silent Spring*, 128–32. *See also* environmentalism; Federal Trade Commission

—BUSINESS ACTIVITIES AND CAREER: achievements and legacy, 12, 14–15, 16, 211–12, 215–16, 217–18; as company president and CEO, 12, 86, 151, 190, 210–12; the Cornucopia Project, 187–88; environmental advocacy in the 1960s, 101, 133–39; foreign travels and activities, 190, 209–11, 229n80; *Organic Gardening* editorship, 12, 72, 103, 116, 122, 151; the regeneration notion, 188–90, 192; and Rodale's mail-order marketing techniques, 172; role in the 1960s FTC action, 12, 86–87, 88. *See also Organic Gardening*

—WRITINGS AND VIEWS OF: on farm worker health hazards, 131–32; on his father and his work, 34, 36, 130, 142; on homesteading, 110–11, 138; in *Organic Gardening*, 116, 128, 131–32, 133, 134–35, 136–39, 237n31; in *Prevention*, 124, 142; on Rodale's goals and social consciousness, 190; syndicated "Organic Living" column and sane living system, 151–55

Rodale consumer community, ix–x, 8, 14–15, 19–20, 38; demographics of, viii, 13–14, 112, 135, 194–95, 220–21; reader-submitted materials in Rodale publications, 244n55. *See also* consumer networks; *Organic Gardening* readers; *Prevention* readers; Rodale marketing techniques

Rodale Cookbook (Albright), 156

Rodale farms: agricultural research at, 45–46, 181; New Farm acquisition, 158; the original farm, 34–35, 36, 45–46, 142, 143–44

Rodale Institute, 6, 191; origins of, 46, 58

Rodale International, 210

Rodale Manufacturing Company, 24, 25–26, 50–51

Rodale marketing techniques: direct-mail operations of the 1950s and 1960s, 79–85, 86, 94–95, 232nn53,54; direct-mail operations of the 1970s and 1980s, 167, 172–75, 176, 194, 197; in the 1970s, 167, 168–76, 178–79, 194; in the 1980s, 182–84, 187, 191–92, 197; in the twenty-first century, 213–14

Rodale Press. *See* Rodale (company); Rodale publications; *specific publications by title*

Rodale publications: book publishing growth in the 1970s, 167; cookbooks,

156, 157, 175; educational materials for environmental groups, 159; 1940s publications and readership, 18, 25, 37–45, 228n28; reader-submitted materials in, 244n55; retail outlets and presence, 150, 197, 232–33n54; *Rodale's Environmental Action Bulletin*, 139–41, 159; thesauri, 25, 226n20; in the twenty-first century, 6, 212–15; use of uncredited articles, 228n53. *See also Organic Gardening*; *Prevention*; *Prevention* books; Rodale (company); Rodale marketing techniques; *other specific book and magazine titles*

Rodale Research Center, 209–10

Rodale Resources Inc., 168

Rodale's Environmental Action Bulletin, 139–41, 159

rototillers, 108, 236n16

Rozell, Bruce and Margilee, 134

Runner's World, 197, 207–8

Russell, Edmund, 118

Russia. *See* Soviet Union

Sane Living in a Mad World: A Guide to the Organic Way of Life (Robert Rodale), 154, 155

Santa Barbara oil spill, 146

Saturday Evening Post, 141–42, 162

Schell, A. F., 43–44

Schor, Juliet, 178

science: Rodale's embrace of ecology in the 1960s, 135–37, 138; the Rodale tendency to vernacular science and dubious evidence, 10, 53, 57–58, 62–69, 94, 129, 130–31, 216. *See also* empiricism; scientific skepticism; vernacular science

scientific research: fluoride trials, 67; the Rodale nonprofit research divisions, 6, 19, 46, 58, 191; *Silent Spring's* grounding in, 129, 130–31. *See also* agricultural research

scientific skepticism, x–xi, 94, 96–97; the Rodales' tendencies to, x–xi, 63, 65–66, 89–90, 94, 136–38

self-improvement culture and literature, 21, 22, 172, 182; healthism, 9, 198–99, 205, 207–8; J. I. Rodale's self-improvement efforts, 21, 22–23, 28. *See also* personal health

Self-Sufficiency Book Club, 170–71

self-sufficiency literature, 170–72

Sellers, Christopher, 121–22
Sharp, Robert, 107
Sherman, Louis, 47
Sibley, Marilyn, 122
Sierra Club, 181
Silent Spring (Carson), x, 101, 121, 125, 126, 128–31, 146, 239–40n76
Simon, Morton, 70, 86
Sinclair, Upton, 128, 200
60 Minutes, 202
sleeping positions, 62, 230n10
Small, Bingham, 47
soap, 62–63
So Human an Animal (Dubos), 154
Soil and Health Foundation, 19, 46, 58, 191
soil health: Commoner's views, 137; early critiques of artificial fertilizers, 30–32; J. I. Rodale's interest in, viii, 18–19, 29–30, 60, 129–30; linked with personal health, viii; linked with public/environmental health, 129–30; linked with social/economic health, 33; *Organic Farming and Gardening's* focus on, 39; post–Dust Bowl concerns about, vii, 29, 30–34, 37, 41
The Solid Gold Mailbox (Weintz), 171–72
Soviet Union, Robert Rodale's visits and interest in, 210, 211
Spock, Marjorie, 121, 125
sports and fitness publications, 167, 197–99. *See also* personal health
Spring, 195–96
Stare, Frederick J., 85
Stark, Salome, 125
Steiner, Rudolf, 40
Stephan, Audrey, 114, 123
Stetler, C. Joseph, 85
Stocking Up, 157
Stoner, Carol Hupping, 157
Stout, Ruth, 107–8, 236n14
Streep, Meryl, 202–3
strontium poisoning, 123–24
sugar, 71
supplements. *See* dietary supplements; vitamins
sustainability, as term, 189
Swoboda, Alois P., 22
The Synonym Finder, 226n20
synthetic chemicals: as focus of the Rodales' critiques, viii–ix, x; health effects of chemical exposure in FTC action arguments, 91–94; J. I. Rodale's

and *Prevention's* critiques of, 58–62, 67–71, 103; organic gardeners' rejection of/concerns about, x, 43–44, 100–102, 112–13, 125–26; *Organic Gardening's* chemical critiques and reporting, 103–4, 112–13, 116–17; post–World War II ubiquity of, vii–viii, 59–60, 100–101, 112–13; Rodale's *Our Poisoned Earth and Sky*, 99–100, 100, 132; synthetic vs. natural vitamins and supplements, 73–74. *See also* agricultural chemicals; environmentalism; fertilizers, chemical; *specific chemicals*

Tanzania, Robert Rodale's visit to, 209–10
Tebbel, John, 49
The Technological Society (Ellul), 137–38, 154–55
technology: new technologies embraced in *Organic Gardening's* pages, 108–10; Rodale ambivalence and advice about, 137–38, 152, 154–55; Rodale's embrace of traditional technologies, 105–6, 158
TEPP (tetraethyl pyrophosphate), 119
Teufel, Robert, 172, 194
thesauri, 25, 226n20
This Pace Is Not Killing Us (J. I. Rodale), 63, 234n80
tobacco advertising, 195
Tomes, Nancy, 96
toxaphene, 119
toxics exposure. *See* agricultural chemicals; pesticides; synthetic chemicals
Tschudy, Donald, 90
Turlington, Mrs. E. A., 107
Turner, Frederick Jackson, 110

The Unsettling of America (Berry), 185
USDA: and the cranberry scare, 128; gypsy moth eradication program (1957), 119–20; 1977 organic methods survey, 187; Rodale's lobbying efforts for organic farming representation, 166

Vegetable Mould and Earthworms (Darwin), 39
The Verb Finder (J. I. Rodale), 25
vernacular science: Commoner's views on, 137; *Organic Gardening* readers as constructors of, 37–39, 42–45, 48–49, 156; *Prevention's* reliance on, 56–58, 62–69, 71, 129, 137. *See also* empiricism; science; scientific skepticism

vitamins and vitamin deficiencies, 62, 73–74, 77–78, 162, 232n51. *See also* diet and nutrition; dietary supplements

Walk, Do Not Run, to the Doctor (J. I. Rodale), 55–56
Washington, DC, J. I. Rodale in, 23–24
The Waste Makers (Packard), 163
water pollution, 133, 135
Weintz, Todd, 172
Weintz, Walter, 171–72
Weissgerber, Rudolf, 75
Whole Earth Catalog, 150

wildlife: pesticide toxicity hazards, 119, 125, 126–27. *See also Silent Spring*
Wiley, Anna Kelton, 17
Wiley, Harvey J., 17
Williams, Raymond, 102
women, as core/target Rodale readers, 194–95, 195–96
Women's Health, 197
The World's Happiest Gardeners, 98–99, 105
World War II, 39–40, 50–51, 118
The Writings of J. I. Rodale (Rodale), 27

Zuckerman, Mary Ellen, 49

Seeking Refuge: Birds and Landscapes of the Pacific Flyway, by Robert M. Wilson

Toxic Archipelago: A History of Industrial Disease in Japan, by Brett L. Walker

Dreaming of Sheep in Navajo Country, by Marsha L. Weisiger

Shaping the Shoreline: Fisheries and Tourism on the Monterey Coast, by Connie Y. Chiang

The Fishermen's Frontier: People and Salmon in Southeast Alaska, by David F. Arnold

Making Mountains: New York City and the Catskills, by David Stradling

Plowed Under: Agriculture and Environment in the Palouse, by Andrew P. Duffin

The Country in the City: The Greening of the San Francisco Bay Area, by Richard A. Walker

Native Seattle: Histories from the Crossing-Over Place, by Coll Thrush

Drawing Lines in the Forest: Creating Wilderness Areas in the Pacific Northwest, by Kevin R. Marsh

Public Power, Private Dams: The Hells Canyon High Dam Controversy, by Karl Boyd Brooks

Windshield Wilderness: Cars, Roads, and Nature in Washington's National Parks, by David Louter

On the Road Again: Montana's Changing Landscape, by William Wyckoff

Wilderness Forever: Howard Zahniser and the Path to the Wilderness Act, by Mark Harvey

The Lost Wolves of Japan, by Brett L. Walker

Landscapes of Conflict: The Oregon Story, 1940–2000, by William G. Robbins

Faith in Nature: Environmentalism as Religious Quest, by Thomas R. Dunlap

The Nature of Gold: An Environmental History of the Klondike Gold Rush, by Kathryn Morse

Where Land and Water Meet: A Western Landscape Transformed, by Nancy Langston

The Rhine: An Eco-Biography, 1815–2000, by Mark Cioc

Driven Wild: How the Fight against Automobiles Launched the Modern Wilderness Movement, by Paul S. Sutter

George Perkins Marsh: Prophet of Conservation, by David Lowenthal

Making Salmon: An Environmental History of the Northwest Fisheries Crisis, by Joseph E. Taylor III

Irrigated Eden: The Making of an Agricultural Landscape in the American West, by Mark Fiege

The Dawn of Conservation Diplomacy: U.S.–Canadian Wildlife Protection Treaties in the Progressive Era, by Kurkpatrick Dorsey

Landscapes of Promise: The Oregon Story, 1800–1940, by William G. Robbins

Forest Dreams, Forest Nightmares: The Paradox of Old Growth in the Inland West, by Nancy Langston

The Natural History of Puget Sound Country, by Arthur R. Kruckeberg